Placemaking

Placemaking

A New Materialist Theory of Pedagogy

Tara Page

EDINBURGH
University Press

Edinburgh University Press is one of the leading university presses in the UK.
We publish academic books and journals in our selected subject areas across the
humanities and social sciences, combining cutting-edge scholarship with high editorial
and production values to produce academic works of lasting importance. For more
information visit our website: edinburghuniversitypress.com

© Tara Page, 2020, 2022

First published in hardback by Edinburgh University Press 2020

Edinburgh University Press Ltd
The Tun – Holyrood Road
12(2f) Jackson's Entry
Edinburgh EH8 8PJ

Typeset in 11/13 Adobe Sabon by
IDSUK (DataConnection) Ltd, and
printed and bound by CPI Group (UK) Ltd, Croydon, CR0 4YY

A CIP record for this book is available from the British Library

ISBN 978 1 4744 2877 4 (hardback)
ISBN 978 1 4744 2878 1 (paperback)
ISBN 978 1 4744 2879 8 (webready PDF)
ISBN 978 1 4744 2880 4 (epub)

The right of Tara Page to be identified as the author of this work has been asserted in
accordance with the Copyright, Designs and Patents Act 1988, and the Copyright and
Related Rights Regulations 2003 (SI No. 2498).

Contents

Acknowledgements

I acknowledge: Braidwood, Australia; Hughenden, Australia; Chudleigh, Australia; Thirton, Australia; Goldsmiths, United Kingdom; Brockley, United Kingdom; the place-worlds that have taught me.

I acknowledge: plates, barbells, racks, knee supports, wrist straps, chalk and my nobulls; the matter that teaches and strengthens – mind, body and spirit.

I acknowledge: Mary, Jenny, Henry, Hettie, Harper, John and Peter, Beckie Coleman, Oseme Edehomo, Rosalyn George, Anna-Hickey Moody, Emma Hoddinott, John Johnston, Lindsay Maguire, Krystyna Martin-Dominguez, Len Platt, Esther Sayers and Becca Watts; the people who love, support, empower and who I have learnt so much from and with.

And Mema, I acknowledge for clarity, strength, humour and love, sometimes tough, but always constant.

Thank you to Emma Caddy, James Dale, Andrew Kirk, Kirsty Woods and Carol Macdonald for their care, patience and understanding.

Thank you to those who granted permissions to reproduce materials and links: National Gallery of Australia, National Gallery of New South Wales and National Gallery of Victoria. Every effort has been made to trace and acknowledge copyright. The author and publisher apologises for any accidental infringement and welcomes information that would redress this situation.

Introduction

It is with trepidation and apprehension that I write this introduction, because this is putting into the world the entangled threads of feelings, thoughts and experiences that I have unconsciously been learning for a very long time. It is also because I have only recently been consciously pulling at and unpicking these threads. When I first heard the term 'hindsight is 20–20', I did not really understand what that meant; hindsight indicating a knowing and learning from and of the past, or history. As I critically reflect on these entangled threads of my artistic, pedagogic and research praxis[1] I now understand and have a 20–20 sight of these threads; of place, bodies, the fascination with stuff-materials making, and a deeper need to bodily know and learn how we are with things, matter, materials with place/s. So, just like the ethnographer Basso's pivotal work with the Apache of North America (Feld and Basso 1996), I am also mapping place.[2] Whereas Basso mapped the stories-words of the Apache ancestors, I am attempting to map the relations and the entanglements of how we make and learn place, and how with the matter of artistic and everyday practice we make and remake place. From this we can learn, know and understand the importance of place, to who we are and also how we are.

As I manoeuvre weaving left, right, around people on the platform with the train tracks disappearing into the distance, a gentle breeze and the sun blinds my left eye. I realise the sun is shining and there is a blue sky in London! People are smiling. It is amazing how a change in the weather dramatically affects people.

I can actually feel London now. Up until now there has been this curtain, only allowing me to see or feel parts of London. But this curtain is not mist, or the constant drizzle and grey cloud blanket. London is being selective in what and how it reveals, when London is ready and when it thinks I am ready I will know.

The sun is blinding my left side as I lean waiting for the East London line, the electronic sign said 10 minutes, it has been 15 minutes, but then this must be 10 minutes London transport time.

Here it comes . . . slowly inching along the platform – never in a hurry – just happy to saunter its rear end along the track. OK, it is the oldest and it takes its time and it is not the most stylish. But to be honest, today I don't care. It is a beautiful day. I am with London and now I can see London. (Page 2006: 1)[3]

'So, where are you from?'; 'You don't sound like you come from here'. As stated above, questions about our experiences of place, and specifically how we make place and have a feeling of belonging, have always been with me; possibly from the embodied experiences of vast open space and great expanses of sky, from horizon to horizon, from my childhood growing up in Australia. However, when embarking on this particular research journey, which coincided with the place-world[4] of London, a very different place-world to those I had known and lived, these questions and fascinations of place and the effect and affects of this embodied knowledge needed to be explored and examined.

Consequently, I am attempting to understand and question the practices of life that are sometimes invisible or hidden, and most of the time taken for granted, because they are sensed, felt, of the body, and are not easily verbalised. As Löfgren and Wilk state, 'sometimes in the inconspicuous practices of daily life, these small repetitive actions can work to subtly change larger social structures, cultural values, and notions of self and society' (2007: 10). With this research I am attempting to take a step towards a better understanding of the relational ways we make place and learn place: placemaking. But also how 'who we are' and 'how we are' are entwined with 'where we are'. Then we can learn from and use these small, hidden, corporeal ways of knowing and understanding because, as Brighouse and Woods assert 'sometimes, very small things make a disproportionate difference . . . Chaos or complexity theory suggests that we may call them butterflies – very context dependent but often the key to great change' (2006: 7).

'Place' can be considered an ambiguous concept; however, I conceive it as eventmental, 'something in process . . . unconfineable to a thing . . . or to a simple location' (Casey 1998: 337), a process with its meanings continually made, performed and learned. A 'sense of place' is an individual's connection to, and their embodied ways of knowing place that is learned from the everyday socio-material practices of their place-world. Consequently, 'belonging' is the feelings of belonging to a group, place or country, and it is through these ways of knowing that identities (group, national and so on) are forged. A 'sense of belonging' is the embodied knowing-making of place that enables these feelings of connection.

This understanding of place as dynamic means that place is an event or process. Aristotle (1983) was the first to state this theoretical understanding of place; the bound relationship of place with body. This premise is pivotal in the resurrection of place and is evident in the work of Kant (1988), Whitehead (1978), Husserl (1970) and especially Merleau-Ponty (1962; 1963). Through an examination of these philosophers' work,

I propose that there can be no place without bodies and that through the practices of the body – perception (sensory, and memory) – with the socio-material, we make and learn place. New materialism supports this exploration and examination of the between spaces of humans and socio-material place-worlds.

This is because new materialism emphasises the connectedness rather than the disconnectedness, or the differences that make a difference that we can then research, question and learn from and with, in order to address and enable a sustainability of human life. Enabling 'the (un) folding of cultural theory – the matter–energy flows of theory formation, the non-linear coding practices, the cutting across matter and signification' (Dolphijn and van der Tuin 2012: 111) means that we can explore and examine the connectedness or entanglement of globalisation, ownership, identity and placial affect and effect to learn how as humans we may sustain life and support deeper relationships with each other and our place-worlds. This can give us a greater understanding of our entanglement with the matter of our place-worlds and maybe even, I hope, a more ethical and respectful relationship, where humans are 'with' place.

Because new materialism posits matter as agentive, indeterminate, constantly forming and reforming in unexpected ways (Coole and Frost 2010), it enables the abandoning of any idea of matter as inert and subject to predictable forces. Matter is always becoming; it 'feels, converses, suffers, desires, yearns and remembers' and, since 'feeling, desiring and experiencing are not singular characteristics or capacities of human consciousness' (Barad in Dolphijn and Van der Tuin 2012: 16), new materialism offers a redefinition of liveness and human–non-human relations and, most importantly for this research assemblage, pedagogy. In order to incorporate such a perspective, Barad explains:

> what is needed is a robust account of the materialization of *all* bodies – 'human' and 'nonhuman' –including agential contributions of all material forces (both 'social' and 'natural'). This will require an understanding of the nature of the relationship between discursive practices and material phenomena; an accounting of 'nonhuman' as well as 'human' forms of agency; and an understanding of the precise causal nature of productive practices that take account of the fullness of matter's implication in its ongoing historicity. (2007: 66)

Bodies and things are then not as separate as we were once taught, and their intra-relationship is vital to how we come to know ourselves as human, and intra-act with our place-worlds and learn from and with our place-worlds.

The body is pivotal to new materialism; it is a complex intra-action (Barad 2007) of the social and affective, where embodiment is a process of encounters, intra-actions with other bodies (Springgay 2008). Thinking about matter matters – if bodies and things are produced together, intertwined, then 'things' and how they act on bodies are co-constitutive of our embodied subjectivity. The concept of intra-action is central to Barad's new materialism, and refers to the movement generated in an encounter of two or more bodies in a process of becoming different:

> The neologism 'intra-action' signifies the mutual constitution of entangled agencies . . . the notion of intra-action recognizes that distinct agencies do not precede, but rather emerge through, their intra-actions. It is important to note that the 'distinct' agencies are only distinct in a relational, not an absolute, sense, that is agencies are only distinct in relation to their mutual entanglement; they don't exist as individual elements. (2007: 33)

New materialism (Alaimo and Hekman 2008; Barad 2007; Braidotti 2013; Barrett and Bolt 2013; Coole and Frost 2010; Hekman 2010) calls for an emphasis on materiality in research; it calls for an embodied, affective, relational understanding of the research process. As a way of exploring the entanglement and co-constitution of matter and subjectivity, new materialism is a methodology, a theoretical framework and a political positioning that emphasises the complex materiality of bodies immersed in social relations of power (Dolphijn and van der Tuin 2012). Inventive methods (Lury and Wakeford 2012), including arts-based (Jagodzinski and Wallin 2013), visual (Pink 2007b; Rose 2012) and embodied/sensory methods (Ingold and Vergunst 2008; Pink 2009; Page 2012b; 2019), are increasingly being mobilised to explore the agency of matter and advance vitalist frameworks. Moving beyond the problem-focused approach of Lury and Wakeford's (2012) engaging intervention into methods, Chapters 1 to 6 work the intra-actions of theory with practice to position the agency of matter as pedagogical. Because matter can teach us, it can teach us to resist dominant discourses, and we can learn new ways of making and learning place and belonging.

Also central to supporting this research and the ways of making and learning have been theories of critical pedagogy (Giroux 2003; hooks 1994) and the work of Freire (1970). Critical pedagogy draws on anarchism, feminism and Marxism, and is a teaching and learning approach that attempts to enable the questioning and challenging of domination, and the beliefs and practices that dominate. Shor defines critical pedagogy as:

> Habits of thought, reading, writing, and speaking which go beneath surface meaning, first impressions, dominant myths, official pronouncements, traditional clichés, received wisdom, and mere opinions, to understand the deep meaning, root causes, social context, ideology, and personal consequences of any action, event, object, process, organization, experience, text, subject matter, policy, mass media, or discourse. (1992: 129)

The three assumptions of critical pedagogy are that praxis can enable social transformation, that learning and teaching are not neutral, and that society can be transformed by the engagement of those who are critically conscious (Grunewald 2003). These assumptions resonate with Barad's (2007) distinction between critique, as an evaluative sensibility, and being critical as reactionary.

However, a critical pedagogical approach also enables thinking through the intra-action of pedagogised identities. Freire states:

> Through dialogue, the teachers-of-the-students and the students-of-the-teachers cease to exist and a new term emerges; teacher-student with student-teacher, the teacher is no longer merely the one who teaches, but the one who is himself [*sic*] taught in dialogue with the students, who in turn while being taught also teach. They become jointly responsible for the process in which all grow. (1970: 80)

I have reworded this statement, replacing the word 'student' with 'learner', and '-of-the' with 'with', which results in the following: Through dialogue, teachers-with-learners and learners-with-teachers cease to exist and a new term emerges; teacher-learner with learner-teacher. The teacher is no longer merely the one who teaches, but the one who is taught in dialogue with the learner who in turn, while being taught also teaches. They become jointly responsible for the process in which all grow. These intra-actions, this 'withness', enables the continual reproduction and renegotiation of learner/teacher/learning, the meanings of which are not predetermined, resulting in the creation of a 'shared place of discovery and learning' (Page 2012a: 73) that is not specific to an educational setting, but, rather, is entangled with wider, global discourses and power relations. These wider, global discourses and power relations are constitutive of pedagogy. Freire explains that this becoming-other is effected through intra-action as 'transformation', where the marked, material change (or becoming) is important. Freire goes on to explain that pedagogy 'becomes the practice of freedom, the means by which men and women deal critically and creatively with reality and discover how to participate in the transformation of their world' (1970: 16). This practice of freedom is 'about how we learn together and make changes together' (Page 2012a: 73), a practice in which learning as responsiveness to matter and to space-time-mattering occurs within the contingencies, differences and diversity of life. Pedagogy can then be conceived as an open, continuously created and recreated practice that is specific to intra-actions of difference that make a difference – not grounded in existing knowledges that attempt to equalise, normalise or fall back on traditions of established values, concepts and practices. A pedagogy that is embodied, material, generative and emancipatory.

Similarly, the use of creative practices, art making in this assemblage, is related to the goal of material thinking, to look beyond the making process and view creative, artistic practices as the making of knowledge; practice with theory; making with thought. Bolt argues that there are many 'materials' through which art 'come[s] into being – the material bodies of artists and theorists, the matter of the medium, the technologies of production and the immaterial bodies of knowledge that form discourse around art' (2012: 7). Also discussing artistic research and new materialisms, Kontturi et al. note:

> questions of materiality have during the past few decades solidly returned or emerged to the agendas of artistic research and art studies as well. In addition to emphasising the active – albeit fundamentally relation-bound – nature of materialities, the notion of intra-action suggests another interesting resonance especially with the burgeoning forms and methodologies of artistic research. By stressing the emergence of agencies, entities and modes of knowledge through relations, it comes close to the underlying objective of artistic research concerning the constant transfers between or co-formations of practice and theory; or of ways of doing, making, feeling, thinking, and conceptualising. (2018: n.p.)

But it is important to emphasise that I am not solely focusing on individual practices of making and learning, nor on the rose-coloured, feelgood, warm and fuzzy of making and learning of place and belonging. This is because there are inequalities of placemaking, and new materialism stresses 'the concrete yet complex materiality of bodies in social relations of power' (Braidotti in Dolphin and Tuin 2012: 21), and so we cannot only focus on the micro yet universal level while ignoring the power of the socio-material of place-worlds.

When there is a loss of connection with place, through individual or collective displacement, Casey (1993) maintains that there is a loss of orientation in the world and that the world becomes mere sites that lack meaning and connection. I argue that this concept of displacement and the rise of the importance of place can be attributed to us searching for a 'sense of place' in an increasingly 'placeless' or non-place-world, where globalisation and technology may have contributed to disbelonging (Casey 1993; Cresswell 2004; Augé 2008). As Nieuwenhuis states:

> Place also increasingly matters as a critique against the flux of capitalism. It can serve as a remedy against the distractions, interferences and displacements caused by the unrestful and distracting circulation of capital. Attention to the air one breathes, to the smell of mud and the sound of waves bursting against the coastline are not signs of conservative nostalgia but are symbols, affects and experiences informing radical ecological critiques against capital's turbulent violence. They form the affects through which we connect to the very place that we call our world. (2016: 314)

Place, the 'where', can often be overlooked and is usually conceived as the backdrop or site where the interesting stuff happens, but it is key in understanding who we are and how we are. 'Where are you from?' – a simple question, yet the answer to this question often refers to someone's birthplace, childhood home or a place that holds significance. The place that is offered in answer to the question is more than a means of orientation, it is a lived place that has meanings and matter that identify and place, because the world really is not global, it is regional.

The idea of globalism, in which people, ideas and products are consistent across the world, is limited (while I acknowledge that McDonalds has had a good crack at it). The reality is that each region will have particularities of matter; the water, the wheat, the weather, the flour and so on of the burger buns – matter matters. So, my aim is not to describe or represent 'place' as an object but to understand and learn the entangled embodied and socio-material ways we know our place-worlds, and how, through everyday and art/s practices, we perform, make and learn place and belonging. Through this praxic assemblage, underpinned by new materialist thought, we can know and understand how matter matters, that the presence, but also the absence of matter is pedagogic. Using the entanglement of images, bodily movement, poetic prose and text, I am attempting to make concepts material, and this may force many of us out of the comfort zone of using the usual words or phrases. But these material articulations have a real potential for novelty and innovation; a new type of reason beyond abstract philosophical thought. This is the 'newness' of this new materialist practice research of understanding and learning placemaking.

Chapter 1 is an assemblage of data of the socio-material embodied ways of making a place-world, the Australian bush. This chapter is an intra-action of the participants and also my own everyday and artistic practices-makings and critical reflections. This intra-action of experiential-embodied prose and art practices-outcomes is a sharing of the senses of place, and to 'work' the differences that make a difference.

This will enable an understanding of the ways of making place, and how through everyday practices with creative-artistic makings place and belonging is made and learned.[5]

From the local to the global, Chapter 2 is an assemblage of the linguistic, poetic, artistic, pedagogic, filmic and geopolitical representations, practices and materiality of a specific place-world, remote Australia. Through mapping the differences that make a difference this analysis demonstrates how the makings of place are made-performed-learned. I use the term 'place-world' to denote a particular place that has specific and particular forms of human and non-human socio-material knowledges, performances and practices. This analysis also demonstrates the power these various mediascapes have, and how the presence, but also the very absence, of matter are pivotal to the pedagogies of national identity and nationhood discourses.

In Chapter 3, I map the theoretical and philosophical concepts of place that I use to underpin and position this assemblage. As there are many theoretical understandings of place with different epistemological underpinnings, in this chapter I position and map how place and the theories of place have been on a winding path through philosophical thought from Aristotle, Newton, Descartes and Kant, in which place was gradually subsumed by space. But by returning to Aristotle's premise of the bound relationship between place and the body, the resurrection of place is enabled through Kant, Whitehead, Husserl and especially Merleau-Ponty and Deleuze. Through examining these theories and philosophers I argue that there can be no place without the body, and that place is continually made through and with the everyday socio-material practices of bodies. So, my place of place is more than a background for action and thought; it is at one with socio-materials practices of the body, a process of embodiment.

However, these ways of knowing and also making place are not produced in isolation; they are produced through social-material engagements, through a continuous process of embodied material learning and teaching. In Chapter 4, I develop a new materialist theory of pedagogy where the intra-actions of humans and matter are pedagogic, an embodied and material pedagogy. This is achieved through the examination of how matter teaches, and how we learn and teach place and belonging.

To understand and question these everyday and artistic practices of life that are sometimes invisible or hidden – and most of the time taken for granted – because they are sensed, felt, of the body, and not easily verbalised, an embodied, affective, relational research approach is needed. The innovative approach of practice research, underpinned by new materialism, that can enable these understandings is discussed in Chapter 5. Additionally, inventive artistic practice methods and a remaking of traditional empirical methods are examined that enable the exploration of the agency of matter and advance vitalist frameworks. By moving beyond the problem-focused approach, this chapter works the intra-actions of theory with practice, practice with theory, to develop new approaches to new materialist-place practice research. The practice research approach also politically positions research practices, emphasising the complex materiality of bodies immersed in social relations of power.

Just as new materialist practice research moves beyond a more traditional idea of research, it also disrupts the practices and discourses that make the identities of researcher-as-subject and participant-as-research object. In Chapter 6 I analyse these intra-actions that can enable the continual reproduction and renegotiation of the positioning of researcher, participant, learner and teacher. I also contend that being 'with', a 'withness', is an ongoing ethical engagement with place-worlds where we take care and have care, and this too is continually made and remade with wider, global discourses and power relations.

To know and learn how we make place we need to know and learn the ways in which bodies intra-act with the socio-material world. These ways are complex and fluid, flexible and subject to change. However, this knowledge of place is not produced in isolation. This is because to be human is to already be materially with place, and to be materially with place is to be human, the entanglement of body with place, place with body. Place is the very experiential fact of our existence, but it is also a necessary one, as it enables the creation-making of meaning and socio-material relations; we know and learn place with embodied and material pedagogies and we also know and learn place from just being with.

Notes

1. Praxis is the process by which a theory, lesson or skill is enacted, embodied or realised. But praxis may also refer to the act of engaging, applying, exercising, realising or practising ideas. Paulo Freire defines praxis in *Pedagogy of the Oppressed* as 'reflection and action directed at the structures to be transformed' (1970: 126). For Freire, through praxis, oppressed people can acquire a critical awareness of their own condition, and, with teacher-students and students-teachers, emancipation is possible. I conceive praxis

as the working of the space between theory with practice and practice with theory. There is no hierarchy and one does not come before the other.

2. Basso, an anthropologist who has done fieldwork among the Western Apache of Arizona for over thirty years, researches the meaning and significance of Apache place names. In working with the Apache people Basso shares the significance of places in the Apache culture and the conceptions of wisdom, manners and morals, and how history are intertwined with place.

3. I have included extracts of my creative writing to share the colour, texture and complexity of this socio-material embodied engagement.

4. A particular place that has specific and particular forms of human and non-human socio-material knowledges, performances and practices.

5. See <https://www.tarapage.org/placemaking>, last accessed 14 January 2020.

CHAPTER 1

Placemaking: The Australian Bush

In this chapter I am sharing the specific experiences-research-learnings, an assemblage if you will, of the entangled empirical and practice research of the socially, embodied and material ways of knowing and learning a specific place-world, the Australian bush. This chapter is an intra-action of the participants' and my own, as artist researcher teacher, placemaking practices, the intra-actions of experiential and embodied practices and outcomes. The aim of this research was to explore and examine specific embodied socio-material ways of knowing place and learn how place is made.

The making of this chapter has been very difficult because I needed to share the colour, texture, sounds, tastes, feelings and so on all of the stuff of placemaking, within the limitations of text. Consequently, I have attempted to layer and weave; entangling the participants and my own ways of knowing, making and learning. My intention is to share our placemaking practices and make something that is rich, complex, layered, intra-woven and three-dimensional. I hope that this may evoke a sense of place (albeit one that may be unfamiliar) rather than, as Feld and Basso assert, 'trying to describe a sense of place, or somehow attempting to characterize it' (1996: 90) that may involve Othering. In this chapter I have included images with the text, at the times at which my own learning intra-acts, becomes entangled with the children's-participants. This usually occurs when we are journeying together or in interviews; however, where the images are separated from the text, it signifies a journeying (both mine and the participants), a continuing progressive sequence where one image is entangled and leads to the next, to be read/viewed collectively, where the spaces between matter.

The beginnings of this research came in the guise of an apparently very simple question: 'So, where are you from?' This seems easy enough to answer, but this question that many ask, usually as small talk when you first meet someone, is difficult for me to answer, as I have lived in and consider myself to be from many different places. So for me, the answer is that all the many places I have lived are where I am from.

Not the simple answer that the questioner might be expecting, or even wanting. From the majority of my childhood spent in a small rural town in Australia, to teaching in remote Australia and in the Yukon in Canada, all of these place-worlds could be described in a very similar way; unending land, open skies, seeing from horizon to horizon and not many people; as my family would ask, 'Why is it always in the middle of nowhere?' But even though these places were similar they were not the same, and I learned so much from the people and the places. I was learning that 'place' is deeply connected and entwined with who and how we are. Consequently, *Placemaking: A New Materialist Theory of Pedagogy* comes from my praxic research and interest in understanding place and the significance of place to who we are and how we are; and so to explore and examine these questions of the entanglement of bodies and place, I needed to return to the place of my childhood. Not the exact place, but a similar place.

Place-world of the Bush

Where was I going to learn how we make place and who was I going to make place with? Having lived and worked in London for almost a decade this was the difficult part. I knew that I needed to research a place-world that had similarities with and could be described as remote and rural, and so Thirton, Queensland, was chosen.[1] I was able to access Thirton and its members with some negotiation through past familial connections and friendships; Thirton was also defined by the ABS (2015) and the state government education department, Education Queensland (2006), as remote/very remote.

At over 107,000 square kilometres (100,000 square miles), Queensland is the second largest state in Australia. Although this makes it six times the area of the United Kingdom, it has only one-fifteenth the population with only two persons per square kilometre (ABS 2016a). Most people live in the southern coastal area, leaving the rest of the state sparsely populated (Fig. 1.1). Queensland is promoted as the 'Sunshine State' and within its borders are the Great Barrier Reef, idyllic beaches, lush tropical rainforests and a harsh, arid interior.[2]

Inland Queensland is mainly agricultural, relying on beef and wool production, and is punctuated by areas of intense mining (ABS 2019). The sparse population of rural Queensland is concentrated in small towns and large ranches, locally known as 'stations' or 'properties'. Traditionally, these have been affluent and owned by generations of established families, with the small rural towns consisting of agricultural support, commercial

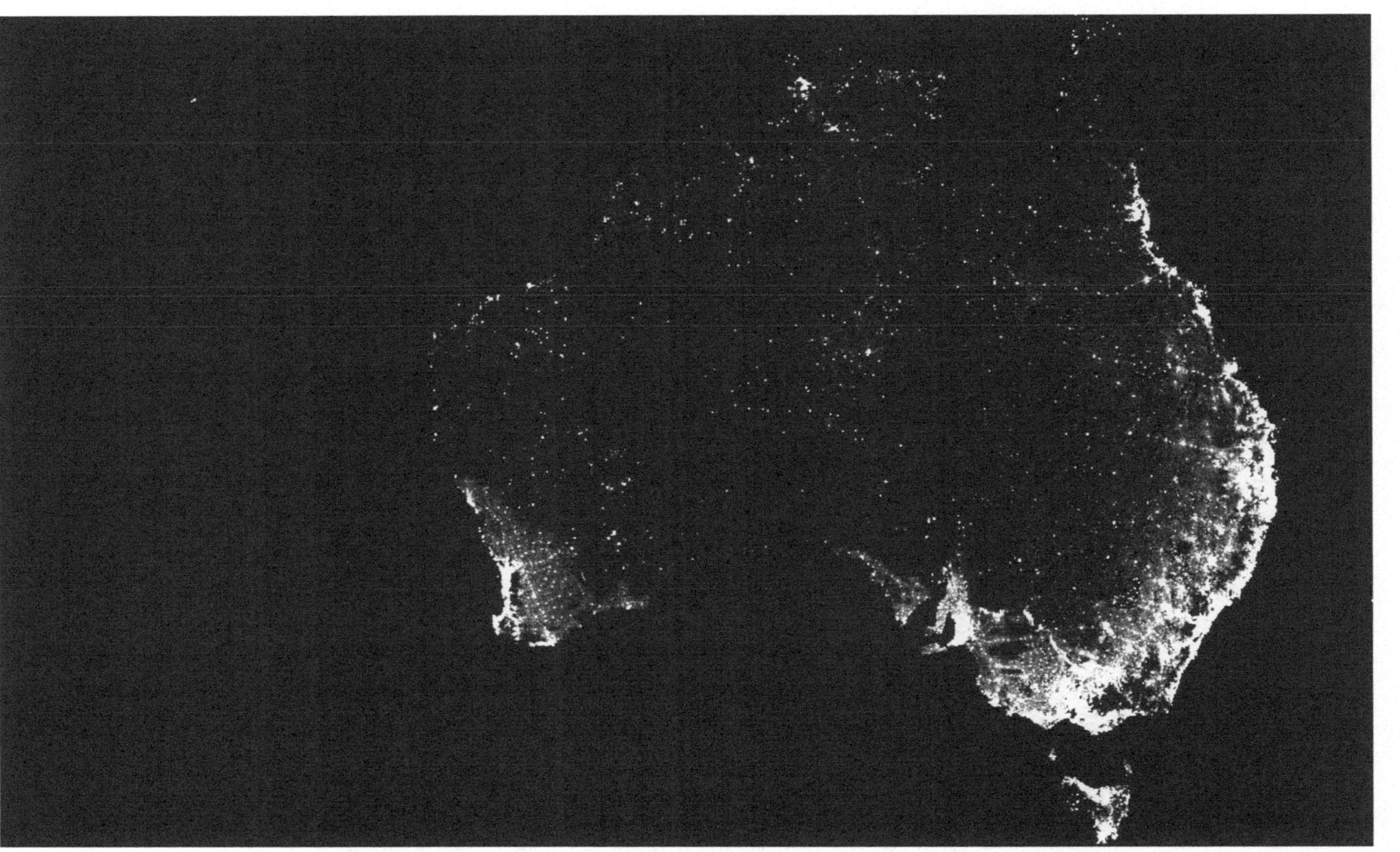

Figure 1.1 Australian Population Grid, 2011 (ABS 2011)

and transport industry workers and their families (ABS 2015). Consequently, the economies of these rural communities are very dependent on the health of the agricultural and mining industries (ABS 2019).

Public education in Queensland is offered and administered by a single, large, state government department, Education Queensland (ABS 2019). Although this large department is centralised in the state capital, Brisbane, school administration is being increasingly decentralised to become the responsibility of both the schools themselves and regional offices (Education Queensland 2003). Thirton, according to the ABS (2013b), is classified as 'very remote'. It is in the south-west of Queensland where the majority of communities are classified as 'remote' or 'very remote' (ABS 2010). This classification highlights the inaccessibility of the region, as distances between towns are considerable and access to services is limited. Additionally, Education Queensland uses a Transfer Rating Scheme to determine the relative weighting given to a school for the purpose of differentiating between applicants for teacher transfer (Education Queensland 2003). The ratings are used to compensate those who transfer to remote areas. Each school is allocated a series of points based on a range of factors (e.g., remoteness, level of community services, complexity of school environment, and so on). There are seven rating levels, with seven being the most remote. Thirton is rated as six. Education Queensland has also developed a new classification system for identifying state schools as rural and remote. This is based on the Ministerial Council on Education, Employment, Training and Youth Affairs Geographic Location Classification (Jones 2000), which drew on the work of the ARIA (see Chapter 2). Within this classification, Thirton is also considered to be very remote.

Thirton has a semi-arid climate with very hot summers and relatively warm, dry winters (ABS 2015). Temperatures commonly reach the low to mid-40s Celsius in summer, while minimum overnight temperatures below freezing are relatively common during winter (ABS 2015). Rainfall is highly seasonal and irregular, with most rain occurring during the summer (October–March), either as heavy thunderstorms or as tropical rain depressions (ABS 2015); rainfall is extremely variable. In 1974 Thirton received 16 inches of rain (400 mm) in a single night and in 2012 had barely 9 inches (225 mm) during the whole year (ABS 2016a). The only predictable conditions are during the August–September period when it is dry (ABS 2015).

This great variety in geographical conditions means that the industries in south-west Queensland also vary. Primary industries, including agriculture and mining, are the largest industry groups in the region. Livestock is the main agricultural industry, with very little vegetable and fruit grown in the area (ABS 2016a). According to ABS (2016a), south-west Queensland has a low population density. The largest town in the region, Paville,[3] has a population of 2,500, and the remainder of the population is widely dispersed, living in small towns, on agricultural properties or around the major mining sites (ABS 2016a). These towns vary dramatically in size, as do the services available to them (ABS 2016a).

Thirton and the surrounding area has a population of 292 (ABS 2016a). Thirton is around 700 kilometres west of Brisbane, and is a major wheat, wool-growing and meat cattle area (ABS 2016a). At the time of the 2006 census, 25 per cent of the population of Bamorrow,[4] the region in which Thirton is located, were aged under 14, with 16 per cent aged between 35 and 44 (ABS 2018). The age profile of Bamorrow differs to that of the Queensland population as a whole, as it has comparatively more children (aged 0–14 years), fewer persons in the younger working-age groups (aged 15–24 years), more in the middle working-age groups (aged 25–49 years) and fewer in the older age groups (over 50 years) (ABS 2018).

The Regional Plan of Bamorrow (DIP 2019) indicates that the issues confronting inhabitants of the region relate to labour supply shortages, due to young people leaving the region or moving to work in other industries. In Bamorrow there is a high proportion of Aboriginal and Torres Strait Islander people (10.3 per cent, 2,530 people), compared to the Queensland average (3.1 per cent) (DIP 2019). The majority of the Indigenous population identify themselves as Aboriginal (approximately 2,500 people) and very few people as Torres Strait Islanders (approximately 30 people) (DIP 2019). Aboriginal people in the region do not live in discrete communities managed by an Indigenous council, but instead inhabit the local government areas and towns (DIP 2019).

There is only one major rural activity centre in the region, Paville, with an approximate population of 2,500 (DIP 2019).[5] Thirton provides a limited range of services, with a single convenience store, a service station and a public bar (from my observations). Individual income levels are higher in Bamorrow; however, the family and household incomes are lower than the state averages (DIP 2019):

- median weekly individual income was $401 in 2001 (Qld average $460)
- median weekly family income was $838 in 2001 (Qld average $871)
- median weekly household income was $688 (Qld average $736).

A total of 28 per cent of the local population were Labourers and Related Workers and 15 per cent were Intermediate Clerical, Sales and Service Workers (ABS 2010b). In Bamorrow, whether Indigenous or non-Indigenous, a higher proportion of people live in disadvantaged circumstances compared to the population of Queensland as a whole. Thirton has a single state primary school catering for students from transition (age 4) to Year 7 (age 12). The closest neighbouring school is in Paville (pre-school–Year 12, P-12, the last year of secondary school), which is approximately 100 kilometres north (Thirton 2019a).

Over half of all state schools in Queensland are classified as remote/very remote (ABS 2013a). As of February 2006 there were 121,520 students enrolled in state schools in remote/very remote Queensland, accounting for 24.8 per cent of the total student population (Education Queensland 2006: iv). In the south-west region of Queensland over 82 per cent of schools are classified as remote/very remote (Education Queensland 2006: v). Thirton State School is described as:

> a small primary school with 30–40 students depending on seasonal employment opportunities. There is a stable population of approximately 30 students. The students of Thirton State School come from varied socio-economic backgrounds and cultures. There are a small number of Aboriginal and Torres Strait Islander students, predominantly from the lands of the Kamilaroi people. Thirton State School operates on a budget made up of local and Government grants with an active Parents and Citizens Association who annually donate for equipment and resources. (Education Queensland 2006: 55)

The teaching staff consists of a teaching principal and one part-time and one full-time teacher. The classes have a mix of age groups in the one classroom. The support staff consists of five teaching assistants, three full-time and two part-time. There is also a part-time administrator (Education Queensland 2006).

The school is located on the main thoroughfare of Thirton and has large grounds with stairs leading to two elevated classrooms. Under the classrooms are the school office, storage, water taps/troughs, refrigerators and covered recreational areas. The refrigerators are provided for pupils' packed lunches from home (as there are limited catering facilities on site), and are necessary due to the year-long high ambient temperatures (Thirton State School 2019a; 2019b). Within the grounds of the school there are two uncovered tennis/netball courts, a large, shadecloth-covered play/sandpit area and a very large, open grassed field bordered by eucalyptus trees. The teaching principal's residence is located within the grounds of the school.[6]

The academic year in Queensland begins at the end of January and ends in early December. The structure of the school year consists of four terms and two semesters per year. The average length of a term is 10–12 weeks, separated by a ten-day/two-week holiday, with the summer/Christmas holidays being six weeks long (Education Queensland 2008). At Thirton State School, the school day in terms 2 and 3 (the cooler and darker months) begins at 9 a.m., with a short break from 11–11.20 a.m. and a longer break from 1–1.45 p.m., finishing at 3 p.m. During terms 1 and 4 (the warmer months) the school day begins at 8.30 a.m. with a longer break from 10.45–11.30 a.m. and a shorter break from 12.45–1.05 p.m., finishing at 2.30 p.m. (Thirton State School 2019b). The rationale for the altered beginning and break times is that in the warmer months pupils begin the school day and have a longer break during the cooler part of the day (Thirton State School 2019b), consequently spending less time in the sun and heat.

The participants of this study included 15 pre-school–Year 7 pupils, aged 3–12 years, their parents, and teaching and support staff at Thirton State School.[7]

Abentures

Initially I had a very specific idea of what I was researching and how I was going to collect the 'data'; easy, or so I thought. One of the many things I have learned in doing/making research is that things change, a lot of things change. The assumptions and expectations you have can be completely blown out of the water. Obviously it is not always as dramatic or drastic as this, but we do need to be open to how we can research with others, bodily and materially. Probably the biggest change-transformation (after Freire and hooks) is you, the researcher; this is because you are continually learning, and so you need to be open, flexible and responsive to all the many experiences and ways that you can research, make and learn.

> Bloody hell, ten long hours of just driving and driving, more road, more red dirt, no cars and an occasional whiff of dead animal. But I'm here now, not too sure where here is but there you go. I followed the directions . . . just a turned off the main road and then turned left again trundling down a dirt track . . . definitely not a road. After a very long ten hours of driving, I had arrived. The children, Jenny aged 6, Henry aged 4 and Hettie, 2, were waiting for me at their house gate; they seemed very apprehensive and quiet when I arrived. Who was this person who had travelled all this way, from England and 'Mummy why does she talk funny?' Their parents explained to them that I lived in London, England, that I sounded funny because I have an English accent, that I would be

staying with them and that I was going to teach and do art with them at their school.

The first morning and I can see the red orange intensity of the sun slowly rising, with its colour blasted across the sky. Slowly a clear blue sky appears as the saturated colour dissipates and the sun rises further above the horizon. There are no clouds and the trees and shearing shed are glowing, as though they are going to explode into flames. It all looks idyllic, just like the tourist images that you see in magazines and newspapers, this is the 'the outback' come have a holiday.

These images and their associations make no difference to the temperature. It is freezing. I have two duvets/doonas and a quilt and am hunkered down, cocooned in wool, cotton and feathers. These old Queenslander[8] houses are absolutely freezing: no insulation, bare floorboards, and corrugated iron roofs. Tendrils of breath were snaking below my nose. I dare not say anything (and I mean moan about the cold) as it has been stated, several times, 'You come from London, you must be used to the cold'. Oh how I love central heating, because walking around inside with two woollen hats and thermal underwear is just not right. (Personal written and audio notes)

The unexpected ways that opened up for me during this research included 'doing jobs' and 'abentures'.

The children are up at 7 a.m. and after brekky (breakfast) it has been decided that I am going with them. At the kitchen table Jenny tells me 'We're gotta do jobs', with Henry nodding beside her, 'C'mon, we've got jobs to do and you can come with us.'[9] The children are really friendly with me and very confident, very different to the shyness and apprehension I saw the day before. Within this place-world the children have certain roles and responsibilities in terms of the daily running and maintenance of the properties they live on, their homes. The jobs that these children perform are part of their everyday life. This 'doing jobs' was not in my plan and I did not think much about it. However, I did decide that it would give me a chance to get to know the children and I thought that this would lead to a shared experience that might 'lead to a very particular closeness and bond' (Lee and Ingold 2006: 69), and the children would also get to know and learn about me. At this stage I thought this would be fairly inconsequential, no big deal. But it was this, on the surface, very simple idea of walking with the children that blew all my assumptions and expectations out of the water. Because what happened was that through the children's inclusion of me in the everyday, socio-material, embodied practices of their place-world I learned how they make and learn place, but I also learned how and why I needed to make place.

Henry and Hettie bolt out of the door, Jenny grabs the camera and follows Henry and Hettie.[10] 'See ya, Mum', is yelled in unison. I quickly get up from the kitchen table, grab my shoes at the back door and try to catch up with them.

'Where are we going?', I yell and Jenny yells back, 'Over to the shearing shed.'

Hettie and Henry have taken off ahead. The distance between the house and the fence surrounding the house is three metres and the area is sparsely grassed, as bore water is used to water this lonely green element in a largely monochromatic red landscape.[11] The earth in this part of Australia is very distinctive, a deep rust red with a very fine texture, like talcum powder. Advertising and tourist information usually describes this part of the world as the Red Centre. This fine dust clearly gets everywhere and is on everything, so that not only is the ground red with occasional spindly straw-coloured tufts of long grass, but so too are the buildings, trees and anything else that stands in the way of this colloquially named 'bull dust'.[12]

Jenny is walking slowly, moving the camera around, taking photos consistently and looking at the large screen on the back. But to me it appears that this is random; Jenny is not really considering the content of the images. I ask her, 'What are you taking photos of?'

'My stuff, where I live.'

'Why do you take photos?'

'So I can remember stuff.'

'Like what?'

'When I go to Grandmas and Poppy's I can remember the dogs and all the stuff, the way it looks, and I can then remember how everything feels, you know my place.'

Here I made the assumption that Jenny was 'taking' photographs randomly, without much consideration; but she was deliberately 'making'[13] the images, while doing 'her jobs', for a purpose. From this experience with Jenny and her brother and sister talking about memories and her place, I started to critically reflect on my own memories of the places of my childhood. The cold, tickling the hairs inside my nose, the stillness with the heavy weight of all the layers of wool on my body and the fog slowly clearing, bringing with it a clarity of every sound (Page 2002: 1). These memories are my embodied ways of knowing, and just like Jenny's, they make the places of our childhood and are our placemaking practices.

Jenny then stopped talking and was very quiet. The hot wind was whipping at my face and arms, and as we neared the shearing shed I could hear Henry and Hettie chatting about the sheep. The shed is about 250 metres from the house and is about the size of four typical English single-storey houses. It is raised from the ground on two-metre high wooden stumps, 'because when the rains come the waters can get pretty high'. The shed looks as though it is about to fall down. The wood is weathered and worn, you can feel the knots and grooves of the grain – no polished or smooth surfaces here. The large nails are the same colour as the earth, but this is rust. As we get closer to the shed I can smell the acrid aroma of sheep shit, but I do not see any lying outside the shed or even in it. As I enter the dark yet pleasingly cool interior, there is a mingle-mangle of smells; of sheep shit, musky sweat (from the shearers) and greasy lanolin (from the wool of the sheep). Harry is moving about the shed explaining and performing the process and practices of shearing.

'We shear the sheep because they need to be sheared. We take the wool off 'em or they will probably get flyblown. They get flyblown when there are flies around their bums and stuff especially when they are really woolly. Then there is where we put 'em after they've been shorn. Bruce does the shearin', he's our shearer.'

Jenny interrupts Henry. 'You know stuff too.'

'Sorry?'

'Well, with the photos you think you know stuff, like what the dogs look like and that but then it changes, you see it different and so you just know it different. You know, all this stuff here, my place.'

Through this conversation Jenny explained that the making of the photographs enabled a deeper knowledge and understanding of 'my place' that went beyond perception, or the photographs as an observational and objectifying product

As I continued to follow Jenny, Henry and Hettie as they went about doing their jobs, they explained to me what they were doing and why it was important. During this time Jenny continued to make photographs and direct and help Henry and Hettie 'doing their jobs'; these included feeding the dogs, putting food and water in the troughs. I listened, occasionally questioned, observed and actively engaged in their practices as they moved through and intra-acted with their socio-material place-world. In other words I offered to help, and Hettie was very keen to direct me, tell what I needed to do and correct me when I was doing it wrong.

Back at the house, after their jobs were done, I asked Jenny if I could look at her photographs. Jenny's photographs were of toys lying outside in the garden, her house, the vegetable garden, the shearing shed, the bore drain, sheep, Henry and Hettie, myself and the surrounding landscape. However, there were also was a lot of photographs of the ground, a lot (Figs 1.2–1.9).[14] I continued go through all of Jenny's photographs, with images of the ground again and again and again;

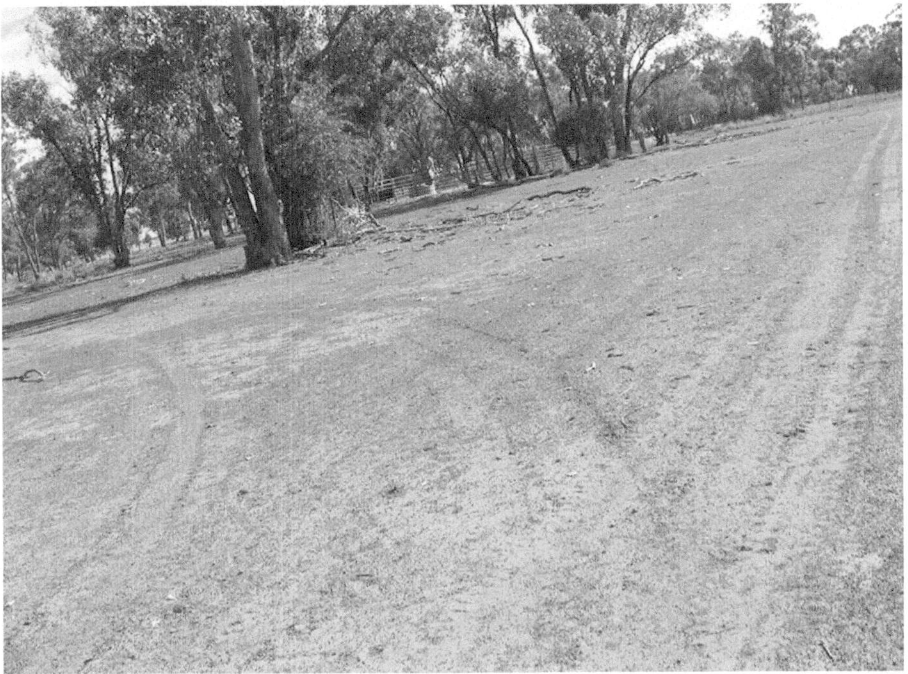

Figure 1.2 Doin' jobs, series, image 1. © Tara Page

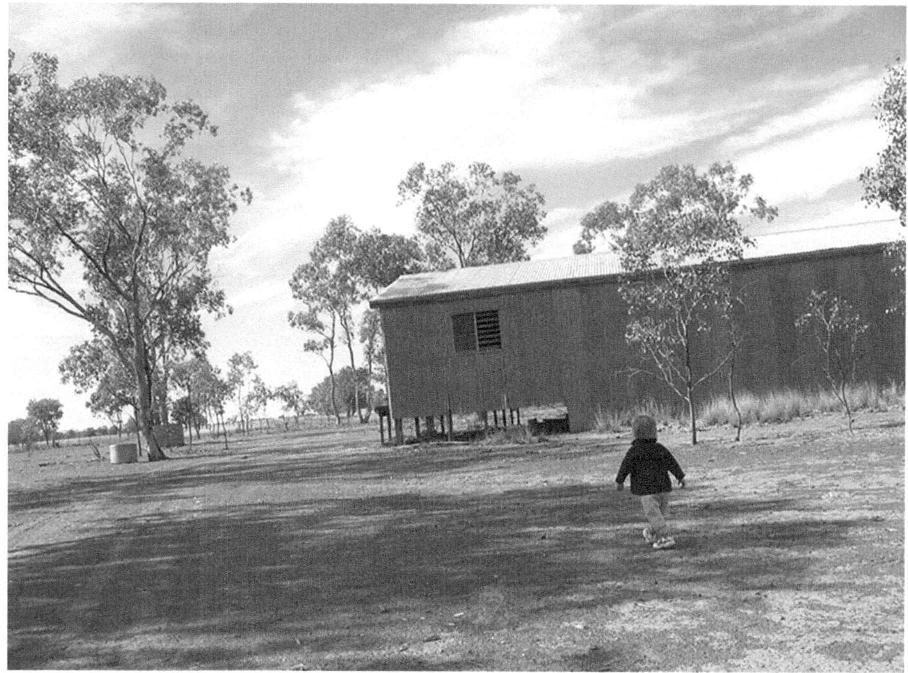

Figure 1.3 Doin' jobs, series, image 2. © Tara Page

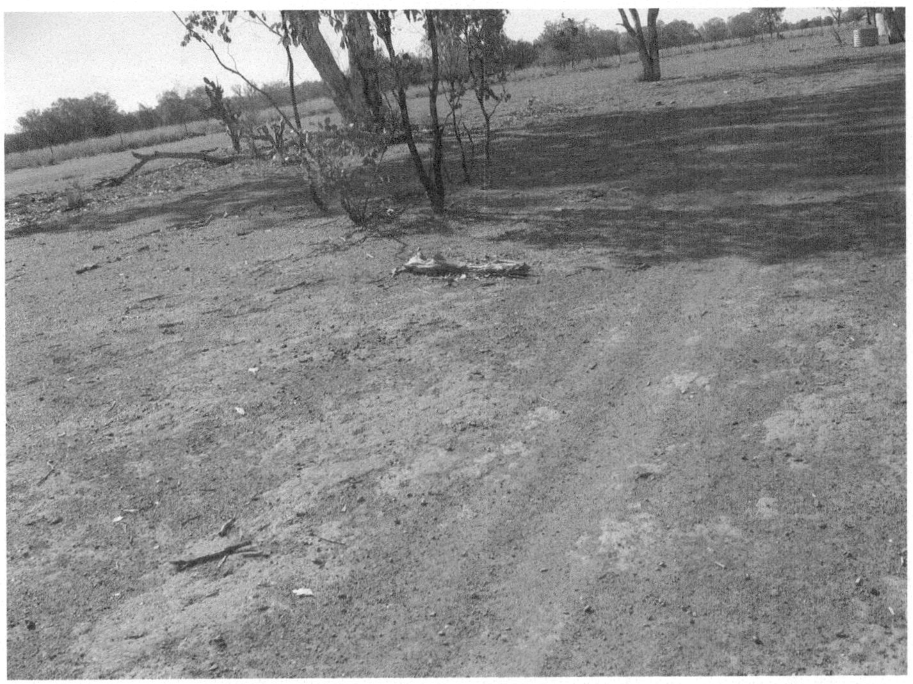

Figure 1.4 Doin' jobs, series, image 3. © Tara Page

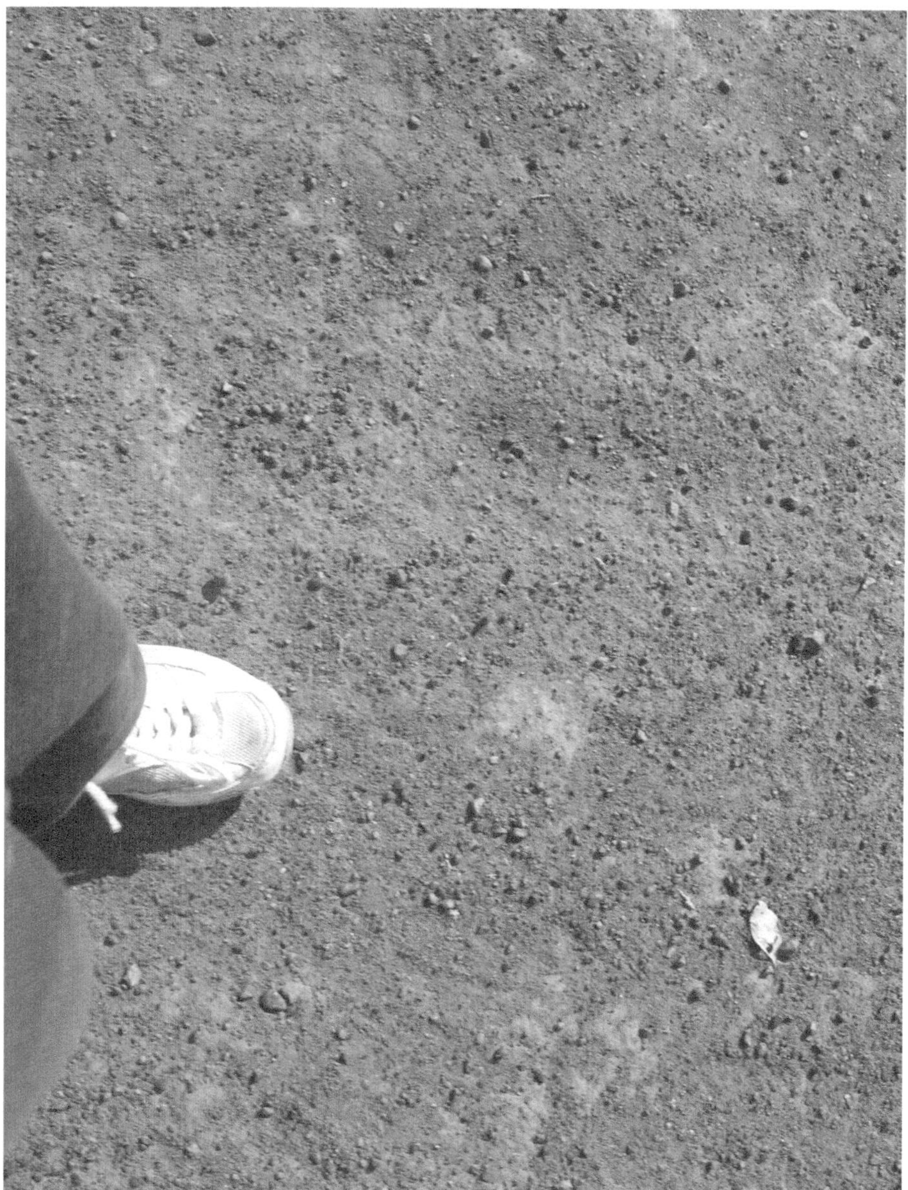

Figure 1.5 Doin' jobs, series, image 4. © Tara Page

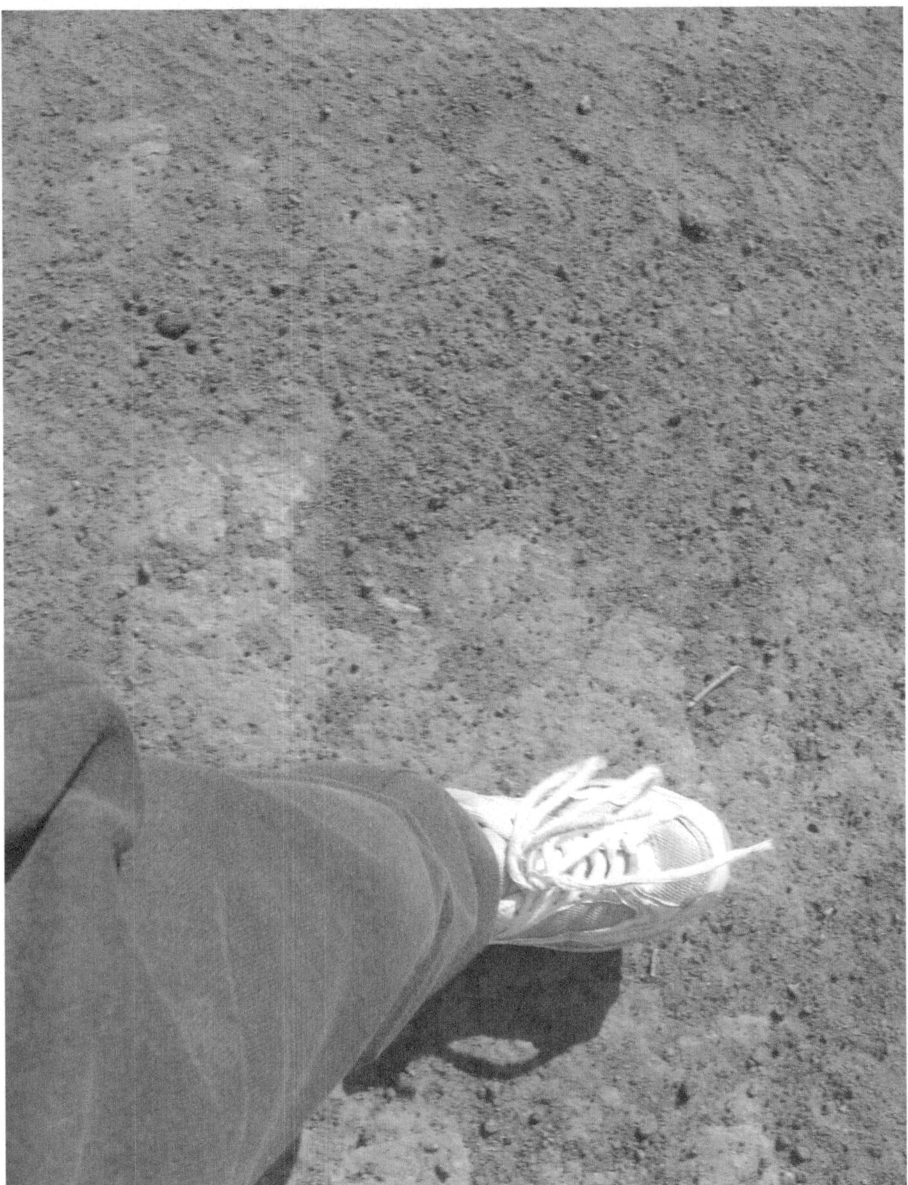

Figure 1.6 Doin' jobs, series, image 5. © Tara Page

Figure 1.7 Doin' jobs, series, image 6. © Tara Page

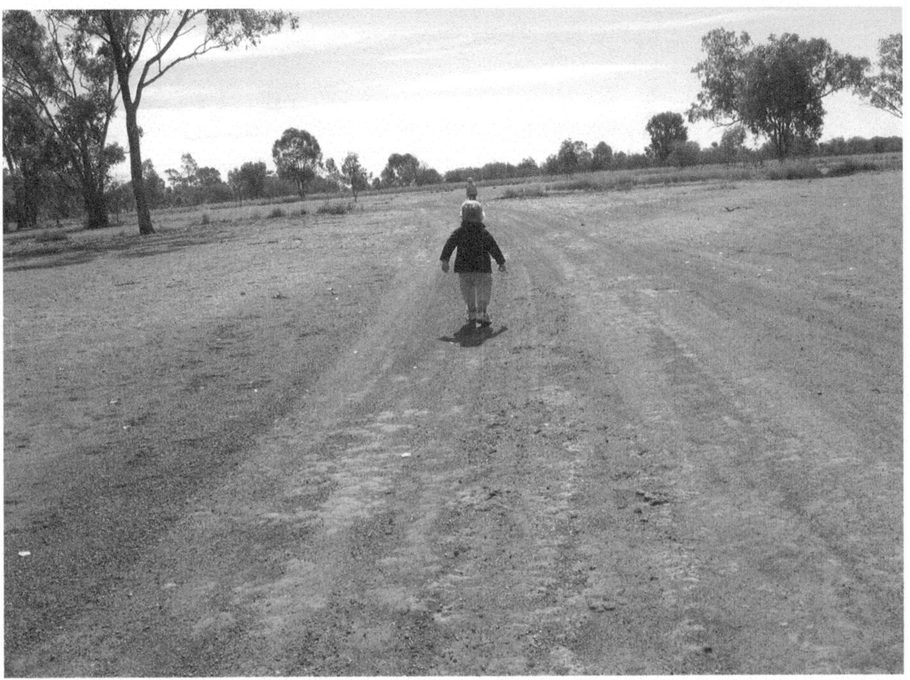

Figure 1.8 Doin' jobs, series, image 7. © Tara Page

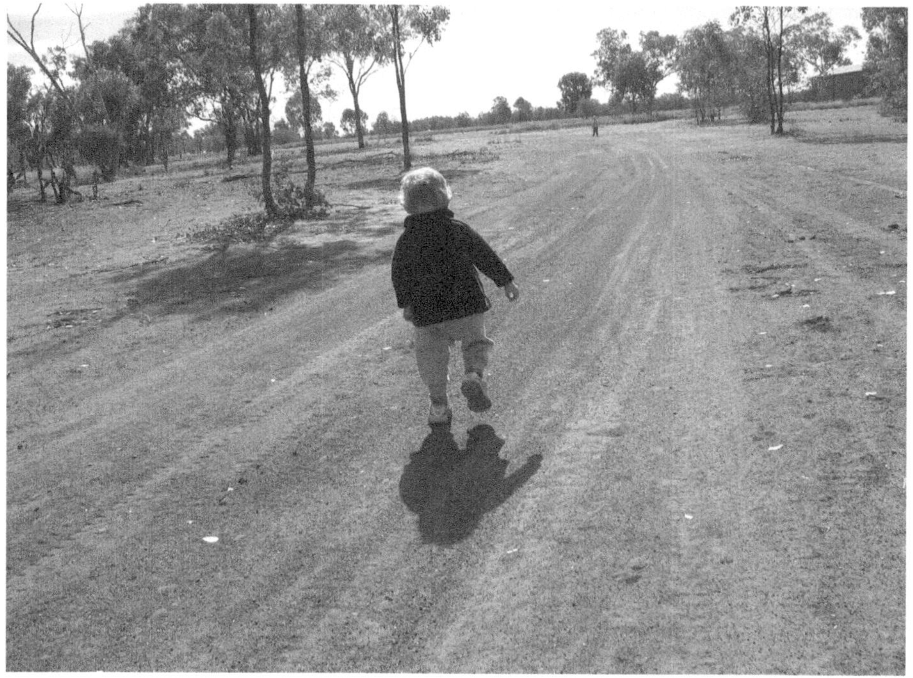

Figure 1.9 Doin' jobs, series, image 8. © Tara Page

red dirt, lumpy red dirt, wet, muddy red dirt, a few leaves with red dirt and so on. I thought that Jenny had accidentally made these photos due to lack of concentration or knowledge of how to use the camera. I asked Jenny why she took so many photographs of the ground. With a withering look and distinct irritation and disdain I was told quite sternly: 'They're not of the ground, they're of tracks.'

Jenny stomped over to me and with a sigh of embodied impatience started to explain: 'Look . . . see, this one's Dad's motorbike, see he is going to the shed. This's Horny [the name of the Merino ram], this's Dad's truck, this is a roo [kangaroo] see . . . Do you see?' Jenny continued to explain to me the specifics of the photographs of the ground, intently telling me what they were. She began to share with me the stories about the tracks. These were narratives, narratives of the between; the bodies that made the tracks with the material of the dirt, the land. I was being taught what the material, the dirt, the markings of the land meant: 'You can know all about them from their tracks. See, you can now know about our place.'

The next morning I wake up freezing cold again; the tip of my nose is cold and wet like a puppy's and I am buzzing from the complete and utter overload, mind, body, spirit, of the previous day. My expectations, my assumptions, my plan of the what and how of my research have all been thrown up in the air. But I know that there is something going on and I just need to relax, not overthink and just go with it and see what happens. As I walk into the kitchen, there is a lot of activity, with Jenny, Henry and Hettie sitting on the kitchen floor with their school backpacks. They are packing water bottles and asking their mother for snacks. I ask what's going on and Henry tells me, 'We're going on an abenture [*sic*], we're going to take you to the red dam.'[15] I assumed that this 'abenture' would be like doing the jobs that we had done the previous day; a short walk, within sight of the house, with some structured activity or purpose. Well it was not. We were gone for over four hours; hence the need for food and water.

The children have their backpacks and hats and insist that I wear a hat too: 'Can't go outside without one.' As we walk Henry and Jenny continue to tell me stories about the events of their place. This was usually triggered by something in the landscape, and Jenny continues to make photographs and films: 'That was where Dad bulldozed, he had to bulldoze all those trees all the way along for the new fence, see . . . you can see it there [indicating the tracks in the ground] it was really muddy and wet. That's why the tracks are so deep and hard.'

'You know you can smell when it's going to rain.'

'Yeah everythin' starts to feel different, everything the air, noises, it's like really heavy.'

'Yeah you can smell it and then feel it and then you can see the real grey clouds comin' in.'

As the children are talking, continuing to explain and teach me about their place, I am concentrating and listening to them. I am watching where they are pointing and how they are intra-acting and communicating their deeply embodied understanding of the land and how fascinating it is. I am entranced by this intra-action between their bodies and the materials of the air, the weather. I then realise that we have been walking for half an hour and I have been so intent on listening and asking questions and trying to understand that I have not been paying attention to where we are going or what direction we have been walking in. I quickly look around and can see nothing: 360 degrees and there is no sign of people or habitation, just a few tall, imposing gum trees in the distance, silvery grey scrubby bushes/grass, red dirt and us – that's it. The wind is blowing hot on my face and I start to feel slightly wobbly. I think to myself, 'Where the hell am I?' and 'What the hell am I doing in this place that feels familiar but doesn't and with three small kids I hardly know?'

The only noise is the children chatting and the barbed wire fence singing as it vibrates in the wind. The air is dry and feels brittle as it heightens every sound and sight and makes the inside of my nose tingle. I smell the soothing, reassuring smell of eucalyptus, mingled with dust and the occasional familiar stink of a dead animal somewhere in the distance. It creeps up on me slowly, but I start to have this feeling, and it is growing, of being totally overwhelmed: there is just so much but at the same time there is nothing. There is bush and scrub and long spindly grasses and the blue, blue sky that goes on forever. The land is flat so you can see from horizon line to horizon line and in between is blue, just blue, blue sky. This blue changes hue and is occasionally interrupted by clouds, but the majority of the time it is just this blanket above you, for miles and miles, all-surrounding and vast. According to John, the children's father, their place is small; 'Out here some would call it a hobby farm, too small to make a decent living out of, but I reckon it's a start . . . it takes about two hours to drive around the fenceline [the boundary of the property]. We've got a couple of dams, a lot of dirt, trees, 1,000 head of sheep, 100 head of cattle and those large bushes, they're our weeds.' It is all so much, but also nothing. I start to feel a sense of loss in this place. It is not a feeling of being lost, but a loss or release of everything that you hold on to so tightly. Because in this place all of that stuff does not matter, it is you and the land and nothing else. Jenny, Henry and Hettie continue to chat, self-assured and confident, still walking, leading me along without any regard for the lack of adults, habitation, or my feelings of anxiety: 'C'mon we're almost there, can't you hear 'em?'

As we near the red dam we disturb a mob of kangaroos; they all bound off together in the same direction, like overgrown mice. I tried to film them but they were too fast. 'Bloody pests', Jenny chimes in as we lose sight of them. 'Eat all the grass, break fences they do. Not good for the sheep, Dad's got a licence to shoot 'em too.'

'Dad skins them, and we use them for rugs in the house, we gave one to Grandma and Poppy as a Christmas present, Grandma calls it Skippy.'[16]

As we open the gate to the 'red paddock' which houses the 'red dam', we hear a high-pitched bleating and the children run over to a sheep that is lying on the ground. 'Have to tell Dad about this one.' I ask what's wrong with it. 'Pregnant probably, . . . that's why it can't get up, too big. Dad'll pick her up in the back of the truck and put her in the yards, you know back at the house.' The children and I settle down on a large dirt mound on the edge of the red dam. It is literally red; red dirt surrounds rust-red water. Cattle have gathered on the far side about 50 metres away, and they are startled by our presence and increase the volume of their lowing. Jenny warns me, 'We don't want to spook them too much – they can charge at you if you aren't careful.' The cattle in this place-world of Australia have always intrigued me. These are not your lovable, benign-looking, long-lashed Jerseys or Friesians, the ones that wander about on lush, grassy, rolling hills in temperate climes. These are predominantly scrawny, see-their-ribs, long-pointed horns, aggressive with camel-like humps on the tops of their necks cattle, made for this place-world, little-to-no-grass, hot and dry.

As the cattle get used to us the lowing decreases; the children are quiet, I assume tired from the 90-minute walk, as they tuck into their packed snacks. I breathe in the light warm air and reflect on my experiences of this place so far and the things and the ways the children have taught me. They have shared with me a deep knowledge and understanding of their place and their everyday practices (Figs 1.10–1.14). They have taught me the very close and complex relationship they have with their socio-material world. Interestingly, as I reflect on this relationship and how the children, in a very short period of time, have been sharing stories, events, experiences and their ways of knowing, learning and making place, I start to feel more comfortable and at ease. I begin to relax; I know this, I have learned this before. I start to feel less alien and alienated and for the first time start to feel truly comfortable.

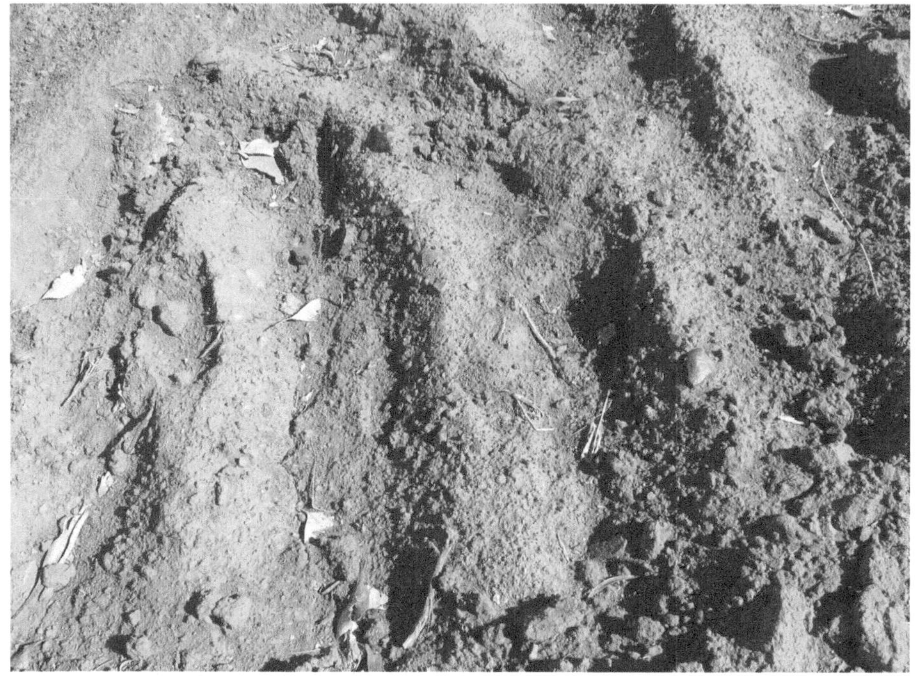

Figure 1.10 An abenture, image 1. © Tara Page

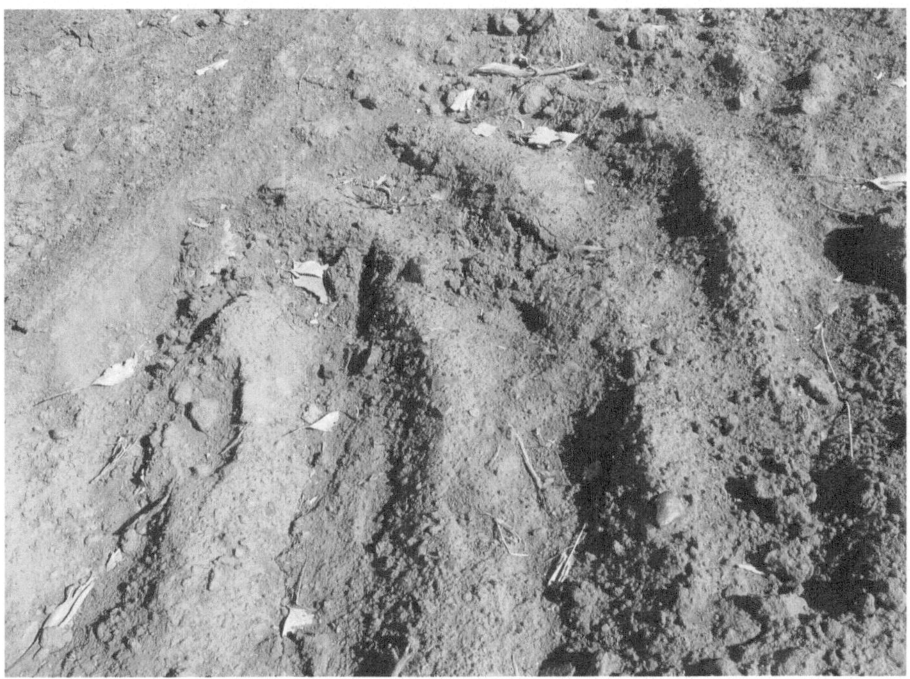

Figure 1.11 An abenture, image 2. © Tara Page

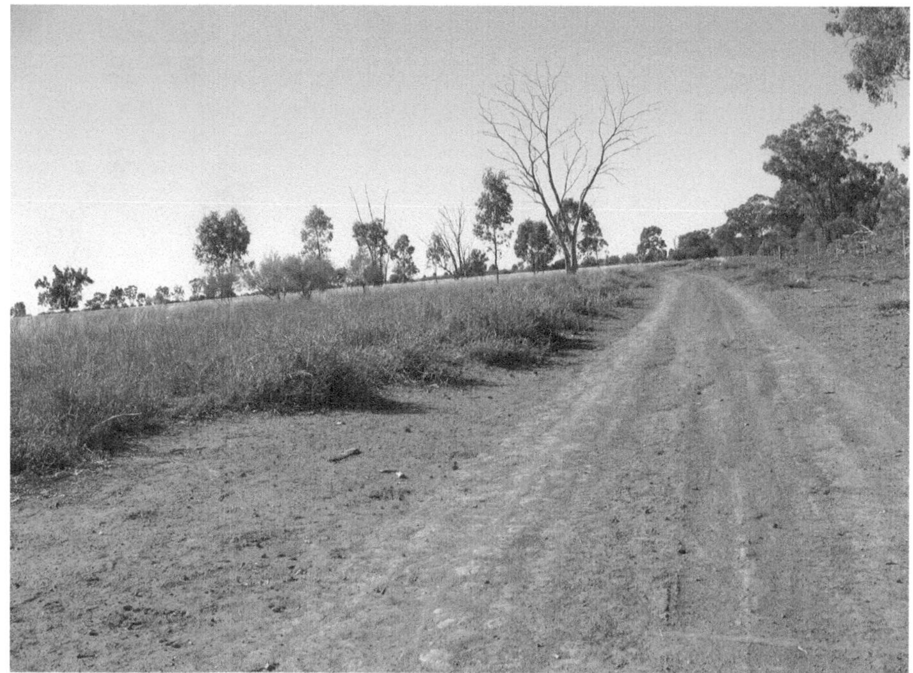

Figure 1.12 An abenture, image 3. © Tara Page

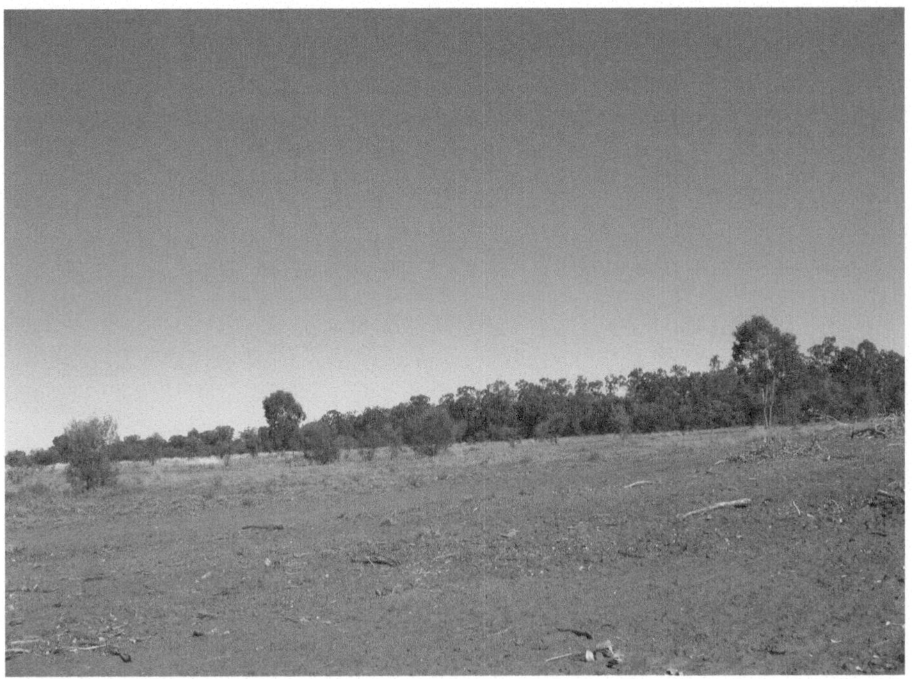

Figure 1.13 An abenture, image 4. © Tara Page

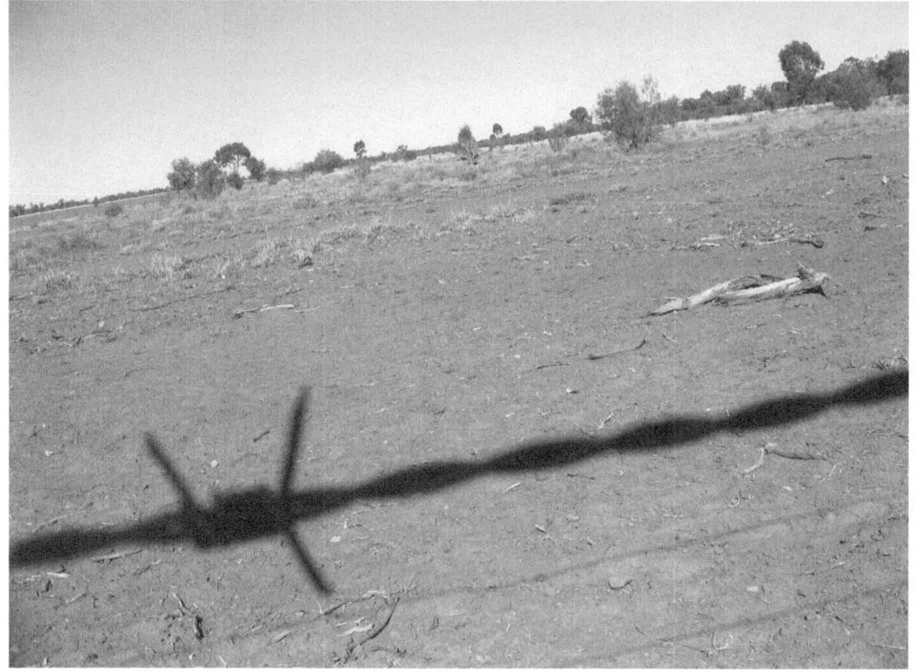

Figure 1.14 An abenture, image 5. © Tara Page

Jenny, Henry and Hettie, all under six years old, performed their jobs and I was the only adult with them. They did not defer to me or ask for permission. They were my teachers, demonstrating and explaining what happens and how things work in their place, sharing their embodied socio-material ways of placemaking with me, the learner. Through doing jobs and going on an 'abenture' together the children shared and taught me their ways of knowing and how they make place. They shared their intra-actions of bodies with matter, and this teaching enabled me to learn from and also participate in their practices, those that shape and define how they know, understand and ultimately make place. As Jenny explained, 'C'mon you can do this too . . . it's important you know . . . you gotta know it too.' Together, Jenny, Henry, Hettie and I made, remade and learned place through the coming together, or the intra-actions of the social with the material and the bodily.

Journeying

The journey to this place-world was very long, both in distance and time. However, it gave me the opportunity to think and critically reflect not only on this research assemblage but also about myself, and what I am doing, and also why I am doing it. A long time driving a car with no radio reception[17] will do that, and there are only so many times you can listen to Madonna's *Immaculate Collection* on CD (Figs 1.15–1.21). But in this place-world, because of the very long distances involved, you have to travel, by car and so on, sometimes for many hours, to get access to what in urban place-worlds is taken for granted. The practices of these journeys make place but also enable learning and so I have collectively called these practices 'journeying'.[18]

I thought that not having driven in three years I would hate it but I am really enjoying the drive to and from school each day. It is about 40 minutes, by car, and it is all dirt, red dirt road and probably only a car and half wide. So, because I haven't driven on dirt roads in a long time, I drive really slowly and always get over one side of the road if another car is coming the other way – very, very rarely will there be another car. You can't follow anyone too closely as you cannot see anything as there is just dust and rocks flying up everywhere. I never really understood the term bull dust. I get the dust bit, but it is more like a fine powder that is impenetrable but that can get everywhere; up your nose, in your ears and that dry caking film in your mouth.

In the mornings I am really careful because of the 'roos; as they are constantly jumping out in front of the car as they bound across the road. Hit one or is it that they hit you and it really damages the car, maybe the roo too, those

As the landscape changed from lush, green, wet, dense with a heavy perfume of frangipanis and wet earth to brittle, dry, brownie red, with nose twitching eucalyptus with a hint of dust I started to get a bit upset crying; remembering what it was like living in this space and how very quickly it became home and my place.

Yet somehow it still is home and my place. It is who I was and now being within this again I am realising it is still who I am. But how has it made me?

Maybe because where I am now is so totally different or that the rural and remote space is totally different and that is what it does to you, you are different, connected, linked, entangled.

All the bared stripped down bones of it all. There are no distractions, not a lot of people, no cacophony of competing noises.

There is a lot of sky, a lot of space and not much in and around you, just you, very, very still. Nothing to lean on, depend on or become dependent on. It is stripped of all the stuff, no grey out here, a lot of back and white..... live or leave.

Figure 1.15 A journey, series, image 1. © Tara Page

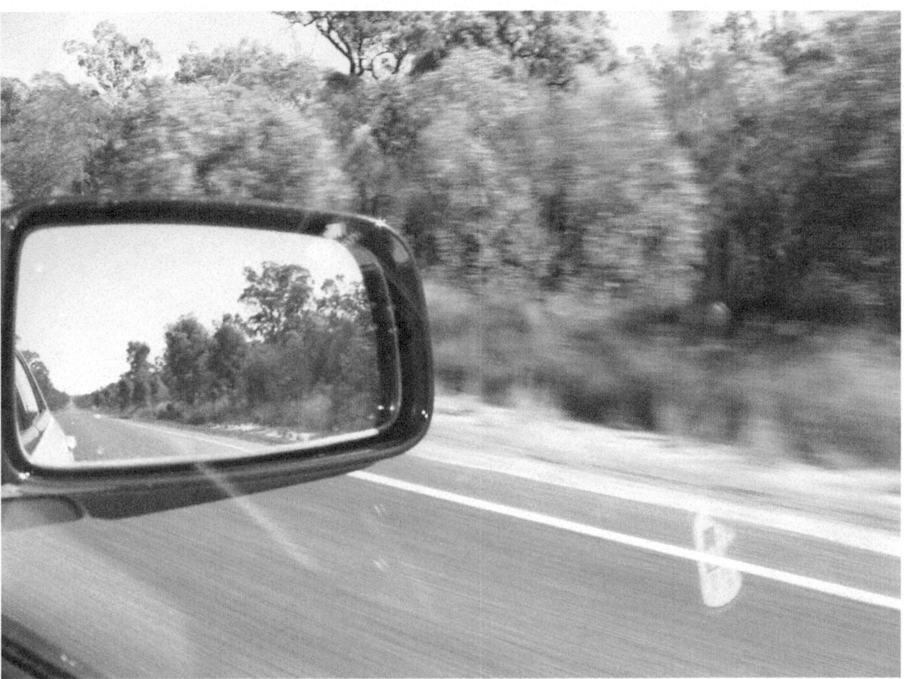

Figure 1.16 A journey, series, image 2. © Tara Page

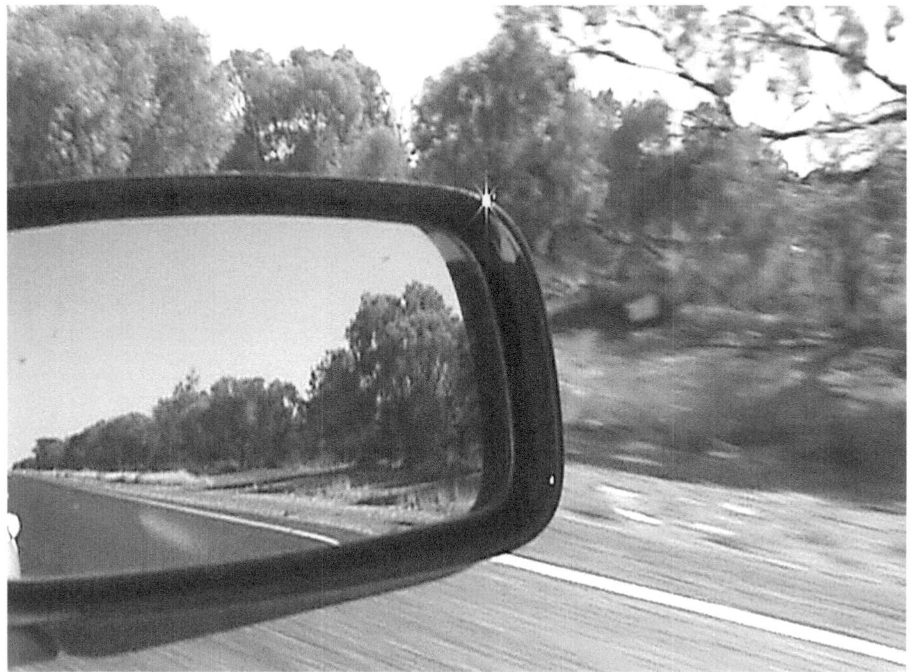

Figure 1.17 A journey, series, image 3. © Tara Page

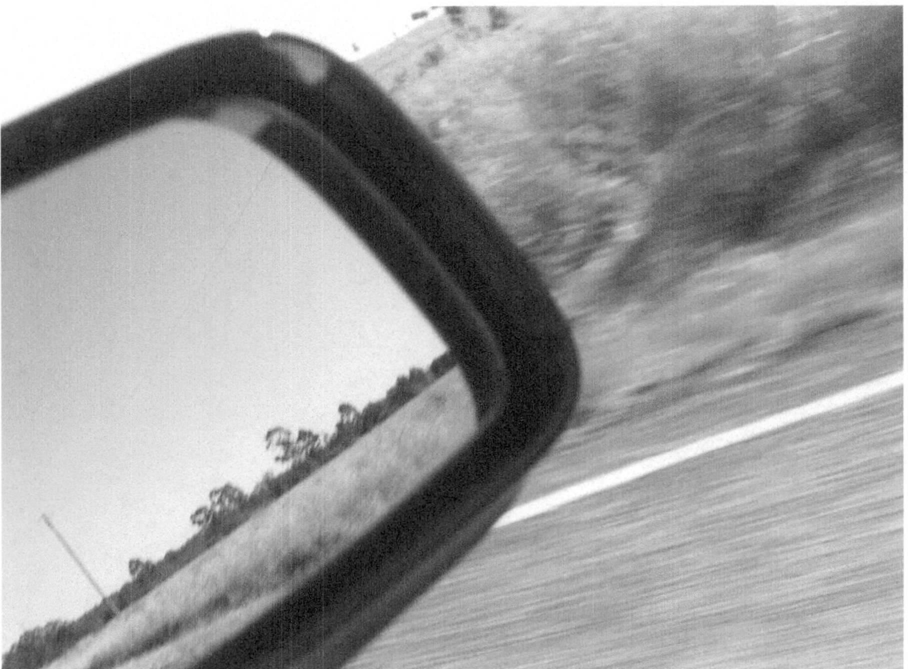

Figure 1.18 A journey, series, image 4. © Tara Page

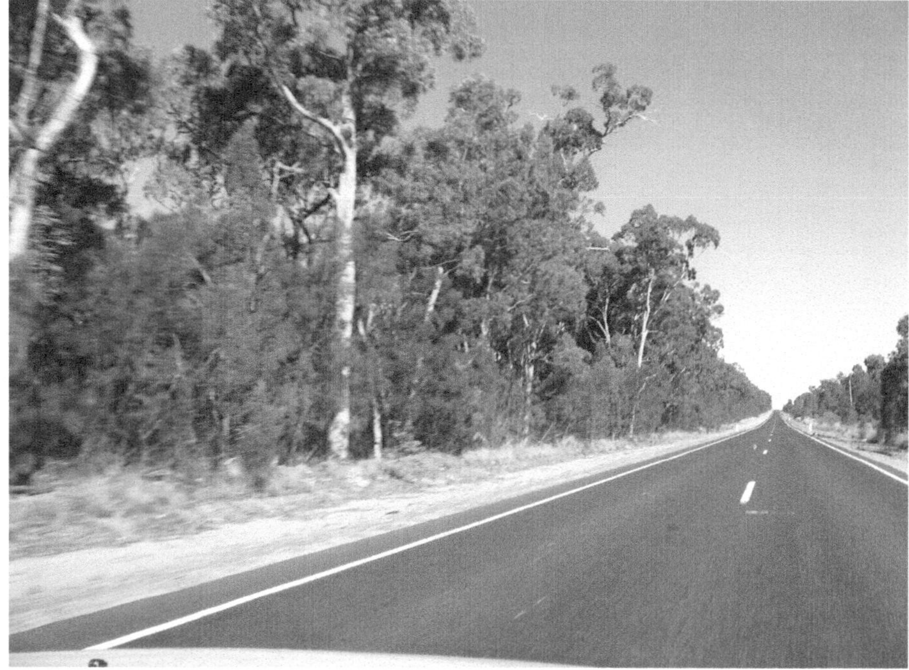

Figure 1.19 A journey, series, image 5. © Tara Page

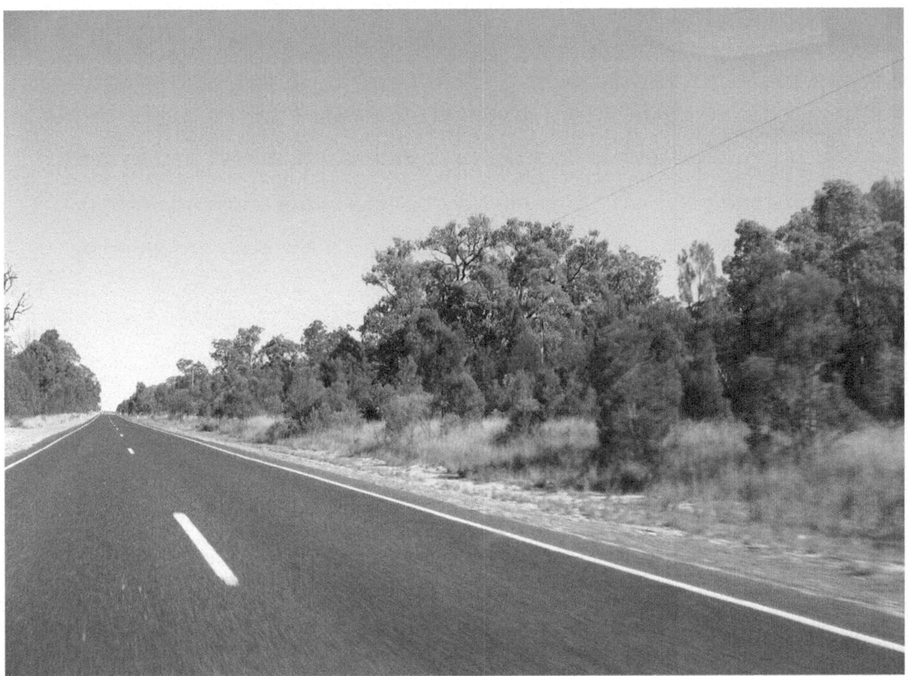

Figure 1.20 A journey, series, image 6. © Tara Page

....OK, Toto we are not in Kansas anymore. What am I doing? And where the hell am I? This feels sort of the same and sort of what I remember, but it is also not the same and not what I imagined or thought. How am I going to do this?

Figure 1.21 A journey, series, image 7. © Tara Page

dead animal smells have to come from something. John was very kind carefully explaining to me the dos and don't of driving, swerving, sudden steering wheel movements is not an option. As you can lose control of the car and go off the road and possibly roll the car. Ah . . . the very intra-actions of bodies and materials; machine and woman, machine and land.

So, the mornings it's kangaroos and the afternoons it is all about emus. They are bloody big awkward birds and cause even more damage than a roo . . . or so I am told. But my experiences of a mob of kangaroos and a flock of emus . . . I will take the roos any day.

The sides of the road are lined with gum trees (eucalyptus). Some of the paddocks are full of long weedy grass and spindly trees, and then there are the ones that have been cleared for growing cotton. It is not a pretty, idyllic landscape but the vastness of nothing and blue sky makes it something. So much has been written about the skies out here, prose, poetry, songs. So, everything I write and say about them has been said or just sounds trite and clichéd. But, there is a whole lot of it out here and it all does overwhelm and is in direct contrast to the landscape, so I suppose that is why it dominates everything I am thinking and feeling. (Personal notes/audio)

I had not really paid attention to the practices of journey/journeying before. Nor had I thought about the significance of what I was doing and why I was doing it. This is probably because I grew up in a very similar place-world, and travelling long distances is just one of those things that you do, that you have to do. This is because of the distances between where you are and where everyone and everything else is; services and facilities you need to access, dentists, doctors, chemists, food shopping and so on. As Mary, one of the children I worked and learned with, said: 'I suppose it's a long way . . . But not really for us cause we do it all the time. You know I don't even think about it, we just do it.' I remember when I lived in a very similar place-world for my first teaching job. I had returned from doing my food shopping and my sister phoned me, asking where I had been all day. I explained that I went food shopping. She said, 'What, all day?' In fact, I had left at 6 a.m., driven the three hours to the supermarket, which opened at 9 a.m., done a little clothes shopping at the two clothing stores, picked up some buttons and fabric at the sewing shop, had an early lunch, and at 12 p.m. when everything closed I drove the three hours back home. Mary was right: you don't think about it, you just do it.

Mary, aged 10, was one of the children I had been teaching and learning with at the local primary school, Thirton State School. From the outset she was very keen and excited and eagerly wanted to learn. Mary talked to me a lot about making photographs at home and was very articulate in explaining to me the meanings but also the purpose of the photographs. She talked a lot, in particular about the journey to and from school each day (Figs 1.22–1.24). The majority of school children, 25 out of 30 (Thirton 2019b) in Thirton travel to school by bus. There are two buses, one heading north and the other south, and the journey to school can take anywhere from 15 to 80 minutes. Mary talked to me about this school day journey:

> These are us kids all of us on the bus that's how we get to school it takes over an hour each way. Some of these would have been good photos; I just don't like that that bit it's a bit blurry and all the stuff moving behind. It's all just as we were going home, out on the highway. That's what I see on the bus, not really exciting, it can be pretty boring cause you see it twice a day and it doesn't change and you are doing it for so long . . . but we talk and muck around and get really noisy so that makes it a bit better. Cause what we are doing and talk about is different every day, so yeah that makes it ok.[19]

> You know out here I get that it's really different, I know because I've seen heaps of pictures of the city and I have been to Tasmingoo. It's not really a city, just feels like a big town really, just a lot more people and more stuff than here. But, here it's different. We've got lots and lots of space so we can do more stuff outside. One time, my Dad, was fixing the tractor and I was like, can I do something, can I help? and he said, you've got 1600 hectares out here go out and do something out there. I suppose, yeah it's a lot of space that we can do stuff.[20]

What is particularly interesting in all our conversations is that Mary did not talk about her place-world as lacking, or the absence of matter. Rather, Mary knew and understood her place as being and having an abundance of land that enabled and supported her placemaking and being.[21]

It was very important to Mary not only to tell me about her 'place', but also to teach me the very particular ways of knowing and learning place. We would have long conversations during which Mary would ask me questions about London and I would ask her questions about making photographs and school and home. But Mary was also very aware of the importance of what we were talking about:

> My Nana said I am really lucky that you came here and that in London they wouldn't know about this stuff. I figured it's really up to me to tell you all this stuff so you can really get it. Then you can know it but then you can tell other people so they can get it to. You know what is like out here.

Mary was very at ease with the film-making that she would use as part of her everyday journeying, such as doing jobs and talking, narrating and explaining.

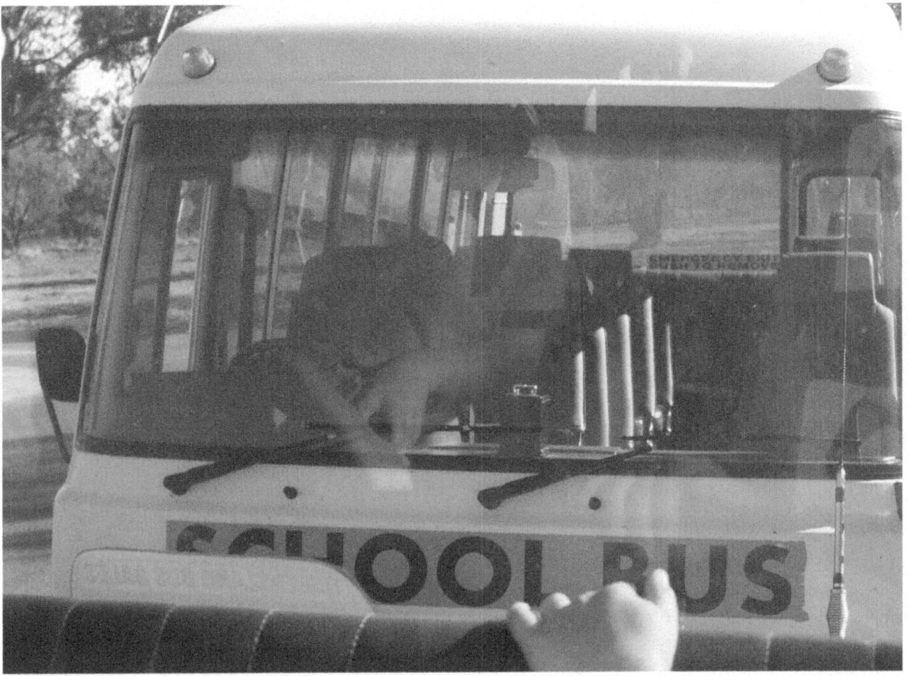

Figure 1.22 Goin' home, series, image 1.

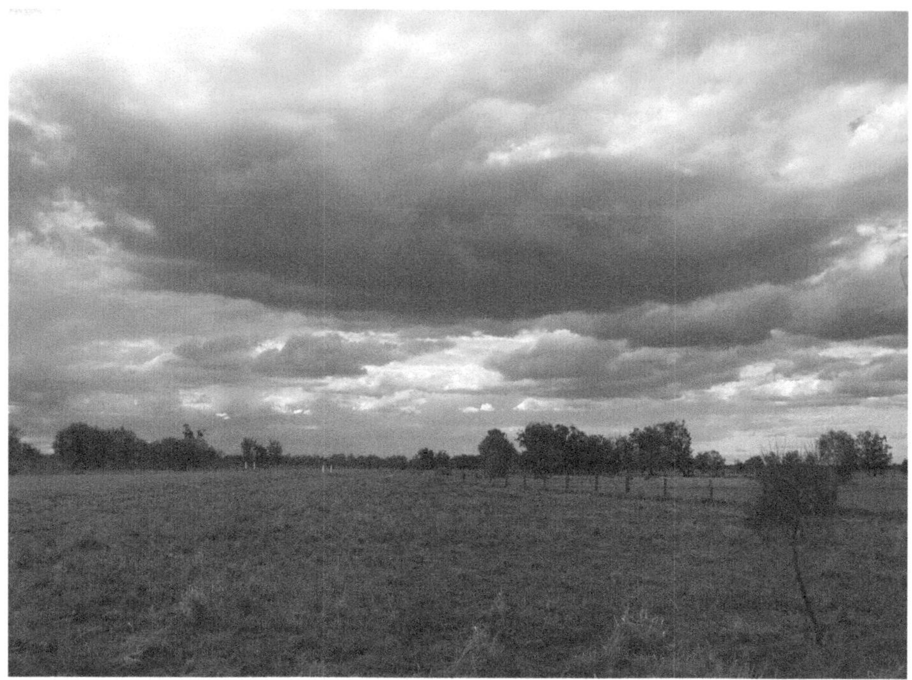

Figure 1.23 Goin' home, series, image 2.

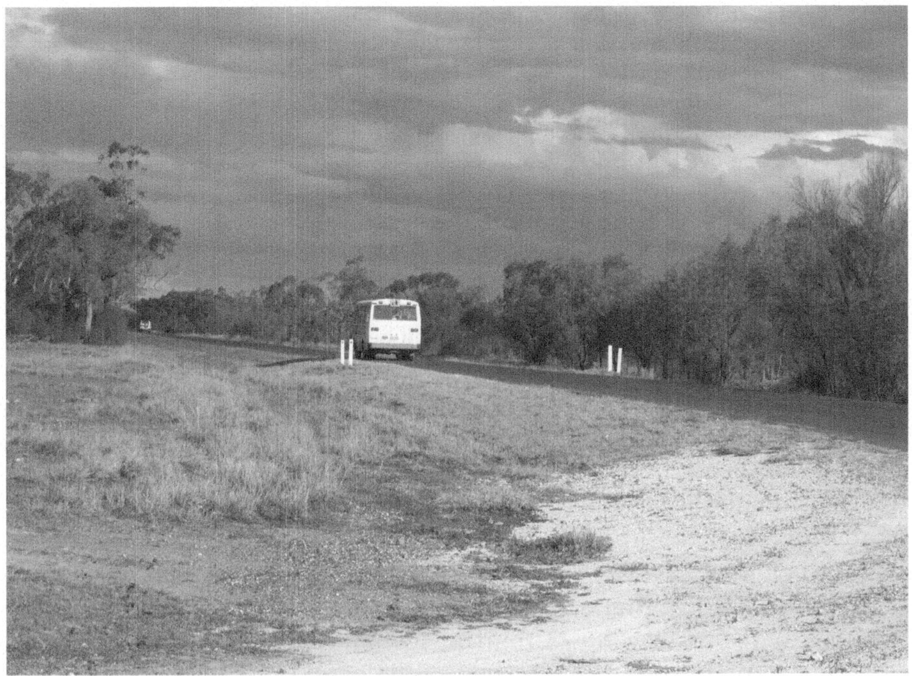

Figure 1.24 Goin' home, series, image 3.

I always started with the camera pointing to me and that's how I usually did it. Because I watch heaps of shows on TV and they always start off introducing, so I thought that's how you do it and I just wanted to share all of it, you know the everyday stuff and that was fun. Other people might think I'm a bit bozo at times but besides from that I think they're pretty good.

I really enjoyed the video, cause you can see where everything is. You know, there's the tree but with me moving and making a film of it you can see where the tree is with the house and where the shed is and the tractor near the tree and the shed. You know all of it, it's all together, not separate. 'Cause it's not separate it's all there together with me and it's more than just what you see. It's all the other stuff too. That's why I am talking. 'Cause then you can understand what it all does, you know. What it does and how it all works together.

These journeying film-making practices enable us to be with Mary, but can also keep us there, teaching us about Mary's bodily 'withness' (Whitehead 1978) with the socio-material place-world. Mary's images, film and journeying stories are not about describing the subject or the object of the journeys, for example the tractor, the tree and so on. Rather, they are about their entanglement; the event, the action between, is what matters. As Mary says, 'It's not separate it's all there together with me. It's more than just what you see, you know. You just know.' Mary's journeying is not only a placemaking practice that makes the very meaning of place, it enables the very meanings of place to be known, understood and also learned in many different and complex ways.

Beauty with Terror

A beautiful morning, cold of course, but there was clarity to the landscape, all raw and clean – a feeling of freshness, everything renewed. 'Big frost this morning, wets everything, won't be much dust' Jenny tells me as she stands at my side. She then hurries ahead of me rushing towards the car. We are all strapped in for the hour long journey to school.

I trundle along slowly, 30 km or thereabouts as I am wary of the mix of slippery dirt roads and speed and also I have someone else's daughter as a passenger. The avenue of gum trees with their grey green bark curling back to reveal fresh white fresh; looks just like skin peeling after a really bad sunburn.

Most of the road, but really just a dirt track is flat. But, deceptively dips, and we are driving through pea-soup fog. It envelops everything, I can't see a thing so I slow down even more, a snail would be proud. I can hear the crunch of the tyres on the rocks and dirt of the track as we slowly eke our way along. I am concentrating on the road directly in front, for anything coming the other way and also on the side of the road keeping the trees parallel, so I don't end up off the road.

'Stop!' Jenny yells from the back. I slam on the brakes and I see it too, a small dark mound waddling across the road. 'What is it?'

> 'Don't know let's go see.' I hear the sound of metal on metal as Jenny slams
> the door, as she rushes up to the waddling mound she excitedly yells at me to
> come quickly.
>
> 'I can't believe it, I have never seen one in the bush before.' I can hear a
> strange snorting and wheezing. As I connect the strange noises with the wad-
> dling mass of knitting needles. I immediately recognize the animal on the Aus-
> tralian five-cent piece – an echidna. It slowly makes its way across to the side
> of the road and up the bank through the grass and scrub, disappearing under a
> dead tree. (Personal notes and audio)

In all my time living in Australia, just like Jenny, I had never seen an echidna outside a zoo. With all my experiences of travelling and living in remote places, the sight and sound of an echidna waddling along the road turned me into an excited seven-year-old. I filmed its journey and was fascinated by its movements, the shape and direction of its quills and how it curled into a tight ball when it sensed our presence. I was so excited.

I thought a lot about the echidna and all the other fascinating and beautiful things of this place-world. Even the daily occurrences when the temperature rises so that the blue of the sky can at times be a little hazy, and that it is at its best in the morning, as the sun comes up. Or at night when the clouds smear the sky as the colour changes to reds, oranges and yellows and the shadows are longer and a softness replaces the hard harsh outlines of the day.

> John's voice broke into my thoughts, 'I experience it everyday and it's beauti-
> ful, I know that. But it does still surprise me. Just when you think you know
> it and think it's yours, it all changes. You can't take it for granted . . . not for
> one second, cause it can get you. You know, that's it lights out, it's not yours.'
> (Personal notes and audio)

This idea of ownership is examined by Gale's (1983; 2005) research with Australian Aboriginal women, who do not consider that they own the land or that it belongs to them, but that they belong to it, the Land. John reiterated this idea of belonging and the land, but also communicated a tension with this idea, a warning that to romanticise or underestimate can have consequences. This tension between land and bodies and the matter of water was shared with me frequently:

> It's dry here and hardly any grass and like heaps of trees and red dirt. I say I
> live in the bush, it's small towns and everybody knows each other and what
> they do and well everyone is friendly and they know each other, but not a lot
> of water. (Mary)

Well I live in a bush town. It's trees and dry, mostly dry all the time and lots of animals, native bush animals like kangaroos and kookaburras and birds and echidnas. Tasmingoo is a city and it's the closest city, it has trees but it's not as dry. They have more water. (Alison)

Midoo[22] is bush too, because it's not huge, you know like as big as Tasmingoo, a city like that. They have a fair few things, more than here but it's still a bush town, real dry. (Harper)

The importance and absence of the matter of water dominates the placemaking practice of those who live with this place-world and as a result the socio-material practices needed to save and preserve water. These include collecting and using bath and shower water, only flushing the toilet when you do a 'number two',[23] and using different waters for different purposes. At Thirton school all the taps have different labels: BORE WATER, TOWN WATER or TANK WATER.

So, Miss, we don't waste this water, because that's the only stuff you can drink. We can only get that water when it rains, which isn't much out here . . . Yeah tank water is the good stuff.

See, you can see two tanks there. Now one is the tank-rain water and the other is the bore water. It's the stuff collected from the school's bore. It has a real strong smell, like rotten eggs. We only use it for washing hands and brushes and stuff, you can boil it too.

Now, town water is from the town tanks. You don't drink that stuff it's got a funny brown colour, tastes funny too. But its OK for washing stuff. (Harper)

Harper was chosen to show me around the school when I first arrived, and as we walked together and she explained the school she talked a lot about her embodied knowledge and understanding of the practices of obtaining, preserving and sharing water, and the impact of a lack of water. The absence of this matter and how important this absence was dominated her explanations. But while we were walking around the school she talked about how they were expecting rain. She then explained to me how she knew it would rain. 'See those huge clouds, see how dark they are. There's darkness but then the light changes and you know rain's comin', it's the first sight of rain.' Jenny also shared an embodied knowledge of the matter of rain. 'Can you smell it? Rain's coming, big storm too'; and Henry said, 'Ants have been going mad the last couple of days, have you seen them.'

Apparently the forecast for Friday and the weekend is rain. Every conversation I have had, child, adult, everyone is consumed by it.

'A front is coming in from the east and we should get rain for three-four days.'

'We really need it too, the tanks are getting low.'

Many conversations centred around the rain forecasted and what needed to be done before the rain comes. There seemed to be a lot of preparations required before the rain, during and then after. John warned me that if it starts to rain while I am at school to head back immediately, 'Don't wait around, get in the car and drive.' I was at a loss, I didn't understand. 'Listen, when we have rain here you just can't drive on the roads, too boggy you need 4WD [four-wheel drive]. You can get stuck for days.'

So, for the last two-three days I have been attempting to help preparing for 'the rain'; bringing cattle in from distant paddocks so they are closer to the house, checking sheep, loading up on supplies/groceries and so on. But there is not a cloud in all this blue sky.

I wake in the middle of the night to the subtle thumping on the iron roof, rain. It does smell different too, damp but not offensive, just wet and clean and everything feels a little duller – not as heightened and sharp. The rhythm is soothing, slowly lulling me back to sleep. I know this.

I wake in the morning to a lot of rain. Even John is still in bed and he stays inside the house, all day. Oh I get it now. All the red dirt, the fine silky dust just turns to mud and sticks to everything. It is very boggy and you just can't go outside.

Here I was thinking, what is the big fuss about, it's just some rain? I even suggested going for a walk, the looks I got I quickly realised that that was not going to happen. 'What, you can't, won't get far.' 'It's like really sticky porridge out there and it just builds up, layer on layer.' 'You'll just get stuck or just keep falling over, it's real slippery.' (Personal research notes/audio)

When I returned to London I shared my photographs and my experiences with a few colleagues, and they all said very similar things: 'Amazing, but how do people live there? It's just all dirt and really dry', or 'Beautiful place, why do people live there, there's nothing there.' This place-world is one that has so much, but at the same time so little: the presence and absence of matter, the tension between beauty and terror. However, those who have grown up learning the placemaking practices of this place-world do not know this, they have not learned this. The terror does not exist for them.

Miss FM [teacher] started to explain the homework that would be due at the end of the week. 'I want you to go into your garden at home like the one in the video we just watched and list all the plants, herbs and vegetables that are growing there.'

Peter, aged 8, called out, 'But Miss, we don't have a veggie garden, we've got trees, sheep and cows and lots and lots of weeds.'

'You've gotta have pretty tough veggie plants to survive out here.' John, aged 10, commented.

'Yeah Miss, life is tough for those sorts of plants and stuff out here, most die.'

'Yeah, a few survive but they mostly all die.'

A titter of giggling spreads through the class. (Personal research notes/audio)

This was the very first lesson I had observed in the school, and John and Peter were calmly telling their teacher why they did not have a veggie garden. I had been living overseas for over ten years and in that time I quickly learned that Australians have a reputation for their direct verbal communication: to the point and very blunt, apparently. Here I was, as an Australian, not necessarily shocked but jolted by the 'matter of factness' of life and death that an eight- and ten-year-old talked about. Initially, this blunt attitude towards life and death was surprising, perhaps because I was surprised at the embodied knowledge and understanding of life and death by very young children. But I quickly learned and continued to learn that the matters of life and death figured strongly in the making of this place-world (Figs 1.25–1.30).

But there is not a tension between life and death because it is part of their placemaking practice. 'What do you mean what do I think, it happens all the time, what can you do. There's nothing to think about?' Similarly, when my art teacher introduced my class to Frederick McCubbin's *Lost* (1866), when I was fifteen years old, she described the imposing and all-encompassing surroundings and the obvious threat that these surroundings conveyed. The entire time I was thinking, 'Where? Are we looking at the same thing?' For me, the painting's smoky blue of the gum (eucalyptus) trees and the way the bark of the tree uncurls reminded me of the places of my early childhood and my own placemaking practices. Mary, Jenny, Henry, Hettie, Harper, John and Peter have shared and taught me their embodied placemaking practices that are made and remade with the very socio-material of this place-world.

In this chapter I have begun to explore and examine the placemaking practices of a specific place-world and how these ways of knowing and understanding are learned and taught. These embodied practices intra-act with the socio-material world, and the very meanings are made and remade individually, but also with others. The children of this place-world taught me the what, how and why of their placemaking, but I was also learning with them. This is because the children were very open in sharing their insights, thoughts and feelings, which were so vivid and sometimes bluntly expressed; I was able to learn and relearn my own ways of placemaking, some new and some old. In a way I was relearning the ways, the practices of my childhood places. It is the children's honesty and deep embodied and material understanding and knowledge that opens up and takes us into their place-world, and conveys the complexity of this particularly place-world. However, this chapter is not about recreating or defining the place-world of the bush or the children's placemaking,

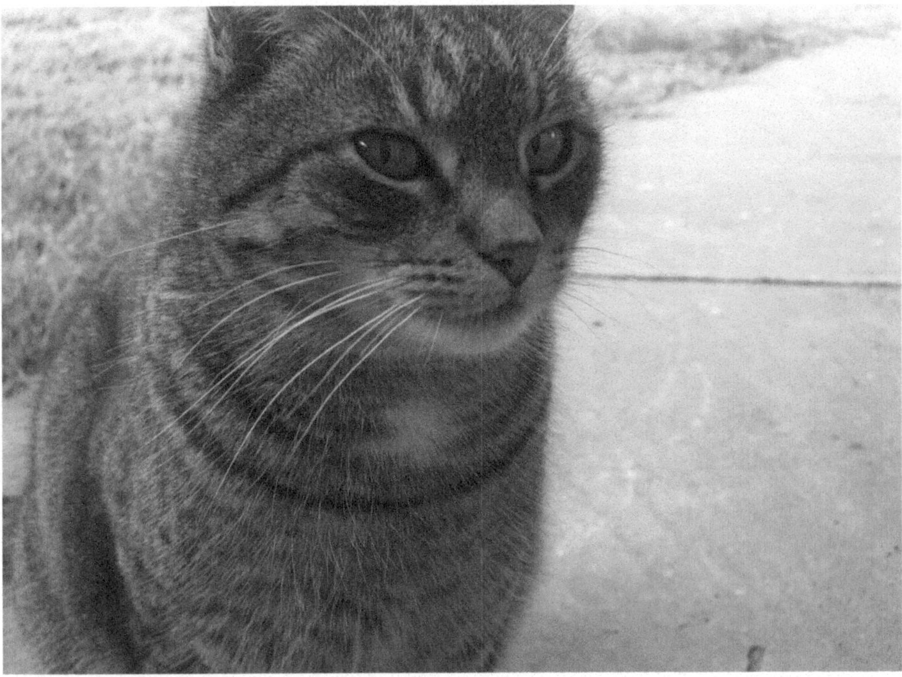

Figure 1.25 'His name is Bows, his father was a housecat and his mother was a feral.'

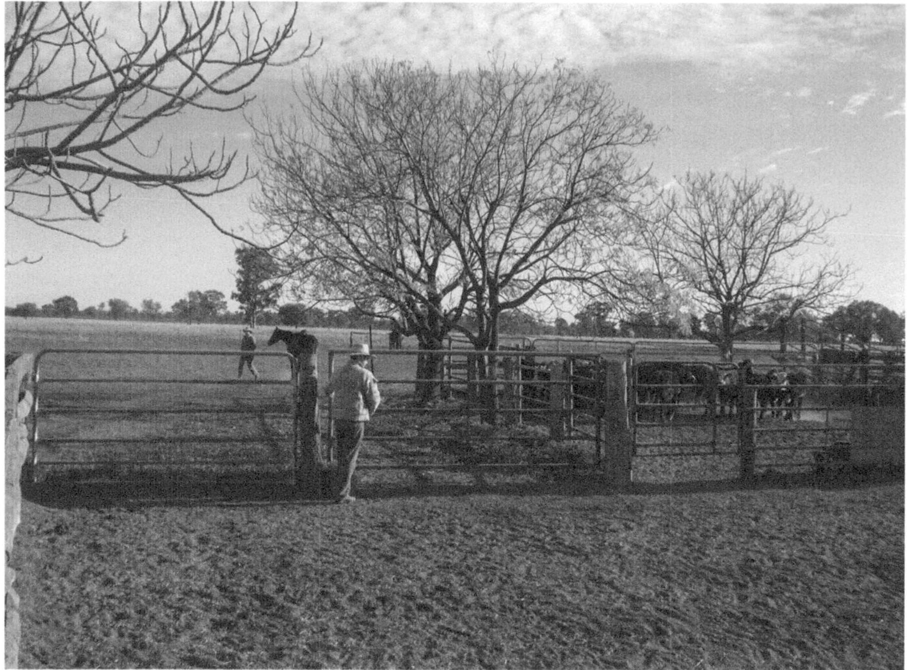

Figure 1.26 'That's like they have to muster. Mustering is sort of like getting a mob of cattle together and taking them from their paddock into the yards and branding and earmarking them and stuff like that.'

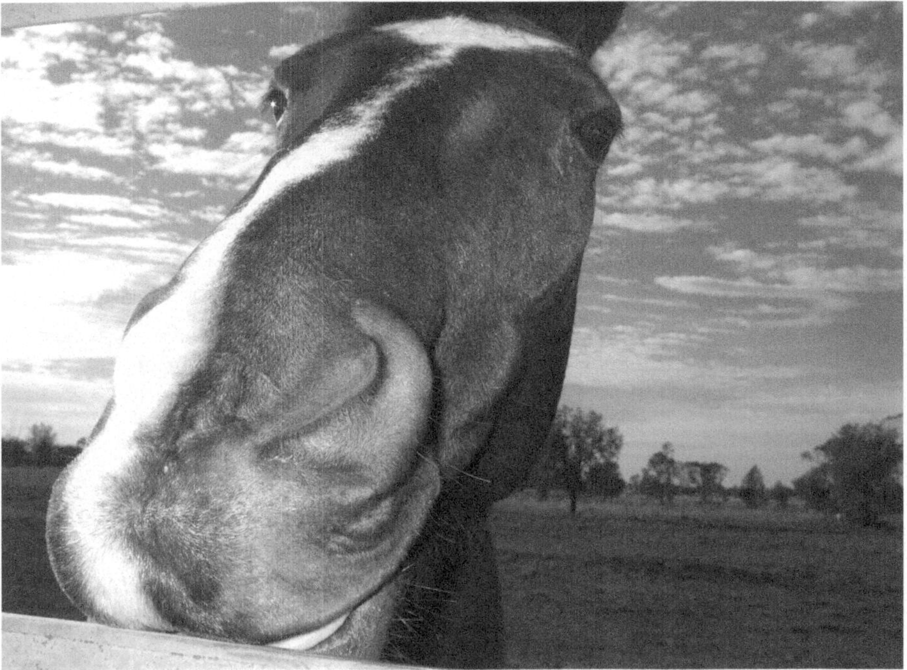

Figure 1.27 'This is Dad's horse, he's a bestest friend he always come around. He's very greedy and he always thinks I have food he comes up close and goes um, um, um, um.'

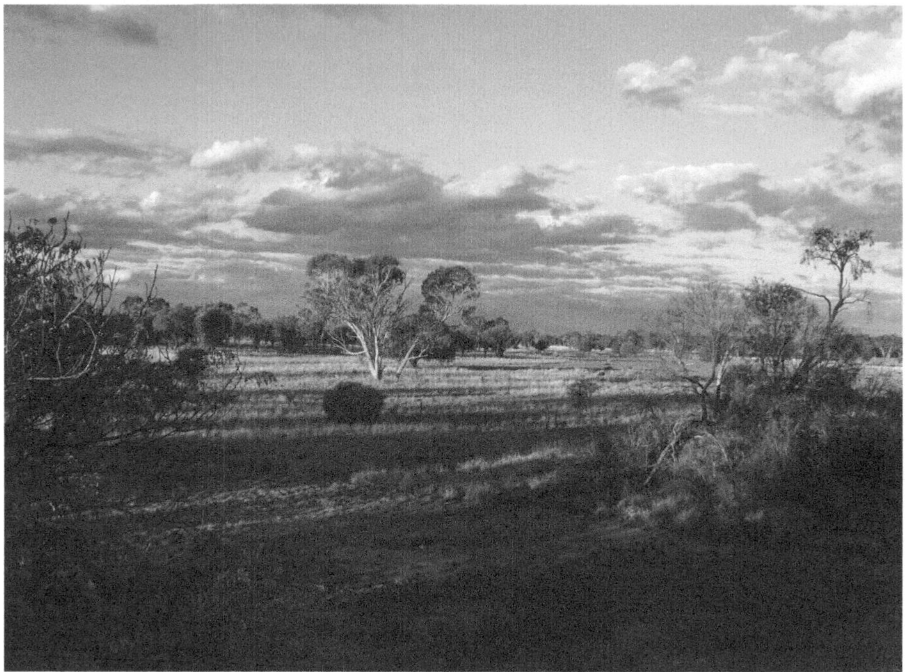

Figure 1.28 'I was walking and 'cause there was heaps of sticks and I had to be careful I didn't trip.'

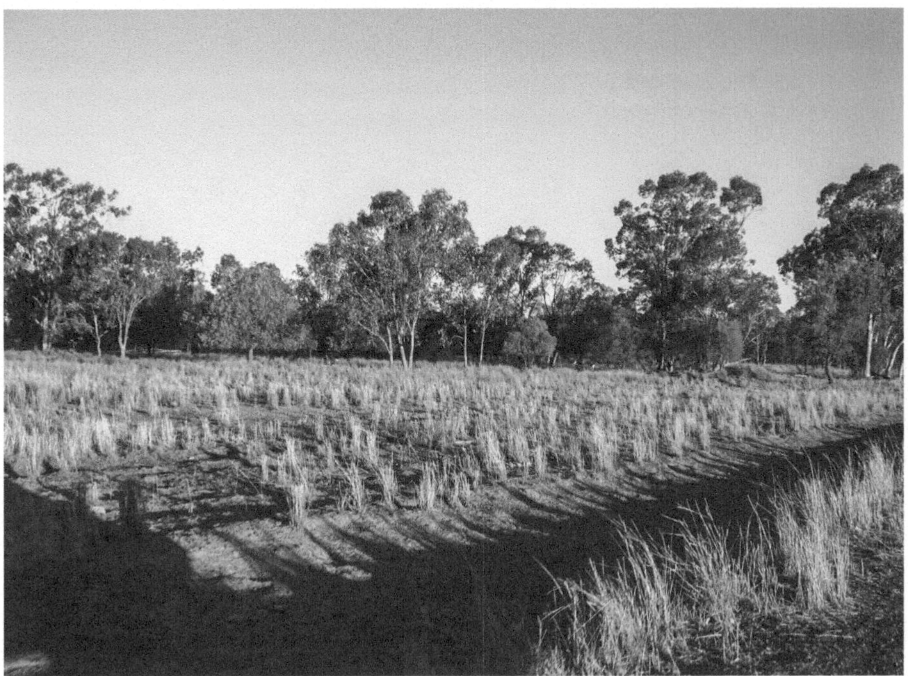

Figure 1.29 'There's no water in the bore drain.'

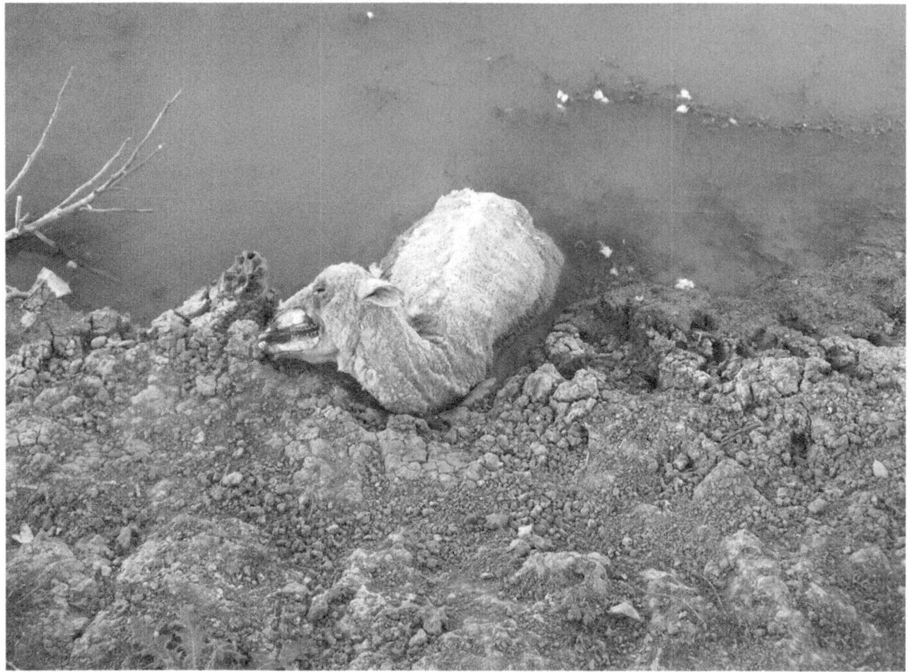

Figure 1.30 'There's a sheep that's been stuck in the dam. We always have them. That one's been there a while so it's got no mouth, no eyes.'

but about understanding and learning the embodied socio-material ways of making place. What is clearly evident in that these ways of knowing, understanding, learning and making place are complex and are entangled with the socio-material; they are not fixed but are fluid, flexible and subject to change. We are continually learning and being taught; making and remaking.

In the next chapter I work the spaces between the linguistic, poetic, artistic, pedagogic, filmic and geopolitical material representations of this place-world, the bush. This examination demonstrates the agency of matter in placemaking, but also exposes how the presence but also the absence of matter is pivotal to the making of a national identity.

Notes

1. Here as elsewhere, the name of the town has been changed to anonymise the participants.
2. See Tourism Australia website, available at <http://www.tourism.australia.com>, last accessed 14 January 2020.
3. Name changed.
4. Name changed.
5. 'Major rural activity centres serve as catchments of subregional to regional significance, with populations of 2000 to 5000 residents. These centres accommodate concentrations of employment, businesses and convenience retail shopping opportunities' (DIP 2019: 8).
6. From observations.
7. To protect the rights of the participants, pseudonyms are used. See journey series, <https://www.tarapage.org/placemaking>, accessed 14 January 2020.
8. 'Queenslander' describes the structure of houses built in Queensland. They usually consist of houses on stilts, which enables airflow beneath the house in order to reduce the temperature inside, and wraparound verandas that are sometimes covered in to provide additional living space (ABS 2019:15).
9. Quotes from participants are shared throughout this chapter, intra-acting with my own notes, capturing our everyday and artistic practices-makings, learnings, critical reflections and conversations.
10. According to Jenny's mother, taking the camera along when they do their jobs has occurred a number of times. The camera is used for family events and so on.
11. Bore water is groundwater that has been accessed by drilling a bore into underground aquifers and pumping to the surface. See <https://www.alkaway.com.au/learning-centre/bore-water/>, last accessed 14 January 2020.

12. 'fine dust found on outback *(qv)* roads/ bullshit *(colloq.)*' (Bickerton 2004: 7).
13. See Chapter 5.
14. See abentures, <https://www.tarapage.org/placemaking>, last accessed 14 January 2020.
15. One of the dams on the property.
16. *Skippy the Bush Kangaroo* (known commonly as *Skippy*) is an Australian television series that aired from 1968 to 1970 about the adventures of a young boy and his highly intelligent pet kangaroo. See <https://en.wikipedia.org/wiki/Skippy_the_Bush_Kangaroo>, last accessed 14 January 2020.
17. There is limited AM/FM radio reception because of the vastness of the country. See <https://www.worldnomads.com/travel-safety/oceania/australia/driving-across-australia>, last accessed 14 January 2020.
18. Journeying goes beyond just 'walking with' – see Chapter 5. It can be journeying to school, doing jobs, or going on an 'abenture'. Journeying is an embodied socio-material practice that enables a way of knowing and learning place as it enables both the time and opportunity to reflect.
19. See goin' home series, <https://www.tarapage.org/placemaking>, last accessed 14 January 2020.
20. See goin' home series, <https://www.tarapage.org/placemaking>, last accessed 14 January 2020.
21. See journeying with Mary – beauty with terror, <https://www.tarapage.org/placemaking>, last accessed 14 January 2020.
22. The closest town to Thirton, population 800.
23. 'If it's yellow let it mellow, if it's brown flush it down.'

CHAPTER 2

The Place-World of the Bush

'The bush', 'the outback', remote Australia: these terms are used to describe a particular Australian place-world that has specific and particular forms of human and non-human socio-material knowledges, performances and practices. This chapter is a deep mapping of the linguistic, poetic, artistic, pedagogic, filmic and geopolitical socio-material representations of this place-world. This deep mapping is an intensive exploration that critically engages with diverse materials – histories, ecologies, poetics, narratives, artefacts, memoirs and so on – and can be used to 'amplify the voices of marginalised stakeholders, both socially and ecologically' (Springett 2015: 624). Using new materialist thinking demonstrates the power of matter, both its absence and presence, in understanding how place is pivotal in pedagogies of national identity and nationhood discourses.

Place-world

Place-world is a particular place that has specific and particular forms of human and non-human socio-material knowledges, performances and practices. A place-world is the intra-action of culture and context; the space between the subject and object of place – more than a site for research or analysis – the meanings and the materiality of this place-world are practised and performed. In other words, the way we experience place, our knowledge of place and how we learn to make place emerge from practices that have value and are valued, and forces produced by intra-acting socio-material networks.

Context can be understood in terms of physical location or positionality 'in a particular time and at a particular place' (Hones 2008: 319). When context is conceived as a physical location it is seen as a fixed setting that is composed of parts that can be broken down and analysed; Seddon (1993) calls this the 'atomist' paradigm. This understanding of context involves individual people, events, phenomena and factors being reduced to data about 'local understandings'.

However, when context is understood to be relational and intra-acting, it becomes a dynamic process where 'the complexification or mediation or spacing of an event, is not in any sense a backdrop to situated human activity but rather is something active, differentially extensive' (Thrift 1996: 3). This relational idea of context can then be understood as 'local understandings' that are 'socially produced through relations of dependence and mutual implication, through relationships established socially and hierarchically between the near and the far, the local and the distant' (Radway 1999: 15). Radway continues this idea of context as relational by challenging the idea of culture as 'the simple function of a fixed, isolated and easily mapped territory' (1999: 15). Culture is not something someone has as a result of being situated at a specific geographic location (McLeod 1987), but is 'a meaning effect produced by the hierarchical relationships established between different spaces and the communities and individuals that give them significance' (Radway 1999: 14).

The population of Australia in terms of religious, cultural and ethnic complexity is diverse (ABS 2019), yet a singular, fixed conception of remote Australia can be said to figure very strongly in the national identity of Australia and Australians. This very specific idea of the place-world of the 'bush' is used to bind Australians together and is also used as proof – a test of being Australian: 'the bush, a sunlit landscape of faded blue hills and cloudless skies and noble gum trees . . . Australians respond to this, as a test of their patriotism, no matter where they originally came from' (White 1981: 86). Using artistic, poetic, filmic, geopolitical, linguistic and pedagogic materials I have mapped these representations/constructions of the place-world of the bush to learn how this place-world is made and remade and also examine how these assemblages are used to affirm, maintain and consolidate a national identity, but also have the power to marginalise and exclude. This chapter is an examination and exploration of the agency of matter in the making of place.

What's in a Name?

'The bush' and 'the outback' are names used to signify the place-world of remote Australia. These appear to be fairly similar; they both denote an area that is sparsely populated, beyond big towns. Outback, or 'the outback', is a noun defined by the *OED* as 'an isolated or sparsely populated inland area, especially in Australia'. 'Bush' is derived from the Dutch word *Bosch* meaning woodland, and the use of the word began in Australia in the nineteenth century (Hughes 1989; Walton 1993). In Australia, 'the bush' has eclipsed the English terms 'woods' and 'forests' as a description of a timbered area and is a generic term to describe all areas away from cities and towns:

> folk who follow a country life are invariably said to live in the bush. Squatters who look after their runs always live in the bush; even though their sheep are pastured on plains . . . nearly every place beyond the influence of the big towns is called 'the bush'. (Hughes 1989: 92)

Language is not only a method of communication but is also a mechanism of power, and the language we use is determined by our relational position in a place-world. The use of terms that may have a similar denotation, such as the bush and the outback, can then position an individual with that place-world, indicating their understanding and knowledge of the place-world and positioning them as either belonging or not belonging – to use ethnographic terms, as being insiders or outsiders. So, when well-meaning people, both in Australia and the UK, would ask me 'How's your research going in the outback?' or 'What's it like in the outback?', they were communicating their relational position with the place-world and their placemaking as outsiders.

In the media, specifically for tourism purposes, the 'outback' is conceived as a place of difference: 'You may not see another human for days but you're guaranteed to stumble across some of the native wildlife that has evolved to survive in the unforgiving outback' (quoted in Ellis 2008: 27).[1] The outback is made as a tourist attraction where tourists, from both overseas and Australia, can visit the non-metropolitan or the exotic Other. The outback is a place-world that you visit, not a place where you live; a place-world where you can experience the different and unusual. The value of this place-world comes from its differences from the metropolitan or non-outback. This idea has strong resonances with traditional ethnography, where researchers ventured to exotic locales and communicated on their return, to the Western world, the lives and cultures of the people in these locales (Price 2005). This strong connection with colonialism and oppression, the objectification of 'natives' and fixed, singular constructions of cultures, is why ethnography has often been criticised (Willis and Trodman 2002).

The use of 'outback' similarly makes and remakes a fixed idea of this place-world, and as Relph contends, it is one that 'involves no awareness of the deep and symbolic . . . it is merely . . . an uncritically accepted stereotype . . . that can be adopted without real involvement'

(1976: 82); nor does it take into account the material power of language. However, 'the bush' is used by insiders, those who live in this place-world of remote Australia, as explained by Angela, one of the children involved in the study discussed in Chapter 1:

> Well I live in the bush. It's trees and dry, mostly dry all the time and lots of animals, native bush animals like kangaroos and kookaburras and birds and echidnas . . . Saying 'the outback' we don't say that, we don't think that, its just the bush or, Thirton is just a bush town.

'The bush' denotes remote Australia but it is also matter that positions the discourse and findings of this research assemblage as authentic and coming from insiders, those that live in/with this particular place-world. The intra-action of the matter of language and the making of place and identity can also be explored with poetic imagery.

The Poetic Bush

Remote Australia was the dominant subject matter of the iconographic poetry of A. B. 'Banjo' Paterson (1864–1941), Henry Lawson (1867–1922) and Dorothea Mackellar (1885–1968). Paterson and Lawson are significant and prominent Australian 'bush poets'; Australian poets who wrote about the bush and Australian rural life during colonial times (Hughes 1989). Paterson's and Lawson's poetry was based on the legends and stories that came from the bush and they used these materials to develop and sustain a particular Australian identity (Hughes 1989). However, there is a tension that exists within their poetry, as they knew and understood the place-world of the bush in very different ways.

Lawson conceived of the struggle with the bush as being central to the Australian identity:

> There is nothing to see, however, and not a soul to meet. You might walk for twenty miles along this track without being able to fix a point in your mind, unless you are a bushman. This is because of the everlasting, maddening sameness of the stunted trees. (Lawson 1901: 2)

Lawson's knowledges and practices of the bush are clearly those of the outsider, as he has not learned the everyday practices required such as 'being able to fix a point in your mind' (Lawson 1901: 2), because if you can you do this then you are of this place, 'you are a bushman' (Lawson 1901: 2). However, rather than constructing the making and learning of these practices of the bush as unnecessary, Lawson conveys that the very struggle to learn and know these ways is what makes a civilised Australian.

In contrast, Paterson was more comfortable and at ease with the bush, as illustrated in 'The Plains':

> A land, as far as the eye can see, where the waving grasses grow
> Or the plains are blackened and burnt and bare, where the false mirages go
> Like shifting symbols of hope deferred – land where you never know.
>
> Land of plenty or land of want, where the grey Companions dance,
> Feast or famine, or hope or fear, and in all things land of chance,
> Where Nature pampers or Nature slays, in her ruthless red romance.
>
> And we catch a sound of a fairy's song, as the wind goes whipping by,
> Or a scent like incense drifts along from the herbage ripe and dry
> Or the dust storms dance on their ballroom floor, where the bones of the cattle
> lie. (Paterson 1987: 2)

Paterson has learned the practices of the bush through attitudes and practices that are characterised by a sense of humour and an intimate knowledge of the bush, but one that is not romantic or idealised: 'Where Nature pampers or Nature slays' a 'land where you never know' (Paterson 1987: 2). Paterson's shares a comfort – a belonging with the entangled extremes of living in this place-world; feast and famine, hope and fear. This knowledge and understanding is also shared in Paterson's most famous poem, the ballad 'Waltzing Matilda' (1895):

> Once a jolly swagman camped by a billabong
> Under the shade of a coolabah tree,
> And he sang as he watched and waited 'til his billy boiled
> You'll come a-Waltzing Matilda, with me.
>
> Waltzing Matilda, Waltzing Matilda
> You'll come a-Waltzing Matilda, with me
> And he sang as he watched and waited 'til his billy boiled,
> You'll come a-Waltzing Matilda, with me.
>
> Down came a jumbuck to drink at that billabong,
> Up jumped the swagman and grabbed him with glee,
> And he sang as he shoved that jumbuck in his tucker bag,
> You'll come a-Waltzing Matilda, with me.
>
> Waltzing Matilda, Waltzing Matilda
> You'll come a-Waltzing Matilda, with me
> And he sang as he shoved that jumbuck in his tucker bag,
> You'll come a-Waltzing Matilda, with me.

> Up rode the squatter, mounted on his thoroughbred,
> Down came the troopers, one, two, three,
> Where's that jolly jumbuck you've got in your tucker bag?
> You'll come a-Waltzing Matilda, with me.
>
> Waltzing Matilda, Waltzing Matilda
> You'll come a-Waltzing Matilda, with me.
> Where's that jolly jumbuck you've got in your tucker bag?
> You'll come a-Waltzing Matilda, with me.
>
> Up jumped the swagman and sprang into the billabong,
> You'll never take me alive, said he,
> And his ghost may be heard as you pass by that billabong,
> You'll come a-Waltzing Matilda, with me.
>
> Waltzing Matilda, Waltzing Matilda
> You'll come a-Waltzing Matilda, with me
> And his ghost may be heard as you pass by that billabong,
> You'll come a-Waltzing Matilda, with me.
> Oh, you'll come a-Waltzing Matilda, with me. (Paterson 1998)

The title of the poem is Australian slang for travelling by foot, 'waltzing' with one's possessions in a 'Matilda' (bag/swag) slung over one's back (Hughes 1989), akin to a colonial backpack. The song narrates the story of a swagman (traveller/itinerant worker) making a drink of tea in a tin with a handle (billy) at a bush camp next to a billabong (small lake/large pond) and catching a jumbuck (sheep) to eat. A squatter (landowner and owner of said sheep) and three troopers (police officers) arrive to arrest the swagman for the theft (a crime punishable by hanging). The swagman drowns himself in, and then haunts, the billabong (Hughes 1989).

This ballad is the official national song of Australia (ABS 2019) and the language in it has not altered in over 115 years. Yet waltzing, swag, swagman, jumbuck, trooper, squatter and billabong are no longer used in everyday Australian vernacular practices. Many Australians who regularly sing this song at national events probably have no idea what they are actually singing about. Paterson's image and the lyrics of 'Waltzing Matilda' are on the Australian 10-dollar note, as well as being serialised on postage stamps issued by Australia Post, the national postal service and network, further demonstrating the persistence and power of the socio-material place-world of the bush in the making of an Australian identity.

The most iconic Australian poem is 'My Country' (1908) by Dorothea Mackellar.

The love of field and coppice,
Of green and shaded lanes.
Of ordered woods and gardens
Is running in your veins,
Strong love of grey-blue distance
Brown streams and soft dim skies
I know but cannot share it,
My love is otherwise.

I love a sunburnt country,
A land of sweeping plains,
Of ragged mountain ranges,
Of droughts and flooding rains.
I love her far horizons,
I love her jewel-sea,
Her beauty and her terror –
The wide brown land for me!

A stark white ring-barked forest
All tragic to the moon,
The sapphire-misted mountains,
The hot gold hush of noon.
Green tangle of the brushes,
Where lithe lianas coil,
And orchids deck the tree-tops
And ferns the warm dark soil.

Core of my heart, my country!
Her pitiless blue sky,
When sick at heart, around us,
We see the cattle die –
But then the grey clouds gather,
And we can bless again
The drumming of an army,
The steady, soaking rain.

Core of my heart, my country!
Land of the Rainbow Gold,
For flood and fire and famine,
She pays us back threefold –
Over the thirsty paddocks,
Watch, after many days,
The filmy veil of greenness
That thickens as we gaze.

An opal-hearted country,
A wilful, lavish land –
All you who have not loved her,

> You will not understand –
> Though earth holds many splendours,
> Wherever I may die,
> I know to what brown country
> My homing thoughts will fly. (Mackellar 1908)

In the first stanza Mackellar shares her knowledge and practices of England; she is sharing an embodied knowledge and understanding of her ancestral home, even though this is idealised and/or a stereotype. In this stanza Mackellar is almost making England Other, sharing an understanding that the Other may be the love of some but that she is rejecting it: 'I know but cannot share it, / My love is otherwise'; she positions a wild grandeur against a coiffured order. Interestingly, the first stanza is relatively unknown, whereas most Australians would be able to recite the second stanza by heart (Spender 1988).

In the second and third stanzas Mackellar describes her love – 'I love a sunburnt country' – and that her practices are that of the insider. She does this through the matter of the landscape: ragged mountain ranges, far horizons, sweeping plains and the climate: sunburnt country, droughts and flooding rains. Mackellar is just not telling the material qualities of the object of the land, she is using poetic imagery of sapphire-misted mountains, the hot gold hush of noon and an opal-hearted country to communicate, to share a deep socio-material narrative that may enable an evocation of place; a making of place. This placemaking can be conceived as idealised and romantic, but Mackellar balances this with practices and knowledges of an insider like Paterson before her, by implying the harshness of this landscape: sunburnt country, flooding rains, fire and famine and a wilful, lavish land. In these stanzas Mackellar communicates her knowledge and understanding of her entanglement with the Land, using the matter of this place-world.

In the fourth and fifth stanzas Mackellar is inclusive of the Australian reader who may share this love, through the use of the pronouns us and we: 'When sick at heart, around us, / We see the cattle die – . . . And we can bless again . . . She pays us back threefold.' However, Mackellar is also exclusive: 'All you who have not loved her, / you will not understand.' The implication is that those who are not Australians cannot understand. This attempts to create a sense of belonging/connection, a strong sense of identification with other Australians through the author's poetic imagery of Australia. In the final stanza, Mackellar returns to the concept of Other, articulating that no matter where she roams or lives her identity will always be Australian: 'Though earth holds many splendours, / Wherever I may die, / I know to what brown country, / My homing thoughts will fly.'

Mackellar, like Paterson and Lawson, uses the matter of language and poetic imagery to make the place-world of the Australian bush, and potentially a universal statement of a nation's connection to the land; and the power of this matter is that it can bind and unify. These poets are sharing their poetic socio-material knowledges and practices of this place-world to make and remake place, and ultimately a sense of belonging. But it is not a sense of belonging to this particular place-world – it is a belonging to and of Australia. The agency of this poetic matter is that it is used to make a very particular Australian national identity. Australian artists have similarly used the matter of the bush to make and remake a particular Australian identity.

The Art of the Bush

The Australian Impressionists Tom Roberts (1856–1931), Frederick McCubbin (1855–1917) and Arthur Streeton (1867–1943) belonged to a group called the Heidelberg School. This term was originally used to describe a small group of artists who painted *plein air* landscapes out-side an area of Melbourne called Heidelberg.[2] However, its scope was later broadened to include the Australian Impressionist artists of the late nineteenth century (Stuart 1993). During my last two years at secondary school I was introduced to the work of Roberts, McCubbin and Stree-ton. My art teacher explained the socio-historical context of these artists and how pivotal they were in seeing, understanding and representing the Australian landscape, not as a mere replication of mother England but as a place that was unique and very different. The artists of the Heidelberg School, McCubbin in particular, focused on the differences of the land-scape flora and fauna of Australia from those of England, but also the differences in the quality of the light.[3] As McCubbin stated, 'Nature under our Australian sky, seems to me like a shy, reserved person . . . but you only have to wait and watch her varying moods, and the light will find all the beauty you can desire'[4] (Stuart 1993: 102). This difference in the qual-ity of the light that McCubbin describes is not something I understood at the time, as I had not experienced this difference.

The first painting I was introduced to was McCubbin's *Lost* (1866).[5] This painting resonated with me, as I remember the smoky blue of the gum (eucalyptus) trees and the way the bark of the tree uncurls, thinking how beautiful the figure of the child was among the yellow long grasses, foliage and branches of the bush, and that she looked as though she was part of the bush. However, my teacher told us the title of the painting and started analysing the image, describing the imposing and all-encompassing surroundings and the obvious threat that these surroundings conveyed. The entire time I was thinking, 'Where? Are we looking at the same work?' Because of my knowledge and understanding of this place-world, I was unable to understand my teacher's interpretation. Yet this is a theme that runs through the work of the Heidelberg School; the making and remaking of the bush as a place of difference from their home place-worlds. This is demonstrated in how the matter of the land – the flora, fauna, the light and weather – is against 'man'. The space between bodies and matter is understood as a conflict, a struggle to live in this land, and the attitudes of rebellion and courage required to survive in this place-world.

> We cannot . . . urge too strongly . . . how requisite it is that we should as soon as possible fill our National Gallery with representative works of our artists and our nation, its early historical scenes, and pictures of the true rude life that must have and did exist in the early days of the colony.[6]

The very matter of this place is entangled with the bodies and has served to maintain the making of the bush, and those that live in the bush as Other. The work of Sir Sidney Nolan (1917–92) and his series of Ned Kelly paintings also makes this idea of the bush and those who live in the bush as Other – rebels, outlaws.

Edward 'Ned' Kelly (1854/55–80) was an Irish-Australian bushranger (Jones 1995), 'a highwayman' (Bickerton 2004: 7) and, to some, a folk hero for his defiance of the colonial authorities. According to Jones, during this period there was social unrest in Australia due to the alleged injustices perpetrated against Irish Catholics by the police and the English and Irish Protestant squatters, 'those who occupied and fenced open land' (Bickerton 2004: 20). Kelly was born in Victoria to an Irish convict father, and as a young man he clashed with the Victoria police. Following an incident at his home in 1878, police parties searched for him in the bush, and after he killed three policemen, the colony proclaimed Kelly and his gang wanted outlaws. A final, violent confrontation with the police took place at Glenrowan, Victoria, with Kelly dressed in homemade plate metal armour and a helmet (Jones 1995). Kelly was eventually captured, sent to gaol and hanged for murder at Old Melbourne Gaol in 1880 (Drewe 1991). His alleged daring and notoriety has made Ned Kelly an iconic figure in Australian history. But it is the very many material reiterations of Kelly in his armour that has made him folkloric, including books (Drewe 1991; Carey 2000), films (*The Story of the Kelly Gang*, dir. Charles Tait, 1906; *Ned Kelly*, dir. Tony Richardson, 1970, with Mick Jagger in the title role; and more recently *Ned Kelly*, dir. Gregor Jordan, 2003, with Heath Ledger as Kelly) and art, as in Nolan's work. But these materials sustain the idea of Ned Kelly more in the mould of Robin Hood, one of 'us' who battles the establishment, rather than an outsider who does not belong, that is, an Irish immigrant.

In Nolan's work, Kelly is painted as independent and defiant, but also as of the land, the embodiment of the bush. Nolan's Kelly is on a horse in an empty landscape with little colour and no other humans. Kelly is depicted as a bold black shape, central and pivotal, but there is no connection between Kelly and the viewer. Kelly faces the landscape; the connection is between him and the landscape.[7] Nolan's paintings in the Ned Kelly series are seen as iconic and would be instantly recognisable to many Australians (Rosenthal 2002). As Reed states:

> Australia has not been an easy country to paint. A number of artists have sensed something of what it holds and one or two . . . but we have waited many years for a mature statement to cover both the landscape and man [*sic*] in relation to the landscape . . . necessitating as it has the most sensitive and profound harmony between symbol, legend and visual impact. (1948: 2)

But Nolan's series is not an attempt to reproduce Kelly or this story. Nor is it a homage to the Ned Kelly legend. It is more a way for Nolan to paint the Australian landscape in new ways, where the story gives meaning but also enables an understanding of this place-world. 'An understanding of landscape was a motivation: I find the desire to paint the landscape involves a wish to hear more of the stories that take place in the landscape' (Nolan 1948: 20). Nolan is attempting to understand place with the matter of painting and his own embodied practice. This demonstrates the concept of intra-actions and entanglement of the relational between bodies and matter. By engaging with and critiquing the matter of narratives and practices we can then understand how place is made and learned, because, as Nolan states, it is about 'a story arising out of the bush and ending in the bush' (1948: 20).

Rosalie Gascoigne (1917–99) also explores the intra-actions of the bodies and matter of the place-world of the bush, but she is more interested in affect. When studying for my undergraduate degree, I attended an artist's talk by Gascoigne in Brisbane, at the Queensland Art Gallery. I was struck with how down to earth she was, but her passion for the Australian landscape was clearly evident as she described what and how she saw the land and her deeply felt experiences of the materials she encountered in her place-world, Canberra, the capital city of Australia. Gascoigne does not make the bush as Other; she wants to share her deep embodied knowledge of the 'land that is clean scoured by the sun and wind and frost' (Edwards 1998: 5). She uses materials, both natural and human-made, that are deeply weathered and then sets them in broad, orderly, yet open configurations.[8] Through her inventive use of the discarded and found materials of her place-world, Gascoigne shares the impact that the Australian landscape can have, literally, on the matter of the bush just as the bush poets Mackellar, Lawson and Paterson did in their poetry.

However, Gascoigne's work is more of a metaphorical vision of her meditative and emotional conceptions of the landscape of home, where I live, my place, where 'I love to roam around, to look, to feel and hear' (Edwards 1998: 5). Gascoigne's artmaking comes from a knowledge and understanding in practice of the place-world of the bush, of the insider, where personal ways of knowing this place-world come from an embodied and material engagement; feeling, hearing, roaming, collecting and making. Through this Gascoigne is making her identity/ies, just as Nolan attempted in his Ned Kelly series, although this representation is of an other.

The Bush in Film

Australian films have similarly used the socio-material place-world of the bush to evoke and convey particular ways of knowing and understanding the bush. In films such as *Mad Max* (dir. George Miller, 1979), *Crocodile Dundee* (dir. Peter Faiman, 1986), *The Adventures of Priscilla, Queen of the Desert* (dir. Stephan Elliot, 1994), *Rabbit-Proof Fence* (dir. Phillip Noyce, 2002) and *Australia* (dir. Baz Luhrmann, 2008), the bush is made in a particular way and is used for different means. In *Australia*, the director, Baz Luhrmann, tries to elicit an emotive connection from the audience and so presents an idealised, remote Australian landscape. He states that:

> This part of Australia, the outback . . . is one of the last places in the world that still conjures mystery, excitement and romance in people's minds and that you need to prepare to be bowled over by her stunning overwhelming power and beauty of the biggest star . . . the ancient continent of Australia. (Robinson 2008: 3)

The 'overwhelming power' and 'the biggest star' status of the 'outback' is evident in the opening scene. A long, panoramic sweep of the camera shows the space of the land continuing to the horizon, undisturbed by marks of human existence, and then a caption flashes up on the screen promising audiences that this is 'where adventure and romance are a way of life'. This filmic matter is used to produce and reproduce remote Australia as unique and exotic through the matter of language, romantic imagery, lighting and the juxtaposition of flora and fauna. It also reproduces this entanglement of beauty and hardship, or as in this film, the adventure and romance of remote Australia, just as Paterson and Mackellar did in their poetry. Lurhmann stated that 'the film truly is about the landscape and how the outdoor experience can have an effect on your soul' and how 'the awesome power of the landscape has the ability to transform and shape character' (Robinson 2008: 3). Again, this entanglement of bodies with matter, and the idea that those who live in these place-worlds are people who are entangled with land, and that the qualities of the matter are qualities of the bodies; unique, independent and defiant, the very embodiment of the bush.

This entanglement of bodies with the matter of this particular place-world was also used in the late 1970s in the film (and eventual trilogy), *Mad Max*. This is an action science fiction fantasy based around the traditional Western genre, telling the story of the breakdown of society, of murder and vengeance in the bush (Dermody and Jacka 1988). An (at the time) unknown Mel Gibson plays the title role of a 'quiet hero'. Basically Gibson's character does not say a lot in the 95 minutes of the film; instead he is the one who will fight the establishment on behalf of the helpless – a modern-day Ned Kelly, a man in the bush against the odds. This embodiment of the bush is further demonstrated, although with much more humour, in the 1986 film *Crocodile Dundee*. In this story a wealthy female reporter hears about the heroic tale of survival of Mick Dundee (Paul Hogan), also known as 'Crocodile Dundee', and flies to the outback to verify his story. As they both travel through 'the outback', retracing his journey of survival, she falls in love with his unpretentious honesty and good-spirited dishonesty. Hogan, like Gibson, also portrays a quiet hero, one who is independent, able to survive in the bush and, of course, protect those around him, although this time it is with a wink and a smile, depicting the Australian 'larrikin' character.[9] This filmic matter embodies the bush in a very particular way, making and teaching a very particular idea of masculinity and maleness; the 'mate', the 'battler', who struggles, albeit quietly, but is also at one with the practices, 'the ways' of the bush. This mythologising further perpetuates the powerful images that have been made and remade by the bush poets Paterson and Lawson, the artists of the Heidelberg School and Nolan's work, as mentioned previously.

One of the reasons for this similarity in the making of filmic matter is that the Australian film industry had a revitalisation in the 1970s, when the government directly bankrolled Australian films. This entanglement of art and politics resulted in the matter of film being used to sustain and consolidate a political agenda of a very particular Australian identity that was used at home and abroad (Dermody and Jacka 1988). The matter of the film was no longer an artistic, cultural or even commercial enterprise but a cog in the assemblage of championing official, conservative, fixed representations of Australian culture and nationhood. Consequently films that presented the nation in a less than favourable light were avoided (Dermody and Jacka 1988).

However, more recently, alternative representations of Australian culture and the bush have come to the fore. Instead of the bush as a place-world of quiet, male heroes and good-natured, male larrikins, the Australian movie industry began to make the bush as a place of rednecks, racists, murderers, homophobes and sexists. *The Adventures of Priscilla, Queen of the Desert* is a comedy/drama based around the journey of three drag queens (two homosexual and one transsexual) travelling across the Australian 'outback' from Sydney to Alice Springs in a tour bus they have named 'Priscilla'. In one scene, the director Stephan Elliot showed outback men watching a Filipino woman shoot ping-pong balls out of her vagina. Another scene depicted one of the main characters being surrounded by a group of 'locals' with the threat of an imminent beating, just because he was gay. This matter also presents a singular and fixed idea of the place-world of the bush, the outback, but now it is one that is uncultured, racist, lewd and intolerant, though still male. This proved very powerful, because many film critics had trouble differentiating fact from stereotypical fiction:

> *The Adventures of Priscilla, Queen of the Desert* went further than any of these in attacking the *Crocodile Dundee* mythology of the essentially harmless heterosexual outback male. These same types of men, usually depicted in bars in Priscilla, can be suspicious, violent, vulgar and extremely intolerant, especially when confronted with alternative definitions of masculinity. (Byrnes 1994: 3)

This matter makes the bush and those who live in the bush in a similar way; there are occasional anomalies, but predominantly the materiality of place makes and teaches particular ideas and ways of this place-world that have become homogenised and fixed, a stereotype. Consequently, there is an assumption that all of the place-worlds that can be named the bush and/or the outback are the same.

The purpose and power of this materiality for placemaking is that it can provide unity, a sense of commonality and belonging. People feel that they not only know this place-world, but that they are sharing this knowing and are therefore part of a nation, affirming the identity of Australia and the socio-materiality of being Australians. Even though these may not be 'true' in practice, they are true in myth; for this reason, belief in the stereotype, belief in the idea is therefore a fact in itself, and is destined to be repeated and used for various sociocultural-economic purposes. Yet while these socio-matterings have the power to make and bring Australians together, they can also be used to exclude, specifically women and Indigenous Australians, from the national identity.

It could be argued that within these discourses the female gender is represented in the form of the Land itself. This is illustrated by Mackellar ('I love her far horizons, / I love her jewel-sea, / Her beauty and her terror'), McCubbin ('you only have to wait and watch her varying moods' [Stuart 1993: 102]) and Luhrmann ('prepare to be bowled over by her stunning overwhelming power' [Robinson 2008: 3]), who all personify Australia as female. The function of female pronouns is to imply a close bond, an innate connection with the landscape, similar to the relationship that Indigenous Australians have. However, this excludes the voices of real women in the making of a national identity, just as it does the voices of Indigenous Australians.

However, the voices of women and indigenous Australians have been acknowledged at the start of this new century in the film *Rabbit-Proof Fence*, which is based on the book *Follow the Rabbit-Proof Fence* by Doris Pilkington Garimara (1996). The film tells the story of three Aboriginal girls who are forcibly taken away from their mother to live in a state-run home and their subsequent escape and journey, when they walk for nine weeks along 1,500 miles (2,400 km) of the Australian rabbit-proof fence to return to their community. The fence of the title, the State Barrier Fence of Western Australia, formerly known as the No. 1 Rabbit-proof Fence, is a pest-exclusion fence built between 1901 and 1907 that stretches 3,253 kilometres, intended to keep rabbits and other agricultural pests out of Western Australian pastoral areas (Broomhall 1991). This film is only one narrative of many experiences of indigenous Australians from the Stolen Generations (Brewster 2007). The Stolen Generations is a term used to describe those children of Australian Aboriginal and Torres Strait Islander descent who were removed from their families by Australian federal and state government agencies and church missions, under Acts of their respective parliaments (Brewster 2007). The removals occurred in the period between approximately 1869 and 1969, although in some places children were still being taken in the 1970s (Brewster 2007). Noyce's film is not only about the voices of the excluded from the bush, that is, female and Indigenous; Noyce also presents the sociopolitical tension that still exists in Australia today between Indigenous and non-Indigenous Australians. Therefore this filmic matter disrupts the previously discussed makings of the bush in the creation of an Australian national identity; hence the bush is made as a place-world that is contested and not fixed or timeless.

Through the deep mapping of poetic, artistic and filmic materials and discourses we can understand and learn how these are made and also how they can be used to produce a particular national identity. However, there is a tension in these materials, because even though they may enable inclusion, they also exclude. The matter of the place-world teaches us and we learn to make place, but the very absence of matter also teaches, as is evident in the political geography of remote Australia.

Where is the Bush?

From my experiences working, living and researching in remote Australia, the official terms, parameters and descriptors of what and where remote Australia is are highly contested. One of the reasons identified by Hugo et al. (1997) is that Australia is a big place and not many people live there. But what is big? The landmass of Australia is equal to that of the 48 contiguous states of the United States. However, the significance of the landmass of Australia comes into perspective when you compare the population of the United States (307,212,000 [CIA 2010]) with that of Australia (21,262,641, where the majority of the population is distributed along the temperate south-eastern coastline in cities and suburbs [ABS 2013a]) (Fig. 2.1). Consequently, not only is Australia a big place with not many people but the majority, including Indigenous Australians, live in either cities or suburbs along or near the coastline.

The Aboriginal and Torres Strait Islander population at the last Australian census made up approximately 2.5 per cent of the overall population (517,174 [ABS 2018]). Contrary to myths and stereotypes, the majority of Indigenous people live in Australian cities, with the highest population living in Sydney; only 8 per cent of Indigenous people live in 'remote' Australia (ABS 2018). However, a person does not stop being Aboriginal or Torres Strait Islander because of where they live. The legal definition provided by the Federal Court declares that 'a person is Indigenous when they are of Aboriginal or Torres Strait Islander descent, that person identifies with the culture and is accepted as such by the community in which they live' (*Gibbs* v. *Capewell* 1995; *Shaw* v. *Wolf* 1999),

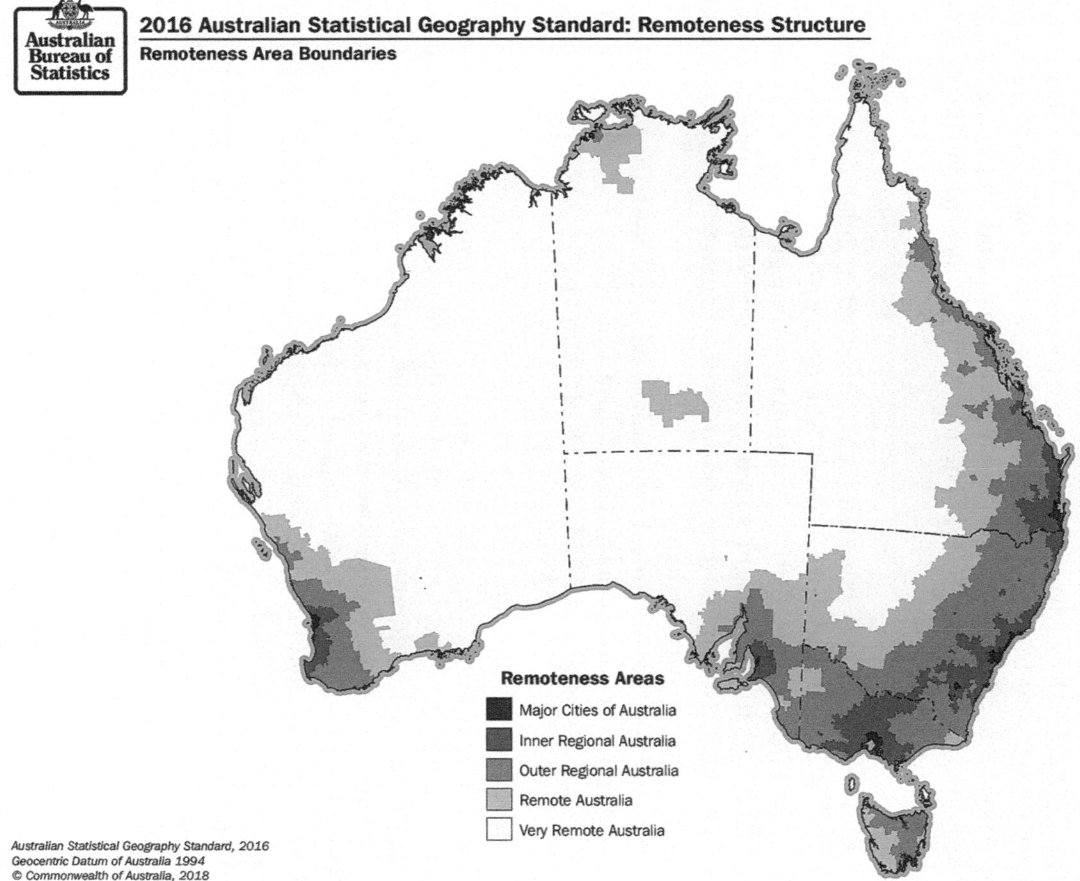

Figure 2.1 Remoteness Australia (ABS 2016)

whether that community is in Nhulunbuy, Bondi or Perth. However, the connection to Land or 'country' is essential to Australian Aboriginal identity, life and culture (Plumwood 2005).

This connection or ownership of 'country' is legally recognised by non-Indigenous Australia through native title, the Australian version of the common law doctrine of Aboriginal title. Native title is 'the recognition by Australian law that Indigenous people have rights and interests to their land that come from their traditional laws and customs' (Russel 2005: 2). Native title can coexist with non-Indigenous proprietary rights, and the Federal Court of Australia mediates claims made by Aboriginal and Torres Strait Islander peoples and makes native title determinations (Russel 2005). The native title concerns the interaction of two systems of law:

- The traditional laws and customs that regulated the lives of Aboriginal and Torres Strait Islanders prior to Australia's colonisation by the British ('customary Aboriginal law'). Although colonisation wrought social changes upon the Aborigines, customary Aboriginal law continues to regulate the lives of many Indigenous Australians.
- The now dominant, English-derived legal system, which was brought to Australia with colonisation, which includes the common law and enacted laws ('Australian law'). (AIATSIS 2012)

However, only Australian laws are enforced directly in Australian courts. Native title is not a concept that forms part of customary Aboriginal law – rather, it is the term adopted to describe the rights to land and water possessed by Indigenous Australians under their customary laws, which have been recognised by the Australian legal system only since 1993 (AIATSIS 2012). For Aboriginal people, their very being is tied to their land. As stated by Gale, 'you whites think you can own the land but you are wrong, it is the land that owns you' and 'our [settler] cultural arrogance, personal greed and complete misunderstanding of the ties that bind people to land are now costing this nation dearly' (2005: 360).

Plumwood (2005) contends that this is evident in Australia through the worst vegetation clearance, land degradation and biodiversity extinction rates in the world. Native title can be possessed by a community or individual depending on the content of the traditional laws and customs, and ranges from land in cities to remote Australia; access and usage rights such as water and so on; and exclusive possession, especially in relation to sacred sites (Russel 2005). An additional issue to the spaces between land, bodies, ownership, law and culture is that the place-world may be considered remote in one part of Australia and may not be considered remote in another.

The Australian Bureau of Statistics (ABS), Australia's national statistical agency, did not have a standard classification of remoteness until 2001. Other classifications allowed quantitative comparisons between 'city' and 'country', but no categorisation existed in relation to remoteness. Before 2001 the Australian Standard Geographical Classification (ASGC) consisted of six parallel structures that divided geographical Australia into different regions and hierarchies of regions, two of which were Urban and Rural (ABS 2013b); there was nothing about remote or isolated. These descriptors did not distinguish between rural areas on the fringe of Sydney, the most populated city in Australia, and rural areas in the centre of Australia, possible the most remote region in the country.

One of the reasons for this is that the ABS used population to distinguish geographical areas (ABS 2016a), which resulted in those townships that had a population of 999 or below, regardless of proximity to metropolitan areas and dominant industries, being classed together as rural. One of the bases for this classification was that the ABS used residential areas of over 1,000 people as data collection points and these areas could not be classified as rural (ABS 2016a). In 1998 a steering committee, formed by the then Commonwealth Department of Health and Aged Care (DH&AC), concluded that the ASGC concept of Urban/ Rural did not encompass all the factors that distinguish the 'city' from the 'country' (DH&AC 2001; ABS 2013b). Additionally, the terminology used, sometimes interchangeably, such as 'urban', 'metropolitan', 'rural', 'regional' or even 'the bush' and 'the outback' needed to be addressed. The steering committee concluded that the critical concept in the geography of Australia is 'remoteness', and that what defines 'city' and 'country' in this context is how far one travels to access goods and services (DH&AC 2001; ABS 2013b).

According to the steering committee, remoteness in terms of distance to travel to access goods and services 'reflects the recognition of the locational disadvantage suffered by Australians residing in areas of low accessibility to services, and that there is a need to embrace different types and standards of government service provision in response to these barriers' (DH&AC 2001: 21). The DH&AC removed the binary of urban and rural, and positioned remoteness on a continuum from accessible to remote and very remote: 'the new Remoteness Structure covers the whole of Australia and classifies Australia into regions which share common characteristics of remoteness' (ABS 2013b: 3). There are now six remoteness areas: 'Major Cities of Australia, Inner Regional Australia, Outer Regional Australia, Remote Australia, Very Remote Australia and Migratory' (Trewin 2001: 3). To determine the remoteness of a place-world, the Accessibility/Remoteness Index of Australia (ARIA) is used, 'where remoteness is defined on the basis of the road distance from any point to the nearest town/service centre in each of five population size classes' (ABS 2013b: 9). The population size of the town or service centre is used as a substitute for the availability of a range of services, and road distance is used as a proxy for the degree of remoteness from those services (Trewin 2001).

It would appear that the ARIA shines a light on the issues of access and equity facing those living in areas of remote and very remote Australia. However, Trewin states very clearly that the

> Remoteness classification, like other statistical geographies, provides a framework for the collection, dissemination and analysis of data. It is not intended to be a 'stand alone' indicator of advantage or disadvantage . . . the Remoteness classification should be used as a framework for statistical analysis and not used as a simplistic answer to complex questions. (2001: 19)

While this suggests that the remoteness classification may not assist in answering complex questions of equity and access, what it does highlight is that the matter of these place-worlds and the spaces between bodies, and the matter of distance and time to travel to facilities and services, is being used as a very powerful geopolitical force. But why did it take until the twenty-first century to develop a standard geographical classification of Australia?

According to the ABS (2013a) and the ARIA, over 86 per cent of Australia's landmass is classified as remote and very remote, with only 2.9 per cent of the population living there. Consequently, an estimated 97 per cent of the total population resides in only 13 per cent of the country, with over two-thirds (65.9 per cent) of this population located in Major Cities and the rest (31.1 per cent) residing in Inner and Outer Regional areas (ABS 2011). It could be argued that the delay in the geographical classification of Australia has more to do with how few people live in remote/very remote Australia, rather than the large proportion of the landmass of Australia that is classified as remote/very remote. The very absence of bodies matters. As stated above, 'Remoteness classification . . . is not intended to be a "stand alone" indicator of advantage or disadvantage' (Trewin 2001: 19). However, the ARIA uses travelling distance from a range of services as a measure. So, if you do not live close to services/facilities such as hospitals, schools and so on that are considered necessary to life and that many would take for granted, then the matter of time and distance from these makes living in these place-worlds a disadvantage. This is because the presence of the matter of time and distance from services renders these place-worlds lacking because of the absence of matter – a range of services. However, if the ARIA were measuring the distance from matter that is considered harmful or negative, such as noise, pollution or conflict, then perhaps living in these place-worlds would be considered advantageous and not lacking.

Geopolitically the place-world of remote Australia is conceived as lacking matter, and as a result is devalued, as evidenced by a historical lack of official definition, the confusion of multiple terms and parameters, and the only recent classification that measures travelling distance from a range of services. This geopolitical matter produces ways of knowing and meanings that in turn create practices of statistics and measurements that are 'expressions of the structure of domination that are consciously and unconsciously reproduced' (Sulkunen 1982: 103). This can be politically understood as creating and maintaining the domination and oppression of those who live in remote Australia. Even though I contend that there are issues with the ARIA as a geopolitical material-method of measuring remoteness, I do acknowledge and appreciate that at least there is a political recognition of the place-worlds of remote and very remote Australia. The matter of place-worlds does matter politically and these geopolitical materials also have an impact on education in the bush.

Education in the Bush

I have lived in the place-world of the bush, and it is through and from these experiences of living but also teaching and learning that I have a deepened understanding of the effect the matter of these place-worlds has on education. I have conducted research with school communities (parents, students and teachers) in these place-worlds (Page 2003; 2007), but there is a paucity of research on education in remote communities and specifically the impact of socio-materiality on education. As previously discussed, the ABS (2013b) developed clear descriptors of what disinguishes the places of remote and rural Australia from the cities of Australia, using distance from services and facilities as a key criterion. The making of these categories is clearly based on the absence of matter, what is lacking or not evident, even though the ABS clearly stipulates that this is not the case (ABS 2016a). This is further illustrated by the landmark policy statement by the Australian Commonwealth Schools Commission in 1988, *Schooling in Rural Australia*: 'Rural Australia was defined as being all of the nation excluding . . . [seven] greater metropolitan regions and, generally, areas within 50 kilometres of those regions. Areas that are outside the 150 kilometre boundary line are classified as isolated' (1988: 24). So, rural Australia is *not* the 'greater metropolitan region', therefore positioning these place-worlds and the people who live there as Other, because the norm is the metropolitan. Because of these geopolitical materials, rural and remote formal education can then be understood as lacking or limited.

The limitations identified by Evans (2003) are the high costs of transport and communication, for example the internet. Access to broadband is limited, and a dial-up connection is charged at long-distance telephone rates (Australian Commonwealth Schools Commission 1988; McKenzie et al. 1996; HREOC 2000a; 2000b; 2000c) and may be highly subsidised. The physical proximity of communities has also been included as a limitation where neighbouring communities have vast distances separating them. Attracting staff to schools in these areas has also been identified as a limitation (Australian Commonwealth Schools Commission 1988; McKenzie et al. 1996; HREOC 2000a; 2000b; 2000c; Turpin et al. 2003), as many people are unwilling to live and work in areas where access to services is restricted and sometimes non-existent (Mills and Gale 2003; Roberts 2004). Without staff, schools cannot offer some subject areas and students may then need to be sent to schools that can provide these subjects. Additionally, many remote communities have high levels of poverty that can then compound the problems already produced by isolation (Australian Commonwealth Schools Commission 1988; HREOC 2000a; 2000b; 2000c; Turpin et al. 2003).

This discourse of lack has also persisted in studies that concentrate on youth experience in rural and remote communities (Danaher et al. 2001; Burnell 2003; McGrath 2001):

> Research generally suggests that between 16 and 20 per cent of children and adolescents have significant mental health problems. The experts tend to agree that in Australia rural youth face the greater risk. They're more likely to commit suicide, to have fatal accidents, and to abuse alcohol. (Wynhausen 1998: 20)

This can then result in a generalised understanding that all young people who live in the bush drink alcohol to excess, have fatal accidents and commit suicide. While not discounting the veracity of these studies, it appears that a deficit model underpins such research, because it implies that non-metropolitan Australia is problematic in comparison to metropolitan Australia. This again results in a singular, homogenised and fixed understanding of this place-world.

There is some educational research that does consider the particulars and specifics of the bush; however, it usually focuses on one pedagogy, that of the School of the Air and distance education (Tynan and O'Neill 2007; Lowrie 2007). This pedagogy is available for students who live in remote and rural areas but do not have daily access to school, that is, the distance to travel to school is too great. However, the majority of school students who live in the place-world of the bush do have daily access to school; over 5,000 schools are located in remote areas, more than 4,000 of which are operated by state education authorities (ABS 2019). These schools have relatively small student enrolments and concomitantly a small teaching staff (Australian Commonwealth Schools Commission 1988; HREOC 2000a; 2000b; 2000c; Turpin et al. 2003).

In 1999/2000 the Human Rights and Equal Opportunity Commission (HREOC) attempted to address the issues of a paucity of research on education in these places and to disrupt the fixed, singular knowledges of pedagogy in the bush (HREOC 2000a; 2000b; 2000c). Chris Sidoti, the Human Rights Commissioner at the time, called these communities 'forgotten', and the aim of the study was to ascertain 'the impact of this forgetting on their basic human rights' (Sidoti 1999). According to the UN Universal Declaration of Human Rights, 'everyone has a right to Education' because it is instrumental in the realisation of personal and political power, and has the ability to break cycles of disadvantage and disempowerment. Education can also be fundamental to the full enjoyment of most other human rights, as well as to the exercise of social responsibilities (including respect for human rights): 'An empowerment right, education is the primary vehicle by which economically and socially marginalized adults and children can lift themselves out of poverty and obtain the means to participate fully in their communities' (United Nations 1948: 13).

However, the HREOC inquiry 'confirmed the disadvantage experienced by rural and remote school students on nearly every indicator of education including availability, accessibility, affordability and acceptability' (2000c: 14). The inquiry confirmed that Australians who live in rural and remote communities 'do not enjoy the right to education' (Sidoti 1999), and made seventy-three recommendations aimed at improving school education in rural and remote Australia (HREOC 2000a; Turpin et al. 2003). Sidoti's speech states that the 'work involves bringing to the attention of the government and the wider community, human rights violations against some of the most disadvantaged people in Australia'. This sociopolitical-material discourse is an attempt to acknowledge the 'forgotten' communities and for them to be seen and heard, making them visible to those who have power to disrupt these deficit discourses and address basic human rights. But if education in the bush is understood as lacking, and an absence of matter, there is a persistence of these socio-material practices and then a failure to see and understand the place-worlds of the bush as dynamic and complex.

These so-called limitations can be made into opportunities that then create potential and become an advantage. Small class sizes are not a limitation because there can be more personalised learning (Luck 2003). The school community (staff, students and parents) are important elements in a community's identity (Hobbs 1994; Wright-Smith 1996), so the smaller the school the stronger the school–wider community links, resulting in the school becoming the hub or a community gathering point (Wyn and Stokes 1998), and a greater entanglement of schools and community. As stated above, a limitation on education in the bush is the small range of subject areas offered; not all rural and remote schools offer art or the arts as part of the secondary curriculum (Australian Commonwealth Schools Commission 1988; Sidoti 1999). However, there are enrichment programmes that actively promote and support art/s education for small and one-teacher schools.

The Priority Country Area Program (PCAP) provides funding to students from geographically isolated areas who have restricted access to educational, social and cultural experiences (Sidoti 1999). The Queensland South West region of PCAP implements cultural activities programmes: art kits and visiting artists. The art kits are loaned to schools for a four-week period. These kits include all the materials and equipment needed for a particular art activity. The activities include screen-printing, marbling, creative paper weaving and so on (PCAP 1996). The visiting artist programme employs artists for four to six weeks at different times of the year (PCAP 1996; 1997). The artists visit PCAP communities, 'spending time, showing, making, talking, giving help and enriching the arts experience for primary and secondary students' (PCAP 1996: 16).

This programme of visiting artists was originally fully funded by PCAP with a budget of $AU50,000 (PCAP 1998). In 1999 the budget was increased to $AU88,000, and schools also contributed to the costs (PCAP 1996; 1998). The Queensland South West PCAP evaluated the programme through a survey, and found that there was a very high level of belief among artists, principals, teachers and parents that the programme was effective and offered quality arts pedagogical experiences (PCAP 1998). However, these socio-material practices of education in the bush produce knowledges and understandings that learning and teaching art is 'only doing and making', and is removed from the everyday. It is something that is only done on special occasions, when an expert comes into the community (Page 2007), and is fun and an adjunct, instead of being an integral component of everyday teaching and learning (Stankiewicz 2001).

Not only is the place-world of remote Australia geopolitically made as lacking, it is also educationally made as lacking. The socio-materiality of this place-world makes pedagogical ways of knowing and meanings that in turn create practices of domination and oppression. So the matter of this place-world of the bush does matter. Because not only does matter teach, a material pedagogy, the matter of the place-world also affects pedagogy. The what and how we teach and learn is effected by where we teach and learn. But we need to consciously and critically disrupt the socio-material practices that enable oppression and singular, fixed ways of knowing, and go beyond the binary of 'bush' and 'city'. This then enables a deep mapping and understanding of the differences of 'where' that can make a difference.

Australia's national image is strongly rooted in a particular socio-material understanding and meaning of the bush, a remote place-world. Australians claim to have a proud history of giving everybody, regardless of location and social circumstance, 'a fair go'. However, as illustrated above, such understandings can be successfully challenged by anyone who is an Indigenous Australian, female and/or who lives in place-worlds that are significantly lacking in the matter that matters geopolitically, ironically the very place that is mythologised, the bush. The place-world of the bush is made and remade though and with socio-cultural materials, practices and discourse. The deep mapping of these linguistic, geopolitical, poetic, filmic, art and education materials and their forces and power relations may promote understandings of how the place-world of the bush is made and remade, but also how it is used to further political and sociocultural agendas of national identity and nationhood. It also demonstrates that these practices and discourses perpetuate and sustain one-dimensional, timeless and fixed meanings, as Gill states: 'practices that promote opacity, insular singularity of place, perspective and life, and diminish variety and complexity by homogenising places are immoral' (2005: 42).

This is because the socio-materiality of place, presence or absence, has the power to include but also to exclude, to identify and contribute to who we are: 'forces that have, over the millennia, shaped that very distinctive Australia . . . kangaroos to gum trees and Aboriginal cultures – are currently working on us, shaping our culture and who we are' (Flannery 2002). Our relationships with place is very pervasive but also complex, and is made, remade and learned through and with broad, big, Political (big P), visible, socio-material practices. But these practices can also be specific, small, political (small p), felt, invisible and of the everyday. But what is place? In the next chapter, I map the theoretical and philosophical journey of place, and clarify the premise and positioning of place for this assemblage, but also the very persistence of place in making who and how we are.

Notes

1. This quote comes from a print campaign for Tourism Australia in the *Metro*, a free newspaper distributed in London.
2. The French term *en plein air* means out of doors and refers to the practice of painting entire finished pictures outside; see <https://www.tate.org.uk/art/art-terms/p/plein-air>, last accessed 14 January 2020.
3. <https://www.theartistsroad.net/articles/australianimpressionists>, last accessed 14 January 2020.
4. Note the genderising and sexualising imagery.
5. See <http://www.ngv.vic.gov.au/explore/collection/work/5975/>, last accessed 14 January 2020.
6. 'Tusque', 'The National Gallery: "On the Line"', *Australian Magazine*, July 1886, <https://www.theartistsroad.net/articles/australianimpressionists>, last accessed 14 January 2020.
7. See <https://nga.gov.au/nolan/>, last accessed 14 January 2020.
8. See <https://www.artgallery.nsw.gov.au/collection/artists/gascoigne-rosalie/>, last accessed 14 January 2020.
9. A 'larrikin' is a person who is given to comical, outlandish behaviour (*OED*). Steve Irwin, the crocodile hunter, was described as a larrikin: 'He was a larrikin: a person who pays little attention to what others think about them, who breaks the rules of social convention and is prone to outlandish behaviour. The thing about Irwin is that he did it with crocodiles' (Lalor and Bodey 2006: 1).

CHAPTER 3

Place

Place is more than a container or background for action, matter and thought. It is at one with the matter-action-thought of the body – a process of embodiment. There are many theoretical understandings of place with different epistemological underpinnings, and because of this theories of place have been on a journey through the history of philosophical thought. In this chapter I map this journey; through this process I have found 'my place', my positioning. Underpinned by new materialism I maintain that there cannot be place without the body, and that place is continually made and remade through the everyday repeated and learned social and material practices of the body. This intra-action of bodies with the socio-material results in our ways of knowing, making and also learning place, emerging in the between of our embodied engagement with the world. But this also suggests that the meanings of place are socially and materially made and learned. Consequently, the way we experience place, our knowledge of place and how we learn to make place emerge from and through repeated practices, and it is through these individual and shared placemaking practices that belonging is performed, and ultimately learned and taught.

But this mapping is by no means finished or comprehensive. It is a beginning that is generative in that I am playing with, or evolving, my positioning, and trying to understand the potential and possibilities of place, where, with everyday practices, our embodied and situated knowledges, the very intra-actions of matter and meaning, can be made visible/known/learned. But what is place? How are the body and place bound together, and how are the meanings of place learned and how do they emerge within, through and from these socio-material relations and practices? According to Casey (1998), we are placed beings to begin with, which means that we are always somewhere, so place can be considered pervasive. However, theoretically it is also very complex and more often than not very ambiguous. Through my examination and mapping of 'place' I have found many philosophers and theorists who have theorised place as a container, a location, a site, a region, an element of space and a process. However, the epistemological underpinnings of these terms vary enormously.

Consequently, I needed to delve into the deep and sometimes dark theoretical waters to understand what place is not, in order to understand and define what it is. But this mapping has also supported an evolving new materialist positioning of place, an understanding of the theoretical history of place where sometimes seemingly heterogeneous scholarship is entangled, because it can be 'the patterns of difference that make a difference' (Dolphijn and van der Tuin 2012: 50), and where the very intra-actions of matter and meaning can be made visible.

The Pervasiveness and Persistence of Place

I begin with Aristotle (following Plato), who recognised place as a key concept and made 'where' one of the ten indispensable categories of every substance: 'wherever we turn in the known universe – we find place awaiting us and shaping any move we might wish to make' (Aristotle 1983: 26). For Aristotle, place is all around, as an inner surface of a container, as something that is bounded and enveloping that has an indispensable role in the universe and comes before all other things. Within this premise, Aristotle's theory also acknowledges the body and its prominent role in place particular to the void, where void is defined as 'place bereft of body' (1983: 26).

Aristotle appears to take a phenomenological as well as a physical approach to place, and deals with place 'in itself', as it contains, and also how it is 'relative to other things' (1983: 12–22) such as the body. In other words, place is conceived as a characteristic of the physical world that defines its physical presence and then, through this presence, actively dynamically surrounds and envelops the body. Through this premise we might think that the omnipotence and power of place is assured, because Aristotle acknowledged the pervasiveness of place in our very being, and that we are not simply 'being', we are always 'being there':

> It has the power to make things be somewhere and to hold and guard them once they are there. Without place, things would not only fail to be located, they would not even be things: they would have no place to be the things they are . . . it would be a loss in a kind of being. (Casey 1998: 71)

However, from the medieval to the early modern era, this phenomenological concept of place was dulled and eventually subsumed by the absolute concept of space, and place was reduced to sites and geometrical points.

When I was first introduced to the concept of place, it was alongside the concept of space. However, when I questioned what the difference was, it was explained to me that the two simply go together, like Forrest Gump's 'peas and carrots'. In a way this is correct, because the rise of the exploration and theorisation of space, and the fall of place, from the sixteenth to the eighteenth centuries was a reaction to Aristotle's phenomenological premise of place, resulting in a progressive mathematisation of nature. This is evident in the work of Newton, Descartes, Locke, Leibniz and Kant, for whom phenomenology was deemed irrelevant, and for a period affect became redundant to philosophical thought. But to understand the theoretical positioning of place I needed to understand how place is 'not' space; specifically how place became subordinate to and absorbed within space, and how it came to be conceived as 'merely momentary subdivisions of a universal space quantitatively determined' (Collingwood 1945: 112).

Newton was perhaps the first to reduce place from the all-pervasive to the relational, place as a part of space, something that determines 'positions and distances' (1962: 6–7), a mathematical point whose position is in relation to other places or to other surrounding points. In this way, Newton conceives of place as having no independent identity or meaning, except for its relationship to space, where it becomes a means of measurement. For Newton, space is an absolute, the backdrop or setting within which physical phenomena occur, 'divested of all inherent differentiations or forces' (1962: I6) and 'abstract, infinite, homogeneous and having its own dimensionality' (1962: I8).

Newton's relational premise of place is supported by Descartes, but this premise of space differs in that space is conceived as an extension of the body. Descartes maintains that our understandings of space can only occur corporeally, because it is 'through the extended body that we understand length, breadth and depth' (1970: 45). Descartes continues Aristotle's premise of the body's necessity in our understandings, but these are quantitative understandings – measurements of space rather than the affects of place. However, Descartes does not support Newton's conception of place as a part of space, as there is a distinction between internal and external place. Internal place is the volume of a body that is determined by the body's size and shape, and external place is the relationship between bodies; place is conceived as an 'hybrid entity: as volumetric, it is like a thing; as situational', but 'it is unthing-like and purely relational' (Casey 1998: 161).

Descartes almost gives place a place by dividing place into external and internal. I argue that Descartes weakens the idea of place because this distinction locates place within space, and external place is still determined by its relative position to other bodies in space. Locke continued this exploration of space as relational, while disagreeing with Descartes' conception of space as an extension of the body. Locke purported that space could include nothing, as in pure space. Locke's idea of pure space results in distance being crucial in determining place, because space is the 'length between two Beings without considering anything else between them' (1975: 167). In other words, place, for Locke, is the distance between two points; for example, the body's distance from another body and then in relation to a third body. This conception results in an understanding that place is not a given, as Casey and Aristotle purport, but is a human convention. Place is then a mode of space that determines distance and position within space (Locke 1975).

Newton's, Descartes' and Locke's progressive mathematisation of nature has resulted in the consistent removal of the qualitative characteristics of place: colour, texture, smell, sound and other sensory qualities that can differentiate place/s. It would seem that that this removal is because these qualities are not necessary in calculating the distance between bodies. As Dean and Millar state: 'place is ever so gradually reduced, elements, characteristics, qualities are removed resulting in the reduction of place to site/situation' (2005: 16). However, the ultimate abstraction of place is achieved by Leibniz.

For Leibniz, place disappears altogether and becomes situation; instead of distance, entities are situated in relation to each other and are therefore 'reflecting and representing each other, other possible locations, and their spatial character, not their metric distance from each other' (Jolley 1984: 78). In other words, for Leibniz, situation is not only the distance between entities but also concerns the space in between such entities, where space is conceived as a 'nexus' of abstractly coordinated positions and reduces place to a position or 'simple location', as 'abstract coordinates' (Leibniz 1956: 1087), upon the axis of analytical space, an 'analysis situs' (1956: 390).

For Newton, Descartes, Locke, Leibniz and later Kant, place becomes a subdivision of space and is dulled, quantified, abstracted and eventually subsumed by space, with space being the backdrop that is all-consuming and absorbing. An additional consequence of this reduction of place in philosophical thought is that the distinctive features, multiple meanings, complexities and affect of place, as asserted by Aristotle, are simplified, homogenised and ultimately made redundant. Place becomes a mere position, a point on the geometrical XYZ axis of space. Ultimately, this reduction and abstraction of place to mathematical coordinates and their relations removes any qualitative aspects or the affect of place, and 'the world becomes a dull affair, soundless, scentless, colourless . . . endless, meaningless' (Dean and Millar 2005: 17); as a result, we do not acknowledge that we are affected by it and nor do we affect it. But place is more than a point or site in space to which we bring ourselves. As Barad, following Ruth Wilson Gilmore (1999), suggests, to replace a politics of location with a politics of possibilities asserts the need to

> dislocate the container model of space, the spatialization of time, and the reification of matter by reconceptualizing the notions of space, time, and matter using an alternative framework that shakes loose the foundational character of notions such as location and opens up a space of agency in which the dynamic intra-play of indeterminacy and determinacy reconfigures the possibilities and impossibilities of the world's becoming such that indeterminacies, contingencies and ambiguities coexist with causality. (2007: 225)

But to support this reconceptualisation of place, there is a need to philosophically and theoretically revisit the first place of place.

Embodiment with Place

The first place of place, as conceived by Aristotle, was centred on the body, as previously discussed, but most importantly the relationship between place and the body. In Aristotle, bodies and things, matter, are not as separate as we were once taught. Rather, their intra-relationship is vital to how we come to know ourselves as humans and how we intra-act with humans and non-humans – animals, climate, land, dirt etc. – to make place. Blackman maps a selection of concepts (and constructs) of the body, including regulated and regulating bodies; communicating bodies; bodies and difference; lived bodies; and the body as enactment. Blackman rejects naturalistic views of bodies 'as entities which are singular, bounded, molar and discretely human in action' (2008: 131) and argues that bodies, knowledge systems, sociability and matter are co-constructed, and that 'the psychological, biological and social are discrete entities that somehow interact' (2008: 131). Using Barad's (2007) premise of intra-action, we can conceive of the body as a complex intra-action of the social and affective; and then embodiment can be conceived as a process of encounters, of intra-actions with other bodies (Springgay 2008). But if bodies and things are made together and are entangled, then 'things' and how they act on bodies are co-constitutive of our embodied subjectivity,[1] and bodies acting on things/matter is also an important part of making subjectivity and therefore making matter matter.

Explaining this idea, Braidotti asserts that the 'enfleshed Deleuzian subject . . . is a folding-in of external influences and a simultaneously unfolding outwards of affects. A mobile entity, an enfleshed sort of memory that repeats. The Deleuzian body is ultimately an embodied memory' (2000: 159). In other words, through the repetitions or practices of bodies with matter, we are making, performing, relating, knowing, remembering, learning and being. However, for Coole and Frost a new materialist approach to embodiment is more phenomenological than Braidotti's Deleuzian embodied memory. Coole and Frost are not only concerned with how power is produced and reproduced by bodies, but they emphasise the 'active, self-transformative, practical aspects of corporeality as it participates in relationships with power' (2010: 19). This new materialist approach, as demonstrated in this assemblage, has clear implications for how we understand the politics and significance of bodies, and the practices, pedagogies and politics of placemaking.

By paying attention to things and the processes of matter, and the intra-actions between human and non-human things and worlds, we can recognise and acknowledge the intertwining of all phenomena: human, non-human, social, physical, material and immaterial. This intertwining 'withness' (Whitehead 1978), or 'mingle and mangle' (Bolt 2012: 3), is where phenomena are entangled – 'the ontological inseparability of intra-acting agencies' (Barad 2007: 338). Whitehead explains this as the way we experience things through and of the body, as in 'we see the contemporary chair, but we see it with our eyes; and we touch the contemporary chair, but we feel it with our hands' (1978: 62).

In other words, intra-actions shift our focus from the subject and/ or the object to their entanglement; the event, the action between (not in-between) is what matters. What is important is the relational, not the subject or the object-matter of the chair, but the event of where and how we bodily experience the chair; the place of the chair as well as our own sense of place, the between, the with. However, 'We do not simply respond to sense perceptions, we activate them even as they activate us. No two experiences can be exactly the same' (Manning 2009: 315). This means that not only are we always with/in bodies, we are always with matter, because 'Bodies are material-discursive phenomena that materialise in intra-action with, and are inseparable from, particular apparatuses of bodily production, that is, practices through which they become intelligible' (Barad 1998: 106). But that means that not only do we make matter, meaning and ultimately place, it also makes us; we are entangled, co-implicated in the generation and formation of knowing, being and the making of place; placemaking.

Husserl (1970) asserts the primacy of the body's role in the constitution and construction of place through the concept of 'kinaesthesia-K', explained as an embodied knowledge or 'the inner experience of the moving or resting body as it feels itself moving or pausing in a given moment' (Stroker 1987: 180). Husserl states that the 'manifold of places is never without K (i.e. a kinaesthetic sensation), nor is any K experienced without the manifold of places being fulfilled in a changing fashion' (Stroker 1987: 180). Consequently, the way we move and feel our own bodies, to use Whitehead's term, prehensions,[2] in a place-world will have a lot to do with how we experience, know and remember that place-world. For example, my own bodily movements, feelings and memories when I am with a particular place-world affects my experiences, my understandings and my sense of place. Through sharing and learning everyday repeated practices, I am able to gain a deeper understanding of the ways of making and learning place, as explored in Chapter 1.

Husserl's writings on place, by way of the body, were mainly exploratory, and at times confusing and conflicting. For example, writing about the idea of place as 'simple location', Husserl uses the words 'place' and 'position' interchangeably, and also asserts that place is always given and not something that changes with our experience of it. But this is in direct opposition to Husserl's premise of K (kinaesthesia), as discussed previously. Husserl also revisits Kant's premise that basic dimensions are rooted in the body (Stroker 1987: 80). However, despite this, Husserl's exploratory premise of the lived body can be pivotal in the ultimate resurrection of place:

> in a quite particular way the living body is constantly in the perceptual field . . . purely in terms of perception, the physical body and living body are essentially different; living body that is understood as the only one which is actually given to me in perception: my own living body. (Husserl 1970: 107)

Merleau-Ponty, in *The Phenomenology of Perception*, further focused Husserl's initial writings on the lived body, and stated that 'the lived body is our general medium for having a world' (1962: 146). Merleau-Ponty attributes this level of importance to the body because it possesses, as Baldwin asserts, 'intentionality of consciousness' (Baldwin 2004: 6) or 'corporeal intentionality' (Merleau-Ponty 1962: 387). This idea is pivotal to my assertion that lived/living body/bodies are entangled with place. That it is 'an intentional arc binding us to the life world we inhabit, replacing the Cartesian mind body dichotomy' (Merleau-Ponty 1962: 136), but also that it is 'the natural subject of perception' (Merleau-Ponty 1962: 208); but this premise of perception goes beyond vision (explored in Chapter 5).

Merleau-Ponty did not explicitly write about place; however, through the premise of 'the lived body', 'our general medium for having a world' (1962: 146), place can be resurrected. This is because this theory of perception enables the idea of place as event, that is, 'if my lived body is the subject, indeed the very source, of expressive and orientated space . . . place cannot be reduced to a sheer position in objective space' (Casey 1998: 231). This means that place can no longer be reduced to a fixed position with defined characteristics and boundaries, in the manner of Newton, Descartes, Locke and Leibniz. Instead, place can be indeterminate in character, with no definite but at the same time many representations. But place can also be imagined (virtual) and remembered, because place can be somewhere we come to, and also somewhere we have been.

This understanding of place is only possible because the body is not an object, but rather 'a system of possible actions, a virtual body with its phenomenal [place] defined by its task [practices] and situation' (Merleau-Ponty 1962: 249–50). This idea of place as phenomenal is similar to Husserl's notion of how we experience place as kinaesthetically felt situations (Stroker 1987). However, there are issues with this premise of the experience of place as only felt. This is because our bodily experiences of place are not only about the affect of place. They are also about how we learn to make place, that is, an embodied, learned knowledge: 'there is a knowledge of place which is reducible to a sort of co-existence with that place, and which is not simple nothing, even though it cannot be conveyed in the form of an objective description or even pointed out without a word being spoken' (Merleau-Ponty 1962: 105).

This knowledge of place is an embodied knowledge, but it is not stored within the body: it is an entanglement of bodies with matter/materials. We can understand embodiment, then, as the practices that are known and learned through and of our body: the knowing body that is with place. Consequently, we cannot be with place without being embodied, and to be embodied is to be with place; there can be no place without the body. As such, we cannot conceive place as a subdivision of an absolute space, or an 'Euclidean grid of identification' (Barad 2007: 240). Place is something particular that has porous boundaries, dynamic orientations and is felt, experienced, known, made and learned with the body.

Deleuze and Guattari similarly address issues of place, the body and movement with their concept of smooth space. In *A Thousand Plateaus* (1980) Deleuze and Guattari differentiate between the ideas of smooth and striated space. Striated space is gridded, linear, metric and produces order and distinct forms, whereas smooth space is heterogeneous and filled with multiplicities that resist and disrupt homogenisation and universality:

> It is a space of contact, of small tactile or manual actions of contact, rather than a visual space like Euclid's striated space . . . a heterogeneous smooth space . . . nonmetric, acentred, with rhizomatic multiplicities . . . that can be explored only by legwork, a non-limited locality. (Deleuze and Guattari 1980: 371)

Even though 'space' is used here, it is clear that with smooth space we have the open, the wandering and continuous becoming of place. Deleuze and Guattari term this the nomad space where there is a wandering, an immersion with the smooth space 'that relies not on points or objects but rather on haecceities, on sets of relations (winds, undulations of snow or sand, the song of the sand or the creaking of ice, the tactile qualities of both)' (1980: 382). This can clearly be conceived as an intra-action of bodies with matter; the matter of the winds, snow or sand, and the bodily of the hearing of the song, of the sound, the creaking of the ice and tactile qualities. But it is through the action, the movement of the body or 'legwork' with matter that we can come to know and learn placemaking, resulting in a clear positioning of Deleuze and Guattari's concept of space as a more materialist understanding of placiality and the importance of embodiment. It is the Deleuze-Guattarian concept of assemblage as a mode of thinking with making, whereby 'nomadic thought' forges 'linkages or connections between different systems of knowledge-formation' (Kaufman and McLean 1998: 5), remaking the way we see, understand and learn for this particular assemblage, place. But this assemblage is also about understanding and learning how subjects are entangled with objects – the spaces between the geo with the bio and the resulting affects and effects.

Sense of Place-belonging: The Working of the Geo with the Bio

Shaviro maintains that the aim of the Deleuze-Guattarian assemblage 'is not a totalization, a definitive tracing of limits, or a final theory of everything. It is rather an expansion of possibilities, an invention of new methods and new perspectives, an active "entertainment" of things, feelings, ideas, and propositions that were previously unavailable to us'

(2009: 148–9). This is pivotal in understanding the materiality of human geography, where there is a rejection of the divide between physical and human geography in favour of their entanglement: 'human–animal and organism–machine relations, in addition to intersubjective relations, [which] appear as constitutive of the self' (Bennett 2010: 164). This has resulted in a greater focus and paying attention to the relationship between the materiality of the geo and the bio of life, and the issues and questions arising from these intra-actions (Casey 1993; Pile and Thrift 1995; Nast and Pile 1998). This not just about meaning but about affect, sensations, that is, sense of place and belonging and how bodies are relational and are woven together with place.

A sense of place can be difficult to define and explain because it is an individual's embodied knowledge of place, 'an intensely personal response . . . which the individual experiences in daily life' (CSIRO 2001: 5). Relph describes it as 'a synaesthetic faculty that combines sight, hearing, smell, movement, touch, imagination, memory, purpose and anticipation. It is both an individual and an intersubjective attribute, closely connected to . . . personal memory and self' (1976: 48). Cresswell contends that we usually have a sense of place developed and learned from how and 'where we lived when we were children' (2004: 8). This idea of our sense of place coming from our embodied practices learned in early childhood may have originated from Bourdieu (1977; 1990a; 1990b), who maintains that the everyday world of social practice is made and learned in early childhood. It is also borne out by de Certeau, who maintains that our everyday practices are destined to 'repeat the joyful and silent experience of childhood' (1984: 109–10). Birkerts further explains this premise:

> no matter what plea or adjustment I make, I cannot catch hold of the peculiar magic of those [childhood] places . . . No effort of will can restore to me that perception that view of the horizon not yet tainted by futility – it runs through me sometimes, but I cannot summon it. And yet everything I would say about place depends on it, and everything I search for in myself involves some deep fantasy of its restoration. My best, truest, I cannot define my terms, self is vitally connected to a few square miles of land. (1986: 54)

Freud, Bachelard and Proust also suggest that to understand the making of place we may need to return, if not in actual fact, then in memory or imagination to the very earliest places we have known.

So, then, to understand how we learn placemaking, we need to return to and understand the embodied practices of our childhood. The pedagogue and cultural critic bell hooks describes a personal placemaking practice of walking: 'I need to live where I can walk . . . Walking, I will establish my presence, as one who is claiming the earth, creating a sense of belonging, a culture of place' (2009: 2). hooks explains how a personal sense of place-belonging is enabled through walking and how this practice came from a childhood where

> I was fascinated by the walkers, by the swinging arms and wide strides they made to swiftly move forward, covering miles in a day but always walking a known terrain, leaving, always coming back to the known reality, walking one clear intent . . . the certainty of knowing one's place. (2009: 2)

I understand and share hooks's desire to revisit and understand these placemaking practices of childhood. As explained in the Introduction, I spent the majority of my childhood in a rural and remote place in Australia, and so I have a sense of place – an embodied knowledge and understanding that was and is made by the my socio-material practices performed with this place. This means that, no matter how geographically remote the place, I have a 'feel for the game': a sense, an embodied knowledge of what is and is not appropriate.

However, during my first year living in London, I struggled with such a densely populated urban place. I remember on my first day of work having to catch the Tube, London's underground public transport network, with so many people all crammed in a metal box. I had to get out at every stop just to catch my breath, and everyone seemed to know where they were going. I remember the signs, the minimal coding by colour and name, having to know the colour and the name of the line I needed: East London, District, Central. I remember thinking: 'Am I heading west or east, what is the final destination?', and reminding myself always to keep to the left, not to talk and most importantly to keep moving! I did not have an embodied knowledge 'of places by direct and continuing acquaintance with them' (Merleau-Ponty 1962: 104) from my lived body. I had to learn and develop new placemaking practices. However, it is important not only to focus on an individual's embodied knowledges and senses of place, but to understand the importance of these socio-material practices, whether art and/or embodied, in understanding the power and politics of place and placemaking. As Casey states, 'the "how" and "who" are intimately linked to the "where" . . . This implacement is as social as it is personal. The idiolocal is not merely . . . individual; it is also collective in character' (1993: 23).

Belonging or a sense of belonging, and Bourdieu's concept of habitus, also offer a way to theorise a sense of belonging, of home, to a group, a place, a land and country. This is because Bourdieu's habitus practices can predispose members of a society to interact in ways consistent with the specific societal norms of their group, their community or even nation. As a consequence of these practices, there is a feeling of ease, of 'fitting in', of belonging. De Certeau maintains that this ease can enable ways to overcome alienation and forge a sense of identity, and I assert a sense of belonging, of being 'home'. As Wenger claims, 'identity in practice is defined socially not merely because it is reified in a social discourse of the self and of social categories, but also because it is produced as lived experience of participation in specific communities' (2005: 151).

Butler maintains that this identity is based on the 'lived experience of participation' or 'performativity' (2003: 12), and that it is our performed actions and behaviours (collective and individual) that constitute and make our identity/ies. Butler explains that performativity is 'not a singular act, for it is always a reiteration of a norm or set of norms, and to the extent that it requires an act-like status in the present, it conceals and dissimulates the conventions of which it is a repetition' (2003:12), Performativity, like habitus, is preconscious. The repeated performance of these norms, as stated by de Certeau, enables communities to achieve a connection to place. These repeated performances can be actual but can also be remembered, so that a sense of belonging is a product or an outcome of these performative (actual and memory) socio-material practices. Thomas Hardy, in *The Woodlanders* (1887), articulated the importance of memory for a sense of belonging, in that to

> know all about those invisible ones of the days gone by, whose feet have traversed the fields . . . what bygone domestic dramas of love, jealousy, revenge, or disappointment have been enacted in the cottages, the mansion, the street or the green. The spot may have beauty, grandeur, salubrity, convenience; but if it lacks memories it will ultimately pall upon him [*sic*] who settles there without opportunity of intercourse with his [*sic*] kind. (1996: 146)

hooks (1990) asserts that this way of understanding home, a sense of belonging, enables the making of both individual and collective identities. This is because for hooks, home was experienced as a place of resistance, an empowering place free from the oppression of the white world beyond her home, 'where one could escape the world of man-made [*sic*] constructions of race and identity' (2009: 7). For hooks, the power of place, of 'home', of belonging, is one that is inclusive and supportive.

However, for hooks home was also

> the place where I was forced to conform to someone else's image of who and what I should be. School was the place where I could forget that self and, through ideas, reinvent myself . . . To be changed by ideas was pure pleasure. But to learn ideas that ran counter to values and beliefs learned at home was to place oneself at risk, to enter the danger zone. (1994: 3)

Rose asserts that home, constructed as 'conflict-free, caring and nurturing and almost mystically venerated' (1993: 56), fails to recognise the differences between people and place and the 'situated realities of historical and spatial sedimentations of power' (Tuck and McKenzie 2015: 36). This is because 'home' can be a place of discrimination, oppression or neglect, with an unequal distribution of power, resources and matter. This can then result in a lack of belonging or 'disbelonging', as examined by Plumwood (2005) and as explored in Chapter 2, where I mapped the 'structuring structures' of a specific place-world and examined how they are used to make and sustain intimate forms of national self-understanding, but also how the power and politics of placemaking practices can 'disconnect certain groups from the national character' (Rose 1996: 34).

In this chapter I have attempted to map the theoretical underpinnings of place, from Aristotle's clear and pervading concept of place and the foci of 'where', the loss of place in the geometrical labyrinth of space (Newton, Locke, Leibniz, Kant), and then the resurrection of place with the body through Whitehead, Husserl and, most notably, Merleau-Ponty. Through this, I have found my place, my theoretical underpinning of place, my positioning, where I feel I fit. My place is everywhere, it is not a quantifiable component of space, nor a fixed, definite representation. It is eventmental, a continuous open practice (Casey 1998; Massey 1997; 2005; Cresswell 2004) that is constituted through, and made with, the body; and

> as such . . . place accomplishes what is begun in body: it possesses an inclusiveness that does not exclude anything but reaches out to everything . . . to all constructed as well as natural things [matter]. It is something for which we continually have to discover or invent new forms of understanding. (Casey 1998: 336)

It is not my intention to classify or pin down place. Instead, as Casey states above, my intention is to 'discover or invent new forms of understanding' and to learn and understand the ways we know and make place, how it is practised, learned and taught. This can then enable 'an unfolding of cultural theory, nonlinear coding practices, cutting across matter and signification' (Dolphijn and van der Tuin 2012: 111), so that we can be conscious of the 'mingle-mangle' of everyday practices and the power and politics of placemaking, and that the matter of place matters.

I have touched on many understandings of place, its various epistemological foundations, and the very complex journey that place has been on in philosophical thought, pulling at the thread of place through the work of Aristotle and then Newton, Descartes and Kant, who enabled the gradual subsuming of place by space, to finally return to Aristotle's premise of the bound relationship between place and the body, leading to the resurrection of place. I argue that there can be no place without the body, and that place is continually made and remade through the everyday social and material practices of the body. Place is more than a background for action, matter and thought. Place is a continuous, open, practised entanglement of life. Conceptualising place as going beyond the social enables a deepened understanding of materiality and an understanding of the multiplicity of human and non-human ways and pedagogies. But this also supports a politics of place to enable us to understand the power and pedagogies of placemaking: the local and the global, the individual and the collective, the embodied and material.

Notes

1. From Deleuze, subjectivity is conceived as 'a specific or collective individuation relating to an event' (1995: 99). Human subjectivity is a collection of dividuations which are activated differently in various machinic arrangements.
2. That is, a basic, extrasensory awareness that all experiences or events have of all earlier experiences-events. These bodily prehensions involve the 'repetition' of the world, and it is through these bodily prehensions 'that the treasures of the past environment are poured into living occasions (events)' (Whitehead 1978: 339).

CHAPTER 4

Embodied and Material Pedagogies

The body and the practices of embodiment are fundamental to our ways of knowing place. However, these ways of knowing and making place are not produced in isolation. They are produced through the continuous practices of embodied and material learning and teaching. In this chapter I develop this new materialist theory of pedagogy where the intra-actions of bodies with matter are conceived as pedagogic: an embodied and material pedagogy. I examine and explore how materials teach and how we learn through a series of dynamic evolving intra-actions that is a continuous open pedagogic practice that is constituted through, and made by, the body with matter/materials to make place.

Generically, pedagogy can be defined as the 'theory and instruction of teaching and learning' that comes from the Greek 'to lead the child' (*OED*). First of all, where is practice in this definition? Also this particular definition of 'leading the child' resonates with Freire's (1970) premise of 'banking education', in which teaching and learning are conceived as processes of transmission where 'students are regarded merely as passive consumers' (hooks 1994: 40). In opposition to this conception, Freire and hooks conceive of pedagogy as a 'union of the mind, body and spirit, not just for striving for knowledge in books, but knowledge about how to live in the world' (hooks 1994: 15), a practice of how to live in the world. Using this idea, pedagogy can then be understood as an entanglement of the body with the world (social and material) that we learn with but that also teaches. Pedagogy, in my definition, is the practices and theories of teaching and learning about how to live with the world, and this can then occur everywhere, not only in the classroom; and it can be also be personal/individual and/or public/collective (Irwin et al. 2009). Ellsworth states that 'specific to pedagogy is the experience of the corporeality of the body's time and space when it is in the midst of learning' (2005: 4) and Barad reminds us that:

Reality is composed not of things-in-themselves or things-behind-phenomena but of all things-in-phenomena. The world is a dynamic process of intra-activity and materialization in the enactment of determinate causal structures with determinate boundaries, properties, meanings, and patterns of marks on bodies. This ongoing flow of agency through which part of the world makes itself differentially intelligible to another part of the world and through which causal structures are stabilized and destabilized does not take place in space and time but happens in the making of spacetime itself. (2007: 140)

As I stated in the previous chapter, the body and the practices of embodiment are core to our ways of knowing, but they are also fundamentally entangled with matter. Yet how does matter teach? This involves the embodied entanglement of matter with pedagogy, that is, the moments when materials and spaces impact on bodies and bodies impact on ideas.

Embodied Pedagogy

In Chapters 1 and 2 I shared the placemaking practices of the place-world of remote Australia, 'the bush'. This place-world is a specific cultural context: a field with a structured social space with rules, practices, values and positions (Bourdieu 1993) that shape and define how people make, know, understand and learn. Therefore, the meanings of this place-world are practised and performed. In other words, the way we experience place, our knowledge of place and how we learn to make place emerge from everyday practices that have social values and forces produced by intra-connected networks. However, they are also made by people with materials in these place-worlds. So, place is not a natural entity; it is made and learned: a socio-material pedagogic event whose meanings emerge from/with the between of bodily-material practices.

But what seems to be missing from Bourdieu's concept of field is the subjective or the individual, because fields, or the field, do not position or make themselves. To address the absence of the individual, Bourdieu developed the concept of the habitus: a lasting and acquired series of attitudes, practices, actions and habits that are 'durable, transposable dispositions, structured structures' (1993: 64) developed by the individual in response to what is required in the field. An example is how you greet someone when you first meet them. This means that there is an intra-action of habitus and field, because individuals possess these dispositions (habitus) that are necessary to participate in the field, but they also give it meaning. By participating in the field, individuals incorporate into their habitus the proper know-how learned from repeated practices that will enable them to function in that field. Such practices may include doing chores, washing up, laundry, as well as performative forms of greeting and social interaction. The repetition of these practices produces what Bourdieu calls a bodily hexis that reflects a positioning in a field, a 'feel for the game' (Thompson 1992: 13), a knowing and being comfortable. In other words, an embodied understanding and knowing of what is and is not appropriate in the circumstances at that time in that place, a sense of belonging.

Bourdieu describes bodily hexis as a 'political mythology realised, embodied, turned into a lasting disposition, a durable manner of standing, speaking and thereby of feeling and thinking' (1992: 13). Consequently, it is the expression of all these factors that make up our habitus, embodied in our physical being, and it is in bodily hexis that the individual combines with the social, because the body is where and how the 'very basics of culture are imprinted and enacted' (Casey 1993: 34). Previously to Bourdieu, Merleau-Ponty used the term 'customary body' (1962: 82) to describe a body that has acquired cultural patterns into its actions and habits; it is 'a matrix of habitual action' (1962: 146). For Bourdieu, the ways in which we relate with our bodies reveal the 'deepest dispositions of the habitus' (1984: 190). This is illustrated by Casey:

> As I know my way around my own house, so I know my way round all the familiar places of my 'habitat': habitual body memory (which underlies an entire set of accustomed and skilful actions) combines with awareness of place . . . Not only do we discover ever new places by means of bodily movement; we find ourselves in the midst of places we already know thanks to the intimate link between their abiding familiarity and our own corporeal habitually. (1998: 233)

However, the issue with this idea is that it suggests that habitus is only performed through and by social practices, what you are saying and doing with other social bodies. But 'things', 'matter', they are 'structuring structures'; Barad explains them as gears in a 'gear assemblage' mechanism:

> (i.e. a gear assemblage in which the gear operations literally work through one another and in which an uneven distribution of forces results in and is the enabling condition for different potentials and performances among the gears), which in an ongoing fashion is being (re)configured/(re)assembled while it is itself in the process of producing other gear assemblages. (2001: 91)

This machinic metaphor illustrates that social practices are embedded in the mechanism of materialisation, and that rather than an intersubjective social environment built on an objective material environment, the world is a material environment characterised by more or less stable physical patterns. This then means that the meanings, the making and the learning of place are not just socially made; they are bodily made and our ways of knowing and learning place emerge with and through our embodied participation in the socio-material world. Therefore, just as we know place through and with the body, we learn placemaking with embodied pedagogies.

But instead of dividing the body into making (practices) and knowing, following Merleau-Ponty, I position the body not as a source of experience and activity but as a source of knowledge. That is, 'the customary body' (Merleau-Ponty 1962: 82) or the knowing body; but the knowing body is also a source of memories, therefore it is also the remembering body. Consequently, through our intra-actions with the socio-material world we learn placemaking through individual and collective embodied (perceptions with memories) practices.

De Certeau maintains that the repetition of the practices of everyday life not only makes place but can also support the making and learning of individual and collective identities. This is demonstrated by Mary's journeying practices (see Chapter 1). These not only enable her to individually know, understand and learn place. They can also enable her to know, understand and learn place with others; to have a sense of belonging to a group, a community, or a country. This is because these repeated and performed practices not only make up but also make individual and collective identities. Butler explains that performativity is 'not a singular act, for it is always a reiteration of a norm or set of norms, and to the extent that it requires an act-like status in the present, it conceals and dissimulates the conventions of which it is a repetition' (2003: 12). These repeated performances can be actual but also remembered: past events, occasions, celebrations, rituals and stories.

As previously discussed, the main premise of Merleau-Ponty's work is the lived body. For Merleau-Ponty, 'the lived body is our general medium for having a world' (1962: 146); this is because it has 'corporeal intentionality' (1962: 387). This is where the lived body intra-acts with the socio-material world and is 'an intentional arc binding us to the life world we inhabit, replacing the Cartesian mind body dichotomy' (1962: 136). The lived body is therefore 'the natural subject of perception' (1962: 208); however, this perception goes beyond vision because perception is achieved through and of the body, and sensation is at the centre of human perception. The anthropologist Ingold, drawing on the ideas of Merleau-Ponty, states that 'the eyes and ears should not be understood as separate keyboards for the registration of sensation but as organs as a whole, in whose movement, within an environment, the activity of perception consists' (2000: 268). Like Whitehead,

Merleau-Ponty maintains that perception is not just a mental or psychological effect; it is the body's orientation in the world and there is a symbiotic relationship between the act of perception and the context of the perceiver, an entanglement if you will. Merleau-Ponty's premise of perception enables us to understand that our embodied perceptions are entangled with the social-material world; it is an intra-action 'of the whole organism in its environment' (1962: 234).

Gibson, an ecological psychologist, similarly placed the body at the centre of perception. Gibson conceived that the body is a perceptual system that 'emphasises the interrelationship between the different senses . . . in perception and the integration of sensory bodily and mental processes' (Rodaway 1994: 19–20). Similarly, Ingold places perception at the centre of his research and further develops Gibson's work through the premise that perception 'is not the achievement of a mind in a body, but of the organism as a whole in its environment, and is tantamount to the organism's own exploratory movement through the world' (2000: 3). Ingold also maintains that

> the perceptual systems not only overlap in their functions, but are also subsumed under a total system of bodily orientation . . . Looking, listening and touching therefore, are not separate activities, they are just different facets of the same activity: that of the whole organism in its environment. (2000: 261)

However, embodied perception does not occur in a vacuum. The anthropologist Howes is critical of the theories of Merleau-Ponty and Gibson, maintaining that their theories are abstracted and that research attuned to embodied perception cannot be achieved acontextually: 'we need to elicit the sensory models of those who you are studying' (2003: 49–50), and '[w]ithout some sense of how the senses are culturally attuned, there is no telling what information the environment affords' (Howes 2005: 144). Even though Merleau-Ponty's and Gibson's premises do not acknowledge the specificity of a socio-material place-world, they do enable us to learn that perception is embodied and entangled with socio-material worlds, because '[a]s places animate the ideas and feelings of persons who attend to them, these same ideas and feelings animate the places on which attention has bestowed' (Feld and Basso 1996: 53). As Whitehead suggests, the body is an active subjective participant in this embodied perception:

> You are in a certain place perceiving things. Your perception takes place where you are, and it is entirely dependent on how your body is functioning. But this functioning of the body in one place exhibits for your cognisance an aspect of

the distant environment, fading away into the general knowledge and there are things beyond. If this cognisance conveys knowledge of a transcendent world, it must be because the event which is the body unifies in itself aspects of the universe. (1978: 92)

This premise of active participation focuses on the body as a 'total event' (Whitehead 1978: 73), as embodied practices that take us into place and enable learning. As Manning explains, sensing and feeling are acts or events that matter:

> A body . . . does not exist – a body is not, it does. To sense is not simply to receive input – it is to invent . . . Sense perceptions are not simply 'out there' to be analyzed by a static body. They are body-events [where] bodies, senses, and worlds recombine to create (invent) new events. (2009: 212)

If we think of these total events as the way that matter teaches us and how we learn with matter, or how matter comes to matter, we can use Whitehead's thinking to theorise bodies as the catalyst of pedagogy. This is because bodies are conceived not as passive, objective perceivers; they are the practices of senses and feelings that inform us, teaching us about current but also past place-worlds, what Whitehead called 'prehensions'. These bodily prehensions involve the 'repetition' of the world, and it is through these bodily prehensions 'that the treasures of the past environment are poured into living occasions (events)' (Whitehead 1978: 339), and can enable placemaking and a sense of belonging.

> It creeps up on me slowly, but I start to have this feeling, and it is growing, of being totally overwhelmed: there is just so much but at the same time there is nothing . . . Jenny, Henry and Hettie continue to chat, self-assured and confident, still walking, leading me along without any regard for the lack of adults, habitation, or my feelings of anxiety . . . as I reflect on how the children, in a very short period of time, have been sharing stories, events, experiences and their ways of knowing, learning and making place, I start to feel more comfortable and at ease. I begin to relax; I know this, I have learned this before. I start to feel less alien and alienated and for the first time start to truly feel comfortable. (Chapter 1)

Because of my bodily prehensions I am intra-acting with this socio-material place-world but also with my past place-worlds; I am learning new placemaking practices but I am also enriching and extending my already learned ways of making place. Manning's research on touch explains how Whitehead's prehensions are embodied, in that

> we sense on top of senses, one sense experience always embedded in another one: cross-modal repetition with a difference. We conceive the world, not

through a linear recomposition of the geometric vectors of our experience, but by the overlapping of the folds of sense-presentation emerging alongside past-ness. (Manning 2009: 215)

It is, then, through an embodied pedagogy (perception with memory) entangled with the socio-material practices of the place-world that we learn placemaking.

An example of this is when the children I was researching with let me help them 'do jobs'. As we were walking together, and they were explaining their jobs and what they had to do, they drew my attention to markings in the dirt and told me that they were tracks made by their Dad on a motorbike heading in the direction of one of their dams, and also tracks from a mob of kangaroos heading in the direction of their neighbour's paddocks. This everyday practice of 'doing jobs' is the children's placemaking, because of the intra-action of the embodied perception of 'tracks' and the embodied memory of past experiences of these material traces of moving bodies. 'Dad on a motorbike', 'a mob of kangaroos': these are 'overlapping folds of sense-presentation' (Manning 2009: 215) emerging with or entangled with pastness.

The children were sharing with me the stories, the narratives, of the between; the bodies that made the tracks with the material of the dirt, the land. I was being taught what the material, the dirt, the markings of the land meant: 'You can know all about them from their tracks. See, you can now know about our place.' Also with their photographs the children taught me the meanings of these socio-material intra-actions, the nuances of direction, depth and location, and I started to learn the seemingly mundane socio-material practices of the children's family, animals, machines and the meanings of movements, purpose and how these are entangled and make place. I was being taught placemaking practices and how it is not about the dirt/the land or the objects/the matter, nor the bodies themselves, but the spaces between.

This placemaking is pedagogic and is inextricable from the invocation, creation and investment of embodied perception with embodied memories, because 'the body imports its own emplaced past into its present' (Casey 1998: 194); just as the body can be conceived as the knowing body it can then also be the source of memories, and is also the remembering body. As hooks states:

We are born and have our being in a place of memory. We chart our lives by everything we remember from the mundane moment to the majestic. We know ourselves through the art and act of remembering. Memories offer us a world where there is no death, where we are sustained by rituals of regard and recollection. (2009: 5)

However, new materialism does not focus solely on individual practices but on the relationalities of matter with bodies. Haraway explains that '[t]hrough their reaching into each other, through their "prehensions" or graspings, beings constitute each other and themselves. Beings do not preexist their relatings' (2003: 6). Connerton's work on collective memory indicates that 'social memory is embedded in the performativity of commemorative ceremonies' (1989: 4) in which bodies are central. Connerton also maintains that through the repeated performance of acts such as walking, journeying, ceremonies and rituals, groups, communities and cultures can share embodied memories or, as Seremetakis refers to them, 'mediation on the historical substance of experience' (1994: 7).

Seremetakis maintains that these embodied memories are not fixed in repetition, but are continually reconstituted through the practices of bringing the past into the present. They then become an inextricable element in our ways of making and learning place, like Whitehead's prehensions, Manning's folds of 'sense-presentation emerging alongside pastness' (2009: 215) and Barad's concept of memory:

> Memory does not reside in the folds of individual brains; rather, memory is the enfoldings of space-time-matter written into the universe, or better, the enfolded articulations of the universe in its mattering. Memory is not a record of a fixed past that can ever be fully erased, written over or recovered (that is, taken away or taken back into one's possession, as if it were a thing that can be owned). And remembering is not a replay of a string of moments, but an enlivening and reconfiguring of past and future that is larger than any individual. Re-membering and re-cognizing [*sic*] do not take care of, or satisfy, or in any way reduce one's responsibilities; rather, like all intra-actions, they extend the entanglements and responsibilities of which one is part. The past is never finished. It cannot be wrapped up like a package, or a scrapbook . . . we never leave it and it never leaves us behind. (2007: ix)

In other words, we fold the past back into the present at every moment, as we encounter 'the now' through our embodied histories and pedagogies, but also through material pedagogies.

Material Pedagogy

> Centering the clay, bringing the small ball into perfect reactivity for throwing, involved a ripple of different movements from hand and wrist, an inclination in the head and neck a slight tautening in the shoulders. It was . . . learning that I could not articulate. (de Waal 2011: 1)

This creative act of learning, of body with the matter of clay (not articulated, but also body with the matter of wheel and water), is what van der

Tuin asserts is an example of Barad's practices of knowing in being (van der Tuin 2014: 262). Explaining the narrative of the sculptor Souriau, van der Tuin explains that it is through the relationships of the clay and the person, in the practice of working with 'the hand, the thumb, the chisel that a statue comes about' (2014: 263), or in the case of de Waal (clay with hand with wrist with head with neck with shoulder) learning comes about. It is through bodies 'with' matter that we are making and learning; it is the intra-actions, the between of bodies with matter that is pedagogic.

From my own experiences with clay and learning to throw on a wheel, I learned how to 'pull the clay' to the point just prior to the collapse of the clay-form I was making. Through and with my body I was learning the feel of the clay, adjusting the speed of the wheel, the exact amount of water I needed to ensure slippage, and adjusting, tweaking, learning the constant and correct pressure and play of clay with my fingers, hands, arms, shoulder, back – my body. The matter – the clay, the wheel, the water – was teaching me what it could and could not do, how far it could be pulled and pushed. The between of body with the matter wherein the matter teaches and we are learning what it can do and what it cannot do; an embodied but also a material pedagogy. With placemaking it is the matter of the place-world, the Land, that teaches and that we learn with.

'You know you can smell when it's going to rain.'

'Yeah everythin' starts to feel different, everything the air, noises, it's like really heavy.'

'Yeah you can smell it and then feel it and then you can see the real grey clouds comin' in.'

But my use of the word Land refers not only to the materiality of place – earth, weather, animals and so on as articulated by the children I was researching with – but to the 'spiritual, emotional and intellectual' (Styres et al. 2013: 37) entanglements. Styres and Zinga state that

> land (the more general term) refers to landscapes as a . . . geographical and physical space that includes earth, rocks and waterways; whereas 'Land' (the proper name indicating a primary relationship) extends beyond a material fixed space. Land is a spiritually infused place [with] interconnected and interdependent relationships, cultural positioning, and is highly contextualised. (2013: 300–1)

Scudder (1979a; 1979b) maintains that Indigenous peoples practise a strong connection with the Land through deeply internalising place, and thus place is entangled with their bodies. Land can then be understood as the intra-actions of socio-material-spiritual-embodied practices, knowledges and pedagogies. Shepard explored these ideas with the Navajo in North America.

> Individual and tribal identities are built up in connection with widely separated places and the paths connecting them. Different places are successfully assimilated and internalised. They become distinct, through unconscious elements of the self, enhanced by mythology and ceremony, generating a network of deep emotional attachments that cements personality. Throughout life those places have a role in the evocation of the self and group consciousness. (1982: 58)

In learning from Indigeous scholars and cultures about the connotative differences between Land, land and place, it is important to not exclude the non-Indigenous and the urban. Styres et al. (2013), Meyer (2008) and Kawagley and Barnhardt (2010) warn against understandings of Indigenous knowledge, practices and pedagogies as static, homogensied and as only learned by those who are authentically Indigenous. Tim Flannery, a leading Australian writer on climate change, stated in a speech to mark Australia Day[1] in 2002 that there is a need for understanding that

> a true people [is created] by developing [learning] deep sustaining roots in the land . . . [as it is] . . . the only thing that we all share. It is at once our inheritance, our sustenance, and the only force ubiquitous and powerful enough to craft [to teach] . . . the land, its climate and creatures and plants defines us . . . These environmental forces . . . are currently working on us . . . and who we are. (Flannery 2002)

This working on us is what Meyer explains as where 'one does not simply learn about the land, we learn best from the land' (2008: 219); this is because Land/place/worlds teach. But it is a teacher of the 'us' not just the 'me'; in other words, these material embodied practices and pedagogies make and make up individual and collective identities. Embodied and material pedagogies are not solely concerned with describing individual sensations/perceptions and pedagogies. This is because these ways of learning and teaching are not made and/or performed in isolation; they are relational, collaborative, they are 'with'.

Wenger developed various theories of learning, including 'knowing in practice' and the 'experience of knowing' (2005: 141, 142). Knowing in practice was originally conceived by Lave and Wenger (1991) as 'situated learning', where learning is no longer a passive process of absorbing factual information (after Freire 1970), but is instead a social and collaborative process whereby theory is entangled with everyday practice with others. These 'communities of practice' (Wenger 2005) are based on apprenticeship communities and enable a way of understanding how practices are learned and knowledge formed and reproduced. However, the situatedness of this learning does not mean it is only specific to a particular place and time (Harris 2007). This is because these collaborative ways of learning are dynamic in bringing into being shared knowledges that can then be learned, taught, recreated and developed by the community as it inducts new members.

An example of this was when I went on an 'abenture' with the children I was researching with. The children shared their knowledge and practices of journeying, teaching me their ways of knowing and making place. They shared with me their material skills, knowledges, understanding and confidence (Page et al. 2011) and together we were able to 'negotiate new meanings' (Wenger 2005: 226). Through journeying and film-making we are with Mary, but these practices also keep us there, teaching us about Mary's bodily 'withness' (Whitehead 1978) with the socio-material place-world. Mary's images, film and journeying stories are not about describing the subject or the object of the journeys, for example the tractor, the tree and so on. Rather, it is about their entanglement; the event, the action between, is what matters. As Mary says 'It's not separate it's all there together with me. It's more than just what you see, you know. You just know.' Mary's journeying is not only a placemaking practice that makes the very meaning of place, it also makes us together; Mary is 'with' me. Mary is entangled, co-implicated in the generation and formation of knowing, making, learning this place-world. As such, place is made and remade on a daily basis; performed and practised, open and changing. This idea is underpinned by my earlier assertion that place is eventmental, a continuous open practice that is constantly changing and that is made through, and of, the body (Whitehead 1978; Merleau-Ponty 1962). This enables the very meanings of place to be known, understood and also learned in many different and complex ways.

But the stories are stories and walking is walking; the children's narratives are not coded messages, and simply having heard the stories is not a way of knowing or making place. These placemaking practices are the narratives entangled with the actual walking 'with' other bodies. Therefore to embody and learn this knowledge it must be practised/learned with others, meaning that Mary's journeying, and Jenny's, Henry's and Hettie's 'doin' jobs' and 'abentures', are not just an adjunct to their knowledge of place. Rather they are embodied socio-material practices and pedagogies that individually but also collectively make and enable the learning of place, just as the place-world of the bush is learned and made through and with the practices of poetry, art, film, pedagogy and geopolitics. The place-world of the bush is also learned, made and remade through and with the reiterations and repetition of embodied and socio-material practices. Consequently, through these intra-actions material pedagogy is continually being made and remade.

As I listened and talked to Mary, sharing and learning from her journeys and stories, light bulbs were going off in my head: 'Oh I get it now.' Mary, like Jenny, Henry and Hettie, was my elder. I had heard the stories and I had seen the journeys (images and films), but it was only through Mary sharing and teaching me her ways of knowing and also my own personal journeying that I came to know and understand journeying as a way of knowing and learning the place-world of the bush. As Casey (1993) maintains, journeys have very little to do with speed, distance and destination; they are more concerned with exploration and depth. Therefore, these performative constructs, the actions and behaviours of practices such as walking and journeying with, constitute and construct individual and also collective identities; and it is through these repeated socio-material bodily performances that we make and learn place. However, individuals can also contribute to multiple communities of practice, either at the same time or at various points during their lifetime, and each place-world will have its own practices and pedagogies that will and can be learned, made and shared.

But not all of these practices and pedagogies will be 'conflict-free, caring and nurturing' (Rose 1993: 56). There may be tensions, conflicts, oppression and domination (Wenger 2005) that can result in isolation, exclusion and disbelonging. This is because, as Handley et al. state:

> Individuals maintain a sense of agency through the adoption and adaptation of different forms of participation and identity construction within different communities. This approach recognizes that attempts to adapt will generate tensions within individuals, and instabilities within the communities in which they participate. These tensions are likely to be continually negotiated. (2006: 653)

These tensions can also be learned and taught from the matter of the place-world:

> I experience it everyday and it's beautiful, I know that. But it still surprises me. Just when you think you know it and think it's yours, it all changes. You can't take it for granted . . . not for one second, cause it can get you. You know, that's it lights out, you are done.

John communicated to me a warning that to romanticise or underestimate this place-world can have dire consequences. This tension between Land and bodies, the place-world of the Australian bush as both beautiful and difficult to live with, figures very strongly in the making of this place-world. In particularly the importance of the matter of water to this place-world:

> It's dry here and hardly any grass and like heaps of trees and red dirt. I say I live in the bush, it's small towns and everybody knows each other and what they do and well everyone is friendly and they know each other, but not a lot of water. (Mary)

> Well I live in a bush town. It's trees and dry, mostly dry all the time and lots of animals, native bush animals like kangaroos and kookaburras and birds and echidnas. Tasmingoo is a city and it's the closest city, it has trees but it's not as dry. They have more water. (Alison)

> Midoo is bush too, because it's not huge, you know like as big as Tasmingoo, a city like that. They have a fair few things, more than here but it's still a bush town, real dry. (Harper)

The importance and absence of the matter of water dominates the place-making practice of those who live with this place-world. They have learned, from a very early age, the importance of water and the lack of water, and as a result the socio-material practices needed to save and preserve water. But the absence of this matter also teaches, as there is a deep embodied knowledge of the possibility of this matter. As Harper explained to me how she knew it would rain, 'See those huge clouds, see how dark they are. There's darkness but then the light changes and you know rain's comin', it's the first sight of rain.' Jenny also shared an embodied knowledge of the matter of rain: 'Can you smell it? Rain's coming, big storm too'; and Henry: 'Ants have been going mad the last couple of days, have you seen them. Goin' to rain.' This place-world is one that has so much but at the same time so little: the presence and absence of matter, the tension between beauty and terror. But what is really interesting is the very space between matters. This is because it is a space of differences, there is a push and pull of the intra-actions of humans and the materiality of this unique landscape, and the very material and embodied pedagogy that is needed to live with this place-world that lacks sustaining matter. While fascinating, these differences support and maintain the making and remaking of the Australian bush, and those who live in the bush, as lacking and as a result devalued. However, those who have grown up learning these placemaking practices, from embodied and material pedagogies, do not know this, they have not learned this. The terror does not exist for them.

The children of this place-world do not articulate a terror, nor a tension between life and death and the issues of survival. Instead they embrace this. 'It's what happens' as they have 'deep sustaining roots in the land' (Flannery 2002). Who they are and how they are, their embodied socio-material practices, are shaped and taught with Land, and as a result Land is entangled with who they are: 'The land does . . . claim us as its own' (Flannery 2002). Rather than knowing and understanding this place-world as something to battle and be at odds with, the children are entangled with Land. This intra-action of bodies with the socio-material of the place-world is a knowledge and understanding 'that it is reducible to a sort of co-existence with place' (Merleau-Ponty 1962: 105). The children know and understand that they are entangled with the Land, they belong to it.

'I'm a bush kid, that's what we are, its what we do, here.'

'What do you mean Henry?'

'Well this is my place, the bush, I'm a bush kid.' Jenny turns around and agrees with Henry. 'Yeah, we will always be bush kids, the bush isn't just where we live, it's . . . you know it's us, here it's us.'

Both Henry and Jenny have learned that they are part of this place-world, the bush. Who they are is where they are and where they are is who they are. As discussed previously, this entanglement of self and place is integral to many Indigenous communities, where placemaking practices (rituals, performances, everyday) constitute and make identity, individually and collectively. But this also occurs through the repetition of these learned and performed practices with others, a connection to place, a sense of belonging, to a community, a culture and so on that is learned (Scudder 1979a; 1979b; Shepard 1982; Gale 2005). But Jenny and Henry have also learned that 'the land . . . owns you' (Gale 2005: 360).

This idea of being owned by the Land is supported by research into the experiences of the Dineh Indians in north-eastern Arizona (Casey 1993). Since 1974 the Dineh, Navajo, have been 'relocated' by the American government, enacting the 1974 Act of Settlement to separate the Navajo from the Hopi (Casey 1993). This forced relocation has resulted in displacement, and I would contend a lack of a sense of belonging and connectedness to the Land. This idea is supported by Scudder, who states that: 'The results of over 25 studies around the world indicate, with no exceptions, that the execution of compulsory relocation among rural populations with strong ties to their land and homes is a traumatic experience' (1979a: 69). This trauma manifests physically and psychologically, as in the case of the Navajo where 'a quarter of those relocated have died, including an unusually high number of suicides. Alcoholism, memory loss [and] depression is also rampant' (Scudder 1979b: 69). Casey (1993) asserts that the Navajo loss of the Land is a loss of life, and that the major cause of these illnesses is the loss of place resulting in a loss of belonging. According to the Navajo, illness is the result of a distorted relationship with the Land: 'To take from the Earth without reciprocating, without having first become a part of the life of the place, is to disrupt a sacred balance and ultimately to grow ill' (Lassiter 1987: 228).

As previously discussed, Australian Aborigines also have this embodied intra-action with the Land, and have also suffered from forced relocation. Gale's research with Australian Aboriginal women describes their experiences and the 'trauma of being removed from their mothers, and their Land and cultural roots that are so embedded in that Land' (2005: 359). For the Aborigines, Tawa asserts:

> Land is not 'landscape' but country – a culturally qualified entity conjoining people, land and myth . . . and it contextualizes a remembrance and renewal of cultural lineage and identity, and the apprenticeship or initiation into the narration of country is fundamental to Indigenous identity. (2002: 45)

This removal from the Land results in a loss of religion, language, cultural history and identity (Wilson 1997). Gale (2005) and Plumwood (2005) also maintain that the decline in Aboriginal health and the high rate of infant mortality and morbidity is because of the trauma of displacement, and I would maintain a resulting sense of disbelonging.

Similarly to, but not the same as, the Indigenous cultures of the Navajo and Australian Aborigines' entanglement with the Land, Mary, Jenny, Henry, Hettie, Harper and John are entangled with the Land. They shared and taught me their embodied placemaking practices that are made and remade with the Land. The very matter of this place-world, the Land, is who they are and as Casey asserts, 'place is what takes place between body and landscape' (1993: 29). It is, then, the very repetition of embodied practices (sometimes everyday, sometimes occasion-special, sometimes individual, sometimes with others, sometimes local, sometimes global) with the socio-material world that makes place. It is through these ways of knowing and understanding that we learn and are taught a sense of belonging to a community, a culture, a nation and Land.

Learning placemaking is not just about developing one's own individual knowledge and practices. It also involves understanding who we are and how and where we are 'with' bodies and matter. Wenger asserts that knowing and learning these ways is not dependent on 'individual dispositions' (Bourdieu 1990b: 64) but on connectedness, or Whitehead's concept of 'withness'; with the embodied socio-material practices of a place-world, 'as happens with people when you live with them . . . resulting in more and more refined knowledge' (de Waal 2011: 1), practices and pedagogies. But these practices and pedagogies are not just of the local and immediate, as Wenger asserts: 'knowing in practice involves an interaction between the local and the global' (2005: 141), or an intra-action of the local with the global.

As discussed previously, I draw on the theories and the premise of critical pedagogy (Giroux 2003; hooks 1984), where pedagogy enables the questioning and challenging of domination, and the beliefs, knowledges and practices that dominate, and can 'become the practice of freedom, the means by which men and women deal critically and creatively with reality and discover how to participate in the transformation of their world' (Freire 1970: 16). Therefore, this practice of freedom is 'about how we learn together and make changes together' (Page 2012a: 73). A practice in which learning as responsiveness to matter and to space-time-mattering occurs within the contingencies, differences and diversity of life that concerns itself not only with relationalities of power, constituted and reproduced by bodies, but also with how bodies participate in/with these relationships (Page 2018). Coole and Frost assert that there is 'increasing acknowledgment within theories of politics – and especially in theories of democracy and citizenship – of the role played by the body as a visceral protagonist within political encounters', and that this 'reveals both the materiality of agency and agentic properties inherent in nature itself' (2010: 19–20). But this sharing and learning from each other is not all rose-coloured and wonderfully uplifting because, in this time of Brexit and increasing global retreat from democracy, we are learning only to look within and embrace protectionism, where we perceive that we own Land and that we need to keep the 'Other' out.

In this chapter I have shared how we may affect matter, but that matter also affects us; the between of bodies with matter is pedagogic. These effects can be profound, although more often they are subtle or hidden. But they are inescapable and are a necessary entanglement that is only altered with different intra-actions of makings of matter. This is because the world really is not global, but regional, as Ganesh maintains in his commentary regarding globalism and eating food: 'We are creatures of our region. It is intra-regional migration that shapes most cities and disturbs domestic politics. It is intra-continental trade that defines most economies', because '[t]oo much hinges on particularities of terroir . . . the regionalism of the world is something you can taste' (2018: 18). This continual making and remaking of place is part of our existence and it is the action between bodies and the matter of place-worlds that matters; just as we know and learn matter pedagogically we also know and learn place just by being.

Placemaking and Being

There can be no place without the body and place is made and remade through embodied and material pedagogies. However, I also contend that there can be no body without place. This is not about a competition or hierarchy regarding what came first, chicken or egg, body or place, but how placemaking, the making of place, is part of who we are, part of our very being. This understanding is possible because matter teaches us through resisting dominant discourses; consequently we are learning new ways of being. It is the entanglements, the between, of the social with the material that matters, and can then enable a deepened understanding of not only materiality, how matter teaches, but also that it is entangled with our very being. These embodied knowledges and practices can then be used to empower and also disrupt the hegemonies and politics of power, because as Bennett asserts, 'matter is an active principle and, though it inhabits us and our inventions, [it] also acts as an outside alien power' (2010: 47).

According to Casey, we are placed beings to begin with and 'without place' we would experience 'a loss of a kind of being' (1998: 71). Aristotle also acknowledges the very pervasiveness of place in our very being, and states that we are not simply being, but that we are 'being there' (1983: 25–6 209a). Malpas maintains that place is a 'necessary part of what it is to be human' (2007: 326), and Merleau-Ponty that 'being is synonymous with being situated' (1962: 252). It would seem that Casey, Aristotle, Malpas and even Merleau-Ponty are suggesting that place is more than the intra-actions of bodies with the socio-material. This is because not only do the practices of placemaking bring together the socio-material of place-worlds, but they are also involved in producing these place-worlds, and so are part of our very being.

Malpas, using Heidegger's philosophies of place in the structure of human existence (Dasein), maintains that place is essential to being in the world because we are 'pre given publicly shared parts of an environing world' (2007: 145). This means that place provides a practical basis for the everyday demands and relations in which human beings are entangled: 'Dasein should be understood . . . as the place which Being requires. Dasein is the "there", hence we could say that Dasein's being is in the strict sense of the word "being-there" (Da-sein)' (Heidegger 1959: 205). In other words, to be human is to already be with place, making place; and to be with place and making place is to be human. Maybe what we need to do is no longer maintain the idea that 'I think therefore I am', and instead acknowledge the place of place with being and reword this to: 'I am with place making place, therefore I am'. By doing this it may be possible to recognise that place/placemaking is the experiential fact of our very existence and is fundamental to the making of meaning and socio-material relations and practices.

However, as discussed previously regarding the idea of Land, Bang et al. would differentiate Western individual connotations of 'I think, therefore I am' from Indigenous tribal connotations of 'we are, therefore I am'. Nonetheless, Bang et al. do extend this ontological difference between place to 'I am, therefore place is' and 'Land is, therefore we are' (2014: 45). The concept of place focuses on the human-individual first, whereas Land is focused on the shared, the collective, the entanglements. However, I do not want to get stuck in an either/or situation where Land and placemaking practices and pedagogies are pitted against each other and one is devalued or dismissed. What really matters are the intra-actions; the between of Land with place, place with Land, and the power relations and politics of these Indigenous but also non-Indigenous ontologies, practices and pedagogies.

This premise of place as being primary to human existence is supported by the research and writing of Gayton (1996) and Measham (2006), who have examined the earliest places of childhood. Measham and Gayton state that our childhood experiences of place form 'primal landscapes' that shape our placemaking practices throughout our life:

> My wife grew up in a seaside community near Seattle and, even though she has no real desire to live near the ocean now, she finds the smell of tide flats and the sound of waves breaking at night to be urgent, compelling messages. It is as if certain sights, sounds and smells bypass the senses and speak directly to her being. (Gayton 1996: 2)

As the children I researched with asserted:

> 'I'm a bush kid, that's what we do.'
>   'Well this is my place, the bush, I'm a bush kid.'
>   'Yeah, we will always be bush kids, the bush is where we live, it's where we are . . . you know it's us.'

This entanglement between our 'primal landscapes', identity formation, identities and placemaking pedagogies is supported by the work of Bourdieu (1977; 1990a; 1990b), Cresswell (2004), de Certeau (1984), Birkerts (1986) and Casey (1993), as discussed in the previous chapter.

But rather than returning to the placemaking practices of our childhood, these primal pedagogies can be conceived as 'learning that is . . . being in place' (Measham 2006: 429), wherein our ways of learning, knowing and making place are part of our human existence and we have not yet unlearned them and they make us. As Gale claims, 'you . . . think you can own the land but you are wrong, it is the land that owns you' (2005: 360); and as Seamus Heaney states, the landscape is both 'humanised and humanising' (1984: 45). As stated previously, we may affect place but place also affects us in deep, sometimes subtle or hidden but always inescapable ways. Bear in mind that this is not an either/or relationship but rather a 'with' relationship, in that

> place . . . is a construction of humanity but a necessary one – one that human life is impossible to conceive of without . . . there was no 'place' before there was humanity but once we came into existence then place did too . . . place is a kind of necessary construction – something we have to construct in order to be human. (Cresswell 2004: 33)

Therefore, just as we know and learn placemaking with embodied and material pedagogies, we also know and learn place just by being. The very places that we make, individually and collectively, come from our everyday practices, the reiteration and repetition of the seemingly mundane but also the rarefied and special. By exploring and examining these practices we can map the ways of making and learning place, placemaking, and develop a deeper knowledge and understanding of place and belonging. This will enable both an individual and collective understanding of the power and politics of place. To know, understand and learn these everyday placemaking practices of life, innovative approaches and methods of research are needed. These methods do not necessarily have to be new; sometimes all that is needed is a reconceptualising of what already exists to support the exploration of the agency of matter, and advance vitalist frameworks and practice with research.

Note

1. 'January 26 (Australia Day) is a time to celebrate and reflect on our national spirit, and the Australia Day Address serves to focus our attention on what that means to all of us. Since 1997 the Address has drawn

on distinguished members from within the community to express their unique perspective on our nation's identity and the diversity of our society. Each year the speaker is encouraged to share their experiences and reflect upon our history and our future, securing the Address as one of the most important Australia Day initiatives' (<https://www.australiaday. com.au/events/australia-day-address/>, last accessed 14 January 2020).

CHAPTER 5

Making and Remaking: The Practice Research of Place

To know, understand and learn the placemaking practices that are often invisible, hidden and mostly taken for granted (because they are of the body and not easily verbalised), an embodied, affective and relational approach is needed. The innovative practice research entanglements of methodologies and methods, underpinned by new materialism, that can enable the exploration of the agency of matter and advance vitalist frameworks are presented and discussed in this chapter. Through moving beyond the problem-focused approach we can work the intra-actions of theory with practice and practice with theory to develop new approaches to making and remaking the processes and outputs of practice research. This approach can also position these research practices politically as it pays attention to the complex materiality of bodies immersed in social relations of power.

The Practice Research of Place

New materialism (Alaimo and Heckman 2008; Barad 2007; Braidotti 2013; Barrett and Bolt 2013; Coole and Frost 2010; Heckman 2010) calls theorists to emphasise materiality in research. Furthermore, it calls for embodied, affective, relational methodologies requiring new ways of approaching and doing research. As Barad states, we need to be

> reconceptualizing the notions of space, time, and matter using an alternative framework that shakes loose the foundational character of notions such as location and opens up a space of agency in which the dynamic intra-play of indeterminacy and determinacy reconfigures the possibilities and impossibilities of the world's becoming such that indeterminacies, contingencies and ambiguities coexist with causality. (2007: 225)

As a way of exploring the entanglements of matter and subjectivity, new materialism is an approach to research that can emphasise and open up ways to understand the complex materiality of bodies immersed in social relations of power (Dolphijn and van der Tuin 2012). However, it is crucial that we do not allow materialist frameworks to de-emphasise the agency of people and politics, and in attempting to know, understand and learn the 'mingle and mangle' (Bolt 2012: 3) of the practices of socio-material life to flatten ontologies. The epistemological underpinnings of new materialism support a way of approaching research; a methodology that rejects dualistic separations of mind from body and of nature from culture. From this position this methodology can support the questioning of how matter comes to matter and the intra-actions of matter with bodies, making with thinking. However, because of this focus, there is a need to go beyond solely text-based research methods and outcomes.

Carter explains that 'the language of creative research is related to the goal of material thinking, and both look beyond the making process to the local reinvention of social relations' (2004: 10). Building on this material transformation through creative process that Carter advocates, Barrett proposes that 'artistic practice be viewed as the production of knowledge or philosophy in action' and specifically argues that 'the emergence of the discipline of practice-led research highlights the crucial interrelationship that exists between theory and practice and the relevance of theoretical and philosophical paradigms' (2007: 1). Similarly, Manning and Massumi assert that 'every practice is a mode of thought, already in the act. To dance: a thinking in movement. To paint: a thinking through color. To perceive in the everyday: a thinking of the world's varied ways of affording itself' (2011: vii). These theories underpinning new materialist practice research as developed by Carter, Barrett and Bolt, Manning and Massumi, and Nelson each, in their own way, argue that the intra-actions of making and concept are important. But this materialisation of a concept can be conceived as complex yet also simple. In an academic place-world, the uncomfortable or awkward reaction to a concept's mattering (through/with image, sound, bodily movement or any combination) is important and needs to be shared. To make concepts materially through/with practice forces us out of the comfort zone of using words or phrases, and jargon cannot be relied upon; each material articulation is created and perceived anew. There is the real potential for uniqueness and innovation; a new type of purpose beyond abstract philosophical thought. This is the 'newness' of new materialist practice research.

There are many terms used to describe an approach to research that uses and/or includes practice, specifically arts-creative practice: practice-led research, practice as research, practice-based research.

All of these position practice in specific and particular ways. Candy (2006) and Barrett and Bolt (2007; 2013) characterise 'practice as research' as an approach that draws on 'multiple fields and pieces together multiple practices in order to provide solutions to concrete and conceptual problems' (Barrett and Bolt 2013: 12). Hickey-Moody relies on Barrett and Bolt, but adds 'practical invention and evaluation, via processes that draw on multiple fields and which piece together multiple practices' (2015: 169). But 'practice research' is a collective bringing together of all these iterations that acknowledges and entangles practice with research. Where and how the practice is positioned and how it is used in the research depends on the questions being asked and the concrete and conceptual problems that need solving. Rather than predetermining the where and how of practice, practice research enables the research, the researcher and those that we are learning and researching 'with' to develop and evolve. Because of this open, dynamic and creative responsive research approach, it is okay to not have all the answers before you begin.

However, it is essential to note that, with practice research, the practice may be the methodology (that is, the approach of the research process) and/or the method (that is, tools to gain information, learning and understanding) and/or the outcome-output of the research (that is, paintings, drawings, performance and so on). Most importantly, practice research is not about isolating, contextualising and deconstructing a product, specifically an artistic product, as it can 'embrace numerous and personal meanings and gives voice to experiences' (Stewart 2007: 132). Practice research is about understanding and learning the sociocultural-material processes and relationships that make these practices and products, enabling us to know, understand and learn. As Crossley maintains, 'meaning is not contained within a form itself, say a painting or a poem' (1996: 71), but it can exist in the between, the intra-actions. As work on non-representational and affective methodologies (Vannini 2015; Coleman and Ringrose 2013; Lury and Wakeford 2012; Back and Puwar 2012; Knudsen and Stage 2015; Lury et al. 2018) indicates, meaning may not always be what is at stake in research, as sensation, feeling, embodiment, intra-activity and engagement may be generated, grasped, understood and intervened in, instead or as well as (see the 2019 *MAI* special issue, 'Feminist New Materialist Practice: The Mattering of Methods').

Sullivan and Stewart have been pivotal in the field of practice research. However, their focus has been 'studio-based inquiry in the visual arts . . . visual research methods grounded within the practices of the studio' (Sullivan 2005: xiii); 'I approach practitioner-based research as a way of working, investigating and theorising what it is to practice in the studio as researcher' (Stewart 2007: 125). This practice research is conducted usually by a lone artist, creating and making in their studio. However, an increasing number of practice researchers are going beyond the place of the studio and researching 'with' bodies with matter (Tolia-Kelly 2007; Irwin et al. 2009; Irwin and Springgay 2008; Page 2019; Palmer and Chalkin 2019; Coleman 2019; Sayers 2019). This is practice research that is embodied and materially engaged.

Clements contends that these practices distance themselves from the traditional focus of individual self-expression and the authority of the institutional gallery system:

> a reflexive, less egocentric and feminine notion of responsive art focusing on wider interaction where artists can participate and re-engage with art and audiences outside the gallery system, for example working with ecological themes and a range of communities in a less individualised and competitive fashion. (2011: 20)

However, hooks claims that the aim of these practices is more than mere participation and inclusion. Rather, they demand a questioning of sociocultural-political conventions and orthodoxies through promoting 'engagements with . . . practices . . . that are defined as on the edge, as pushing limits, disturbing the conventional, acceptable politics of representation' (1994: 4–5), and are consequently pedagogic. Similarly a socio-materially engaged practice research is the practices, processes and outcomes that support the exploration and examination of the effects and affects of our social-material world, which can promote debate, disruption and social change of

> the neglected . . . the forgotten . . . the irrational, the insignificant, the repressed, the borderline, the eccentric, the sublimated, the rejected, the non-essential, the marginal, the peripheral, the excluded, the silenced, the accidental, the deferred, the disjointed. . . everything 'the modern age has never cared to understand in any particular detail, with any sort of specificity'. (Nelson 1987: 217)

Irwin et al. (2009) and Irwin and Springgay (2008) were pivotal in developing a rhizomatic methodology for practice research specifically in the field of education that is attentive to the between of art making, researching and teaching: a/r/tography, 'where meanings reside in the simultaneous use of language, images, materials, situations, space and time' and where 'theory is understood as a critical exchange that is reflective, responsive and relational. Theory-as-practice-as-process-as complication' that 'is an embodied, living space of inquiry' (Irwin and Springgay 2008: 106). Irwin et al. used this approach in their research with the community of Richmond, British Columbia. The aim of the research was to use practice to explore ideas of identity, place, displacement, community and the changing environment of the city, 'what it means to feel at home' (Irwin et al. 2009: 62), using collective artistic and educational praxis: 'as artist educators we initiated several community-engaged arts projects, working from the premise that the arts are powerful forces for rearranging and re-engaging patterns of community through public art and public pedagogy' (2009: 62). A variety of practices, such as personal narratives, artefacts, photographs and videos, were produced, all focusing on the concepts of 'home' and 'away'. Irwin et al. maintain that this overlapping of 'art' and 'graphy' (2009: 63) enables relationships through a process of dialogue, and underpinned by the critical pedagogy of Freire (2000), they assert that everyone becomes co-authors of actions performed on and in the world, and that art practices create continuous making and remaking of place.

Through the methodology and methods of practice research, the community of Richmond created places of learning where the relationships between people and place and thereby the space of community could be examined and explored (Irwin et al. 2009). However, Irwin et al. assert that it is important that this approach is not constructed as a particular visual style or visual presentation. Instead, it is about social purpose, because 'education cannot be limited to personal achievement' and must 'involve social understanding and contribution' (2009: 68). This practice-research methodology enables a process of embodied exchange and relations that are learned through and with socio-material engagements, an embodied and material pedagogy with others.

Usually studies of place in the social sciences use the methodology of ethnography (Rodman 2003; Grasseni 2004; Pink 2008; Berger 2016). While there is a strong history of this research approach, it can come with its share of problems, as discussed below. Clifford and Marcus, writing in the 1980s, prompted an interesting idea of ethnography in art practice (see also Schneider and Wright 2010; Coles 2000; Foster 1996). But I would also suggest that a growing development is not of ethnography in art practice, but more 'with', an entanglement, and that this can enable a more expansive premise of ethnography with practice research or an ethnographic practice research. In order to do this we can use new materialist diffraction that enables us to 'work' the spaces between the assumptions and philosophical and epistemological underpinnings of ethnography with practice research. Fetterman claims that ethnography 'is the art and science of describing a group or culture, the study of how people see, understand and experience their cultural world' (1989: 1). I would suggest that, historically, the 'science' has well and truly been 'worked' and that the 'art' needs a more thorough workout.

As the younger sibling of anthropology, ethnography has a history of 'Othering', and has been the methodology of choice for researchers venturing to exotic locales to describe and communicate to the Western world the lives and cultures of these people (Price 2005). Ethnography's strong connection with colonialism, imperialistic judgements and the objectification of 'natives' from other cultures is one of its problems (Willis and Trodman 2002). Fine (1994) contends that classic ethnographers have a tendency to portray events from the alien view of the researcher and consequently judge rather than describe.

However, contemporary forms of ethnography, such as critical ethnography, go beyond viewing culture as a descriptive object and the practices of 'Othering'. These forms of disrupted[1] ethnography openly declare the ideological productions and reproductions of culture, and attempt to produce reflexive, ideologically open texts (Koro-Ljungberg and Greckhamer 2005). Critical ethnography uses an intentional and planned theoretical framework that views culture through particular political and critical lenses (Dressman 2006), but also acknowledges that knowledge can be 'reproduced, remapped and decentred' (Koro-Ljungberg and Greckhamer 2005: 293). But critical ethnography also conceives of the researcher as part of the world being studied; not only does the researcher affect the cultural context, the cultural context affects the researcher (Koro-Ljungberg and Greckhamer 2005).[2]

A consequence of this epistemological underpinning and one of the criticisms levelled at critical ethnography is that its data and findings are too subjective (Collier and Collier 1996; Becker 1958; 1986). However, by acknowledging and embracing the subjective and the reflexive, and the fact that data is placial and that the researcher is part of the socio-material world, this criticism can be addressed. But to work the spaces between we need to be explicit about the nature of the reflexivity that initiated and framed the research, embrace subjectivity, critique the place-world that is being researched, following Barad's premise of critique, and also reflect not only on the products of this participation but also on the practices and processes of the socio-material. However, is this enough when the usual outcome of ethnography is text-based?

Historically, the main outcome of ethnography is thick description, where witnessing and observing are translated into written language: the human experience is transformed into linguistic descriptions and so culture is represented through the medium of words, becoming 'a science of words' (Mead 1975: 5). This can be problematic because 'language is doing the work of the eyes' (Tyler 1986: 137). The use of images in ethnographic research has been hotly debated since the turn of the twentieth century, and there are many conflicting views on their value (Holliday 2000; Chaplin 1994). Many of these debates regarding the use of still and moving images focus on images as a supplementary method, a way of documenting or confirming text descriptions, as in Frank's (1969) study of US culture, Berger and Mohr's (1975; 1982) portrait of intra-European labour-based migrancy and Lévi-Strauss's (1995) fieldwork in Brazil between 1935 and 1939. The problem with this scientific-realist approach is that the images are considered as a support to observations, and as such are made as an observation of reality and an adjunct to the written text (Plummer 1983; Collier and Collier 1996; Walker 1993; Emmison and Smith 2000). Furthermore, these images and films have traditionally been used to capture the 'noble savagery' of exotic cultures, diminishing the political context and serving to confirm racist stereotypes (Marks 1995; Singh 1992; Ball and Smith 1992).

By acknowledging 'the polysemic quality of the image' (Harper 2003: 244) – its many connotations and interpretations and the making of meaning – images and films (whether of the researcher and/or participant) can be used to create and enable dialogues around multiple meanings rather than claiming representational authenticity.[3] Examples include the meanings of the body for female prostitutes through performance art (O'Neill et al. 2002); the changes in traditional dairy communities in Maine and Minnesota using archival images (Harper 2003); encounters with organic materials where the images enable a witness in understanding environmental changes (Hunter 2019); and literally following the matter of glitter, to see where it goes and what it does, methodologically, politically, affectively within a research assemblage (Coleman 2019).

An ethnographic practice research, underpinned by new materialism, that acknowledges and embraces the artistic and the subjective can reveal many layers of meaning that can then enrich our knowledge and understanding of the world. It can also strengthen the broader social-material structures and processes that empower, and reveal and understand those that disempower. But we can use more than the visual to know and learn. New materialist practice-research approaches can enable very subtle, nuanced but also complex data to be known and learned, which can teach us about human difference and similarity. This

entails taking a series of conceptual and practical steps that allow the researcher
to rethink both established and new participatory and collaborative research

> techniques in terms of . . . meanings, values, ways of knowing and practices
> [embodiment]. It involves the researcher self-consciously and reflexively attend-
> ing to the senses [bodies] throughout the research process. (Pink 2009: 10)

Pink acknowledges that embodied practice is not about a prescriptive way of conducting research or about favouring one type of data or method. Instead, it is about being 'open to multiple ways of knowing and to the exploration of and reflection on new routes to knowledge' (2009: 8). This sensoriality, or the 'sensorial turn' (Howes 2003: xii) has been addressed within the academic fields of human geography, social and cultural anthropology and sociology.

Simmel's seminal work 'Sociology of the Senses', originally published in 1907, focused on the sensory perception of others and the key role this plays in human interaction. Largey and Watson (2006) and Low (2005) built on Simmel's premise through focusing their research on the examination of smell and social interaction. Bull (2000), however, went in another direction, focusing on sound and how sound is an invisible presence in everyday life. Hindmarsh and Pilnick (2007) and Lammer (2007) also used sociological approaches to explore social and multisensory interactions in clinical contexts. Sensoriality has also been examined within the field of human geography by Tuan (1977) and Porteus (1990), who examined the different modalities of sensory experience with reference to how the environment and landscape is experienced. This work drew on existing social studies, philosophy and literature, and was strongly opposed to solely focusing on the visual: 'vision drives out the other senses' (Porteus 1990: 5).

Rodaway offers a more integrated conception of the role of the senses in geographical understanding, conceiving of 'the sense both as relationship to a world and the sense as themselves a kind of structuring of space and defining of place' (1994: 4). Rodaway shares this conceptual thread with the social and cultural anthropologists Howes, Classen (Howes and Classen (1991; Howes 2005), Stoller (1989; 1997), Feld and Basso (Feld 1982; Feld and Basso 1996), who primarily mapped a cross-cultural comparison of how sense experience varies from one culture to the next and the meanings and emphasis attached to each modality of perception. However, there have been some criticisms of these approaches, since their focus is on the collective sensory and the senses as cultural models rather than on the specificity of practice and experience (Ingold 2000).

Rather than focusing on one sense and isolating and deconstructing one sense as product or object, a new materialist practice research and studies of place and placemaking acknowledge that embodiment, perceptions and memories are fundamental to how we learn, understand and present lives, experiences, values and socio-material worlds. They can be conceived as intra-acting, entangled if you will, and so this approach, this methodology, can support inquiries into place and how the ways of knowing and learning placemaking are embodied and material. But this approach can also support an engagement with the politics of placemaking. This understanding of the politics of place can be learned through an analysis of existing knowledges and presentations such as poetry, artworks, film and so on. But we can also gain insights into how corporeal socio-material experiences and knowledges, from everyday practices and ideologies, form part of our sociocultural-material knowledges. This is demonstrated in the cultural geographer Tolia-Kelly's research on participants' embodied interdependencies with the landscape.

The aim of Tolia-Kelly's (2007) research was to create a sensory archive and reflect the ideal landscapes of belonging, citizenship and home for South Asian women. Tolia-Kelly used collaborative practice-research methods to explore how the landscape of the Lake District National Park in England was 'experienced beyond the frame of a singular English sensibility by working with migrants from Eastern Europe, India, Ireland and Scotland' (2007: 329). The research methods employed were drawing and painting, and also walking and talking with the participants (the participants and Tolia-Kelly took walks through the Lake District), through biographical, memory and art-based workshops in which the participants produced collages of their own 'valued landscapes' (2007: 330). Tolia-Kelly claims that these practices and methods enabled 'a set of affective registers that are not normally encountered' with regard to this particular landscape, and that the aim of these practices was to 'make tangible a divergent set of sensory responses to this landscape and show how affect and emotion are experienced' (2007: 331). Tolia-Kelly's emphasis on the multiple and varied connections to place and land that shape belonging, identity and citizenship contribute to the knowledge and understanding of the value of race, land and memory for postcolonial migrants living in Britain.

Pink (2004; 2005b; 2006) has also examined how everyday and seemingly mundane practices make identities and moralities when researching people's cleaning, home decorating and laundry practices: 'an exploration of multisensory relationships to the materialities and environments of everyday lives, and the feelings about them' (Pink 2009: 19). Through practice-research methods and interviews, Pink explored how participants thought about different embodied modalities as ways of understanding cleanliness through the absence or presence of matter, namely dirt. Through a multiphase exploration, Pink was able to 'build a picture of when different people thought that the smell, feel and visual appearance of their laundry became an important signifier of its cleanliness' (2005b: 80). Through analysing the participant responses, Pink assessed how the participants constructed their self-identities through their embodied practices with the materiality of their laundry, but also how the participants then made moral judgements about the embodied cleaning practices of others.

Ivinson and Renold (2013) similarly explored how subjectivities are affectively tied to place and time through ethnographic research on young people's everyday lives in a semi-rural, post-industrial locale. Through focusing on one teenage girl's inventive socio-material practices, Ivinson and Renold share moments in time to explore how conscious and unconscious affective relations repeat and rupture sedimented gendered histories of placemaking. However, using Deleuze and Guattari's concept of the full and empty body without organs, Ivinson and Renold argue that making visible young people's nascent becomings is to focus on their existing socio-material makings, doings and imaginings, so that there is not a loss of the very sense of place that makes them feel both safe and alive.

In the above examples these scholars demonstrate how the various ways in which we embody the world (individually, generationally, through gender, through ethnicity, through class, and materially) impact on how we know, understand and ultimately live our lives. Similarly, with my research I focus on the entanglement of bodies (mine with the participants) and the sociocultural matterings of a particular place-world. This deep mapping enables an insight into how we learn these ways of knowing and understanding, but also how our identities, who we are, are entangled with the power and politics of embodied material practices. These ways of knowing also offer us routes into understanding how people socially-materially intra-act. These scholars also use a variety of methods that can be theorised as placemaking practices, as they enable an understanding and learning of how people make place through a range of embodied creative-artistic material practices.

Methods for the Practice Research of Place

Inventive methods (Lury and Wakeford 2012) including arts-based (Jagodzinski and Wallin 2013), visual (Pink 2007b; Rose 2012) and embodied or sensory (Pink 2009; Ingold and Vergunst 2008; Page 2012a; 20102b) are increasingly being used to explore the agency of matter and advance vitalist frameworks. These methods enable an exploration and examination of the entanglement of all phenomena; human, non-human, social, physical, material and immaterial. In my experience there is no one way, no one single tool/method that can enable this, and, just as Barad (2007) calls for a reconceptualising of approaches to research, I call for a reconceptualising of empirical methods. This reconceptualising is not solely about inventing new methods; it can be more a remaking of methods for the twenty-first century. Increasingly there is work that is beginning to explore and develop a range of research methods and practices that both put new materialist concepts to work, and reflect back on them, reshaping what new materialism is, what it does, and what it can do (Coleman et al. 2019). Springgay (2015) asserts that these ways of researching should be termed techniques rather than methods or tools, as techniques are processual, emergent and continually reinvent themselves or remake themselves. But entangling practice with method is to see them as doing/makings.

In the social sciences, methods are often considered the practice of research, or the practical aspects of research; and in the arts and humanities, practice is also sometimes seen as a method or as an approach. In both of these conceptions, there is an activity through which something is produced/made. But by drawing on recent developments in the social sciences that see methods as inventive (Lury and Wakeford 2012; Coleman 2009), performative or enactive (Law and Urry 2004), they become part of the social worlds they study: 'they are constituted by the social world of which they are a part' and 'they help to constitute that social [material] world' (Law et al. 2011: 4). Consequently, methods are politicised and methods make worlds, and so what methods might 'we' want to make? This understanding of methods challenges the idea of methods as neutral tools for applying theory, resulting in a divide between theory, method and the focus of a research project (Law et al. 2011). At the same time this challenges the understanding of the empirical world as 'out there', waiting to be studied, a passive, inert object that the human animates. Understanding method in this way, through new materialism, enables us to consider how the human is only part of a research assemblage and how matter is also active in research.

Active participation and events

In the majority of social science studies of specific place-worlds, cultures and so on, ethnography is the methodology of choice, and in classic ethnography the researcher is the primary tool for collecting data. The data is usually collected from an emic, or insider's, perspective (Kottak 2006), and the research methods have to facilitate thick description and be able to tap into local points of view. The usual methods of ethnography are those of human interaction; participant observation and interviews.

Participant observation in empirical research is used as a conscious decision to get close to the participants within the setting (Genzuk 2003). However, this method can also be conceived as an opportunity to access lived experiences that incorporate but also transcend language. Atkinson et al. (2007), who used participant observation to reveal how embodied phenomena were culturally significant to a given group of participants, exemplifies this. In their study, Atkinson et al. were attempting to understand sensory codes within cultural and social systems, but this was done through 'the visual . . . the most important mode of understanding' (2007: 180). However, this method privileges the visual, and results in a lack of attention to the experiential, the embodied.

During a discussion with a postgraduate student regarding their choice of methods for research with young people in a secondary school, I queried why the student felt the need to collect only written observations. I asked: 'Why do you need these detailed minute-by-minute accounts of what happened with the young people and what they did and did not do? Where are you? Where is the learning?' The student's response was 'I write it all down 'cause then I can compare and contrast what happened with the other class and then I can measure it and then I can prove they have learned it. 'Cause if you don't see it how do you know they have learned it, how do you know?' But if we reconceive, remake participant observation as a method in which we actively participate with/in socio-material practices, subjectivities and explanations, it can then become an embodied way to know, understand and learn 'with', where we are working the spaces between bodies and the socio-material.

This is demonstrated in Okely's research on the 'changing conditions and experience of the aged in rural France' (1994: 44). Okely, through actively participating in everyday practices with participants, was able to find routes into understanding biographical experiences, both in the present but also in the past, stating that 'my residence in the villages and work on a small farm similar to those the aged had once known, gave embodied knowledge of something of their past' (1994: 44). Consequently, active participation can be a method that supports the accessing of 'knowledge beyond language', an embodied-material knowledge of 'bodily movement, its vigour, stillness or unsteadiness is . . . absorbed' (1994: 45).

Similarly, Coleman's work with teenage girls was focused on developing methods for engaging futures (e.g. Coleman 2017b), where in workshops Coleman actively participated with 13–14-year-old girls in collaging imaginations of their futures. Coleman (2019) conceives collaging as accessible and an enjoyable method for working with materials and for exploring the relations between bodies and ideas. But Coleman also draws attention to the active participation of materials in this research process and develops ways of following as a way of responding to the liveliness of a thing, that is, glitter. Through outlining the revealing routes via which glitter might be followed, Coleman considers not only the material properties but also the affect of glitter: 'the aim was to literally follow glitter, to see where it goes and what it does, methodologically, politically, affectively' (2019: n.p.).

This method of active participation, of bodies and/with matter, is underpinned by Whitehead's premise that the body is not just an objective perceiver for the registration of direction or even sensation, but is instead actively participating with the practices of perception. Therefore, learning ways of knowing and understanding through active participation can occur 'with' our own embodied experiences, through sharing socio-material practices, but also with materials. Stoller maintains that researchers need 'to open themselves up to others and absorb their worlds' (1997: 23) and this method can also 'work' the disruption of practices of Othering. This method of active participation not only enables the learning and sharing of embodied socio-material experiences and practices, it is also enables us, as researchers, to place ourselves and be part of the research assemblage and begin to know and learn about our own placemaking practices.

In social science research, interviews can be conceived as 'social interactions structured by both researcher and participant' (Marcus 1998: 112). During the interview process, the participants' responses form a verbal exchange from which an interviewer seeks to elicit personal knowledge, experiences, beliefs, opinions, perceptions and ideas that cannot be directly observed (Burns 1997). Talking plays a central role in the interview (Oakley 2000; Seale 1998; Rapley 2004), which is constructed as a social event (Seale 1998) where 'two people, often relative strangers, sit down and talk about a specific topic' (Rapley 2004: 15) that attempts to 'imitate conversations' (Oakley 2000: 200). However, interviews can also be remade, just like participant observation, because they can be so much more than mere face-to-face conversations. Interviews can be remade as socio-material embodied events, in which experiences and knowledges can be shared and taught through metaphor, memories, gesture, touching, smells, sounds, images and tastes. I remember one very intense conversation with a group of participants where we hotly debated and discussed the qualities of a good pie: pastry-buttery, melt in the mouth, filling-chunky with some sauce but too much. By recognising and acknowledging the intra-action of bodies with the social material world, interviews as a research method can then go beyond mere description and become events, and like active participation they are productive of place. That is, they make place.

These practice methods can become a way of making place because it is where researcher and participant together create 'a shared place of discovery and learning' (Page 2012a: 73):

> the interview is a process through which verbal, experiential, emotional, sensory, material, social and other encounters are brought together. This process creates a place from which the researcher can better understand how the interviewee experiences her or his world . . . this way offers a means of understanding the interview encounter as a place-event. (Pink 2009: 95)

The interview, or to rename it, the event, then becomes a way of sharing, understanding and learning the placemaking of others, but it can also become a way to learn about our own ways of placemaking as researchers 'through collaborative and reflexive exploration' (Pink 2009: 83). This was clearly evident when I collaborated with participants in making photographs and the mapping of place through the sharing of practices. This collaboration was not about displaying and showing off our photographs, but rather was a way to share our understanding and learning. Together we were reflecting, defining, explaining and communicating our embodied matterings, but we were also making place. However, this reconceptualising/remaking of methods does not magically change this way of collecting of data; that is, 'I think about it differently, therefore it is different.' Everything, from the way we approach these methods, to developing relationships, the language used and so on, needs to be considered but also continually made, remade, learned.

This corporeal approach to practice-research methods is a feminist research approach, which Rubin and Rubin explain 'humanizes both researcher and the interviewee' (Rubin and Rubin 2005: 26). It also empowers by enabling people to 'talk back' (Rubin and Rubin 2005: 26) and we can hear the voices of those who have been or have felt silenced.[4] Rubin and Rubin maintain that a feminist research approach acknowledges the emotive nature of the interview and the need for researchers to be reflexive about their own emotions and experiences. A process of 'reflexive interviewing' (Marcus 1998: 110)

means that there can be flexibility in the interviewing process, because
the discussion follows whatever direction might be appropriate, rather
than a predetermined agenda. For example, when I researched with
participants (children, students, parents and teachers), we all talked
and shared at length our views about various topics and experiences
(Page et al. 2011; Page 2012b). This made possible open expressions
of all of our, theirs and mine, ways of knowing and understanding,
which are not always relevant to the research. But these conversations
did not aimlessly wander, because I would come back to questions
that would gradually support a probing of ideas and so on, which
I thought were relevant or problematic in terms of the research, but
also in terms of my own understandings and pedagogy; hooks (1981)
calls this technique 'funnelling'. However, the participants also 'fun-
nelled' the conversations through asking their own questions, similarly probing ideas that they thought were relevant or problematic
in terms of their understandings and ways of knowing and learning.

It is because of this acknowledgement, negotiating and fluidity of
power relations that positionality and non-unitary subjectivity (Sands
1996) can be performed within the reflexive interview. Positionality comprises the biases, experiences and interpersonal contexts that
we (researcher and participants) bring to the research process (hooks
1984). Non-unitary subjectivity is the 'multiple subject positions people occupy which influence the formation of subjectivity' (Bloom 1998:
3). This can be achieved through conceiving the interview as an event
where there is an intra-action of bodies (researcher with participant)
with place, whose subjectivities are multiple, fluid and complex, and
manifest and alter in different socio-material worlds, moments and
time. 'Othering' may then be interrupted because the interview is a
socio-material event, and the affects and effects of the power relations
of these intra-actions can be examined and mapped.

However, interview-events are not just about the content of the talking, as stated earlier; rather they are shared, performed, embodied, socio-
material narratives of life. During the interview both researchers and
participants continue to be active participants in their socio-material
place-worlds, sharing and learning from and with each other stories and
practices. Braidotti maintains that 'neo-materialism' as 'a method, is a
conceptual frame and a political stand, which refuses the linguistic paradigm, stressing instead the concrete yet complex materiality of bodies
immersed in social relations of power' (Braidotti in Dolphijn and van
der Tuin 2012: 21). This is demonstrated in Spinney's (2006) research, in
which participants share stories about their lives while cycling alongside

each other, or Pink's (2004; 2005b) research regarding laundry practices, when the participants would prepare and share cups of tea during the interview. Having lived in the UK for over a decade, I returned to Australia to do research, and, during an interview, a participant commented, 'Some of your words are real Pommie and then you say others and you sound just like us.' This statement about my sounding both Australian and Pommie (English) started a discussion about travelling and sharing experiences and stories about living overseas and what I missed about Australia.

Interviews are, then, made and remade as socio-material events that are actively engaged, performed and embodied; researcher 'with' participant, participant with researcher. During these events, the participants 'with' researcher/s are narrating, performing, communicating (verbally and non-verbally through metaphor, gesture, movement), sharing and presenting. Together, we are learning and teaching our embodied ways of knowing and learning our socio-material place-world, making and negotiating our identities and, ultimately, making place. As stated above, sometimes with research all we need is a little bit of refurbishment. However, sometimes the old ways just do not cut it and we need to be inventive, open and responsive to the development of new methods.

Walking with and making

Walking with is a sustained movement method that can enable participation in and learning of particular placemaking practices. Similar methods have been used by Springgay (2011; 2016), Springgay and Truman (2017; 2018; 2019b), Pink (2009), Lee and Ingold (2006) and Kusenbach (2003). Lee and Ingold describe their method as 'participant observation in the form of sharing walks with a variety of people' (2006: 68). Kusenbach terms the method 'go-along' and describes this as 'a hybrid between the interview and participant observation where you are able to apprehend and comprehend the ephemeral, embodied and reflexive aspects of lived experience as grounded in place' (2003: 456). Kusenbach used the go-along as an ethnographic research tool in a collaborative ethnographic study that explored how residents in urban neighbourhoods understand local environmental issues, and how their daily activities and social interactions relate to these understandings. Kusenbach describes the process of the go-along as 'accompanying informants' (2003: 457), but this is problematic as accompanying can create a distance from participants; a positioning of the researcher outside the research process that results in Othering discourses and practice. Also Kusenbach does not include any personal thoughts regarding the experiences; there is no acknowledging or recognition of the self within the research process. Kusenbach also conceives of these 'trips' as 'natural' (2003: 457). However, the method of 'walking with' is not 'natural'; it has been developed and learned in a particular socio-material place-world, with specific rules, values and positions. This method is not a hybrid: it is a method that supports a sharing of embodied and material pedagogies, that enables a knowledge and understanding, but also a learning of the intra-actions of bodies with with bodies with matter.

Springgay's and Truman's work on public walking research-creation events is curated by *WalkingLab*, a queer, feminist collaboration.[5] Through organising international walking projects and collaborating with artists and scholars, Springgay and Truman aim to complicate and rupture the white-cis-hetero-ableist-patriarchal canon of walking scholarship. However, the aim of their walking research-creation methodologies is not to analyse the walking events in a traditional interpretative fashion, or to explain how the walks were experienced. Springgay and Truman (2019) consider the ways that these walking projects 'enact' different (as in non-humanist-centric) materialities, bodies and temporalities.

Older studies involving walking or running with research participants describe the enhanced relationship that this enabled; for example, Turnbull (1961) recounts his approval by the Mbuti Pygmies and his acceptance because of his ability to walk through the forest; Geertz (1973) describes having to run away from a police raid after a cockfight with the local people. However, more recent work has been done on the history of walking (Solnit 2001), the ethnography of walking (Ingold and Vergunst 2008) and the role of walking in ethnography (Lee and Ingold 2006), where 'sharing or creating a walking rhythm with other people can lead to a very particular closeness and bond between people involved' (Lee and Ingold 2006: 69). This is because when we are 'walking with', we are learning and being taught, explicitly and implicitly, sharing the ways bodies with bodies with matter know and understand. Lund describes walking as:

> a bodily movement that not only connects the body to the ground, but also includes different postures, speeds, rhythms . . . that . . . shape the tactile interactions between the moving body and the ground, and play a fundamental part in how the surroundings are sensually experienced. (2005: 28)

Springgay and Truman similarly assert that their walking research-creation opens up socio-material intra-actions between human and non-human entities, but that it also needs to

> become accountable to Indigenous knowledges and sovereignty to Land, consider the geosocial formations of the more-than-human, prioritize affective subjectivities, and emphasize movement that is not about moving from one point to another but about the endless proliferation of absolute movement. (2019a: n.p.)

This entanglement of walking with, placemaking and pedagogy is integral to many Indigenous communities, such the Malaysian Batek, Canadian Dene and Australian Aborigines.

Tuck-Po's (2008) research on the walking of the Batek people of Malaysia – forest-dwelling hunter-gatherers – claims that there is no division between knowledge and movement. According to Tuck-Po, the Batek teach their children the art of negotiating the forest not through the imposition of rules or getting them to follow the adults, but by allowing the children to take the lead and enabling them to find and learn their own way:

> For the Batek, walking comprises a suite of bodily performances that include observing, monitoring, remembering, talking, listening, touching, crouching and climbing. And it is through these performances . . . that their knowledge is forged. Movement, here, is not adjunct to knowledge, the movement of walking is itself a way of knowing. (Tuck-Po 2008: 26)

Additionally, Legat's (2008) research into walking with the hunter-gatherers of the north-west of Canada, the Tåîchô (Dogrib) Dene people, in their forest environment describes the link between knowledge and walking and also the intra-action of walking, talking (storytelling) and learning. Legat came to see the entanglement of telling stories and walking as a form of placemaking, and that Dene children grow up listening to stories about walks and paths; 'relations with places are initiated as soon as children first hear the narratives' (2008: 36). Then, as the children grow older, they walk the very same paths they had heard of through stories: 'the period between listening to stories and walking them marks an in-between phase of learning during which people who have heard "talk" do not yet know the "truth" or reality of a narrative' (2008: 37). From these observations, Legat states that walking is 'the experience that binds narrative to the acquisition of personal knowledge' (2008: 35), or the practice that 'validates the reality of the past in the present' (2008: 35). As Tuck-Po states:

> Talking and walking are inseparable . . . If walking creates the path and if walk-
> ing itself is an act of sociality, then can the path have any meaning without the
> stories of the people using it? . . . Paths are social phenomena, and are remem-
> bered in relation to social events. (2008: 26)

The entanglement of narration and walking as placemaking is also
evident in Australian Aboriginal culture. Tawa's (2002) research with
the Ngaanyatjarra communities around Patjarr and Warbarton Ranges
in the Gibson Desert of Western Australian found that the practices of
walking are not simply moving through but moving with, and being
aware of the speeds and shapes of movement and of the various systems
and networks that operate in the country;

> Walking . . . is a process of reading, in great detail, its current state and
> condition – its ecology, geology, meteorology, astronomy . . . this prepares a
> caring for country through various adjustments made in terms of cultural and
> environmental practices, behaviours and protocols necessary for its sustain-
> ment – ranging from ceremonial activities, to hunting and gathering, and fire
> management practices. (Tawa 2002: 48)

For the Ngaanyatjarra, the practice of walking with narration is about
learning to care, keep and tend to the country. But it is also about
remembering and recollecting the various relationships and configurations of the country, and confirming familial lineage and cultural links
to communities and regions (Graham 1999; Tawa 2002).

The songlines of Aboriginal culture are among the best-known examples of the Indigenous entanglement of movement and narrative, and are
sometimes referred to as The Dreaming or Dreaming-tracks:

> each totemic ancestor, while traveling through the country, was thought to have
> scattered a trail of words and musical notes along the line of his/her footprints
> . . . and these Dreaming-tracks lay over the land as 'ways' of communication
> between the most far flung tribes. (Huggan 1991: 62)

These narratives, whether spoken or performed (singing, dancing), are
used as maps and directions and are a way for communities to identify
who has the right to live in an area, and the sacred ways/rituals and so
on associated with them (Myers 1986; James 2008; Long 2008). For
Australian Aborigines,[6] 'Walking initiates a remembrance of genealogi-
cal, mythical and geographical networks of inheritance and descent and
announces that experience through narration' (Tawa 2002: 48); and,
like the Dene and the Batek, these practices and embodied and material
pedagogy cannot be disentangled.

Similarly, going on an 'abenture' enabled me to begin to learn and understand how the children of a particular place-world make and learn place. I listened, occasionally questioned, observed and actively engaged in their practices as they moved through and intra-acted with their socio-material place-world. The children directed me, told me what I needed to do and corrected me when I was doing it wrong. As de Certeau (1984) maintains, through everyday habitual processes and practices of movement we come to familiarise ourselves with place. We begin to know place, make place and start to learn and make meanings with and of that place-world. But what I also learned was the very multiplicities of bodies and matter bound together; what we smell, hear, see, taste and feel, and also the very things, the stuff, that we just know but maybe cannot explain or communicate. Through sharing these intra-actions, whether going on abentures, doin' jobs or making photography and films, I started to develop a greater understanding and knowledge of how we can make and learn place.

As stated previously, the use of photographs and films in research is quite common, but usually in the form of illustrations, cultural texts, representations of ethnographic data, documentary videos or multimedia online texts (Banks 1992; Harper 2003; O'Neill et al. 2002; Ruby 1981; 2000; Pink 2006; 2007b). However, these are usually used to represent experiences/places rather than, as Pink suggests, to convey experiences:

> When the lone ethnographer is working with her or his own materials, these materials become meaningful in terms of the ethnographer's whole biographical experience of the research process. In this situation, the materials help to evoke the sensorality of the research encounter itself (and concomitant memories and imaginaries), rather than just suggesting, for instance, textures and smells. In contrast, in representations, such as ethnographic film, this biographical and cultural contextualisation is problematically missing. The viewer must grasp at her or his own experiences and memories and engage her or his imagination in trying to reach the . . . experience of others. (2009: 100)

However, making (photographs and film) is a practice-research method that can enable the sharing and learning of embodied and material knowledges and understandings, instead of a representation of them. Barad maintains that 'the move toward performative alternatives to representation shifts the focus from questions of correspondence between descriptions and reality (e.g., do they mirror nature or culture?) to matters of practices/doings/actions' (2003: 802). I use making rather than taking when I refer to film and photography to reframe/remake these practices away from representations or illustrations of reality/truth to 'making . . . as a process of growth' (Ingold 2013: 13), where the maker participates with the socio-material, bringing together the forces of the socio-material; as Hickey-Moody states, 'making itself re-machines the world in which the making occurs' (2015: 180).

MacDougall supports this idea of audiovisual practices as makings, using the work of Merleau-Ponty, and emphasising how 'Filmmaking requires interaction [intra-actions] of the body with the world in registering qualities of texture and shape, which do not exist independently of such encounters and that the world is not apart from, but around and within the filmmaker and the viewer' (2006: 50). The apparatus of the camera not only enables ways of experiencing our socio-material worlds, but it is an intra-action of the camera with the body that we are making and remaking. MacDougall extends this premise to images and conceives them as 'not just the images of other bodies; they are also the images of the body behind the camera and its relations with the world'. These are then reflexive as they 'refer back to the photographer at the moment of their creation . . . further locating the author in relation to the subjects' (2006: 3). In other words, photography and film-making are embodied active entanglements that are placemaking practices. This is because place is made and remade through the intra-actions of bodies and the material of the research event; and then place is made with the apparatus of the camera and the matter of image, not as a representation but as a presentation of an experienced reality. However, it is not about each individual image and its content – traditionally composing the subject matter, angle, lighting and so on, which is individually analysed and mined for meaning. As Jenny shared with me, she understands the photographs as collectively intra-acting, the spaces between the making of the photographs and the space between the photographic objects themselves. As Bolt maintains, 'the material practice of art has real material effects and there could possibly be a mutual exchange between the matter of bodies and the image of bodies' (2004: 168). The material practice of Jenny's photography and the matter of the photographic object are not a visual index, a representation that is deconstructed after the research or fieldwork is conducted in another place (Prosser 1998; Ball and Smith 1992). It is an artistic, creative practice-making that can be explored as a site for inquiry where there are 'creative and critical features of artistic knowing' (Sullivan 2005: 62) that embrace numerous and personal meanings and give voice to experiences (Stewart 2007), affect and sensations.

As explored in Chapter 2, the Australian artists Tom Roberts, Arthur Streeton, Frederick McCubbin, Sidney Nolan and Rosalie Gascoigne also made and remade place with their art making (practice and product). This is particularly true of the work and practices of Nolan and Gascoigne; Gascoigne makes a metaphorical vision of her meditative and emotional conceptions of place, of home, the bush, just as Nolan did in his 'Ned Kelly' series. Although Nolan's work recounts another's narrative, it is nonetheless 'a story arising out of the bush and ending in the bush' (Nolan 1948: 20). However, Gascoigne's and Nolan's making also enables and supports our ways of knowing and understanding their knowledge and understandings of the place-world of the bush. The contemporary practices of artists Laurie Anderson (b. 1947), Ingrid Pollard (b. 1953) and Francis Alys (b. 1959) also evoke a sense of place and therefore a knowledge and understanding of making place and the importance of 'where' to who and how they are. However, it is important to emphasise that in new materialist practice research, art products are not privileged over art practices; it is about the 'space between' product with practice. As Sullivan asserts, it 'is not so much about trying to describe visual content'; rather, the intent is 'to understand how those who make' (2005: 63) make meanings, ideas and so on.

This premise of making, specifically photography as an embodied socio-material production of knowledge, is in direct contradiction to Bourdieu (Bourdieu and Bourdieu 2004), Stokes (1992) and Van House et al. (2004), who maintain that the personal production of photographs mainly occurs on special social occasions: birthdays, weddings, holidays, highlighting and memorialising events. However, these ideas are now outdated, because photographs and films are becoming something we are able to make every day, because of the increased availability and accessibility of mobile phones with cameras, digital photography and platforms that support the sharing and curating of photography and films (for example, YouTube, Instagram, Snapchat and Facebook). Holland (2000) and Murray (2008) assert that because the technology and the means of production have moved into the realm of the everyday, the meanings of photographs and of photography have also changed. They are not always concerned with special or rarefied moments, as Bourdieu and Van House et al. maintain, but are 'more alive, immediate, fleeting' (Murray 2008: 151); the collective, and so how we make, know and learn, has also transformed.

This means that making photography and film, the practices and outcomes, like walking with, active participation and events, can be used as methods to explore and examine the socio-materiality of our place-worlds. But they are not passive recordings or representations; they are active, embodied, collaborative ways of researching and learning that can support the examination and exploration of place-worlds; the between of socio-material relations, practices and pedagogies. This can then enable new knowledge and understandings of how we make and learn place. However, once we have used these methods, these techniques 'to collect data', what then? What does all this data mean and how can we share the felt, the invisible, the nuanced?

Analysis and Sharing of Practice Research

With new materialism, the focus is the intra-actions of the subject and/ or the object to the event; the action between is what matters. As such, this key premise of new materialism also needs to be part of the analysis of all the information/data that has been gathered. Taguchi details diffractive analysis as

> a transcorporeal process of becoming-minoritarian with the data, the researcher is attentive to those bodymind faculties that register smell, touch, level, temperature, pressure, tension and force in the interconnections emerging in between different matter, matter and discourse, in the event of engagement with data. (2012: 267)

As Downey (2005; 2007) maintains, analysis does not just involve the cognitive, it also involves the physiological and the affective; it is not just in our minds but it is embodied. Therefore, practice-research analysis is not solely focused on the data but addresses how the data is entangled together with theory. I also maintain that there is not a separate stage or procedural steps/rules of analysis, or a distinction to be made between gathering the data (traditionally called data collection) and analysing it. This is because research and learning with the research materials, bodies with matter, is continually made and remade; it is an ongoing praxic entanglement.

This lack of analytical explicitness can be, as Pink explains, 'an intuitive, messy and sometime serendipitous task' (2009: 119). But this also enables a research process that is open, reflexive, flexible and responsive to innovative practices and the potential and possibilities of the unknown and unknowable. In other words, a research process that is pedagogical and reflexive because, no matter how much preparation you have done, the books you have read, and the expectations you may have, unforeseen and unplanned opportunities and experiences may arise; and it is important to acknowledge but most importantly be open to learning from and with them.

However, not only does a new materialist diffractive analysis enable a mapping of the between of the embodied socio-material experiences/

practices of research with the practices of academia, it can also be conceived as placemaking. This is because, through a continuous process of analysis of the intra-actions of perceptions, memories, embodied experiences, socio-material practices with theory, the power relations of place-worlds can be known and made meaningful and can then be framed as abstracted knowledge, where issues and questions can be debated and/or translated into policies and emancipatory practices. But how can we present, or better yet share, these knowledges, these practices, when they are often nuanced, subtle and of the body?

The sharing of these praxic entanglements of practice research, like the previous discussion regarding representation and performativity, highlights a tension particularly in academia, where the dominant and traditional presentation is written text. Pink maintains that 'scholarly writing remains a central, and I believe crucial, medium for the description, evocation, argument and theoretical debating of . . . research' (2009: 132). As an artist researcher teacher, I maintain that if the purpose of presenting and/or sharing research is to enable 'description, evocation, argument and theoretical debating', but also to learn about our socio-material worlds, it is essential to seek ways that not only produce scholarship but do so in ways that are appropriate but also accessible. It does not have to be a choice of either one or the other.

While academic writing as a genre is slowly evolving and developing to support the sharing of practice research, so too are advances in technology that can enable more inclusive and appropriate ways of sharing (see Coleman et al. 2019). In Chapter 1 I attempted to address these issues by entangling my own experiential and embodied prose and making (practices and products) with that of the participants. In doing so, I attempted to share the practices and pedagogies of placemaking, while also evoking a particular place-world. As Areses Huertas et al. state, regarding written texts:

> It can make you feel something or think something or take you to that place or to revisit that place . . . Like Heaney's poetry where through language he communicates how places and landscapes make us human but also we make these landscapes human . . . a very poetic use of language, and when you say that then you've got a book that takes you to those places it is because it coalesces language and memory. You can smell the earth. You can hear the shovel going into the turf and you know that woman down the road. It's that sort of beautiful use of language of soulful pictures and experiences. (2012: 17)

While Stoller (2004) maintains that written text can never achieve the full experiential awareness that video recordings, images, sound recordings or scent can, I contend that Sutton's work (2006) on modern cooking practices has been able to share an embodied experience both descriptively and analytically through interweaving analysis, information about participants, descriptions of the practices, participants' quotes and commentary, links to research and theory, and both Sutton's and the participants' images. Sutton has done this through moving the narrative between a range of voices and focusing on the spaces between, on the differences that make a difference. I have learned from Sutton's work and have attempted to entangle written text in a range of voices: theoretical, descriptive, autobiographical, participants' narrative, with my own and the participants' photographs and films.[7] I have intentionally sought to share textures, colour, forms and embodied experiences in an attempt to enable an embodied knowledge and understanding. I have attempted to share what it 'feels' like to be with this socio-material place-world. Additionally, as the 'reader' engages with this work, their own theoretical and biographical threads may also become entangled.

However, for these ways of researching and presenting to be shared and disseminated widely requires researchers, editors and publishers to find new ways of supporting and disseminating research beyond text-based chapters and articles. Coleman et al., in their special issue of *MAI: Feminism & Visual Culture* entitled 'Feminist New Materialist Practice: The Mattering of Methods' (2019), do just that, bringing together a collection of international feminist academics and artists working in and across the social sciences, arts and humanities to examine the relevance and productiveness of new materialisms in doing and/or making research. This collection contains work that

> entangles practice with research, theory with practice, bodies with methods and ultimately cut through disciplinary boundaries . . . entangle[s] text and multimedia (still and moving images), requiring us to become 'readers' and 'viewers' of practice in multiple ways. This inclusion of 'not the usual' contributions, we suggest, is crucial to demonstrate the breadth of work that is emerging in feminist new materialisms, and to highlight the significance of practice to this field. (Coleman et al. 2019: n.p.)

However, the editors of the special issue also share the difficulties and challenges in the publication of research that includes multimedia work, but also the issues of the invisible labour of academics and financial viability for publishing companies (Coleman et al. 2019).[8]

In this chapter I have tackled the complexities of the methodologies, methods, analysis and the presenting/sharing of practice research of placemaking. I have mapped the between of the methodologies of a/r/tography and critical contemporary, visual and sensory ethnography, and their philosophical and epistemological underpinnings. The premise of remaking the usual research methods of participant observation and interviews to that of active participation and embodied placed events has also been explored, with new methods of walking with and making. I maintain that an evolving and continuous reflexive and analytical engagement can result in an embodied placial research process where practice is entangled with analysis. Analysis is not a separate stage, and, through entangling written text in and from a range of voices with practices and products of practice, a socio-material engaged exploration of the complex but also subtle ways of knowing and learning place can be enabled.

Notes

1. 'The term disruption is used to refer to the theoretical approaches that differ from classical ethnography' (Koro-Ljungberg and Greckhamer 2005: 286).

2. As Calhoun states, knowing and understanding 'social life requires our active engagement in its games' (2000: 710). However, through these processes I started to feel that critical ethnography was not able to fully support who I am as an artist teacher, or enable a greater breadth of outcomes and practices that the participants and I could and did make.

3. One of the first studies that incorporated photographs into the text and used photographs to generate theory was Bateson and Mead's (1942) study of Balinese culture. Here the name of the study defined the purpose of the images: *Balinese Character: A Photographic Analysis*, and the photographs show performed rituals and everyday activities and routines. These still images were used in the same way as time-lapse images, to record the events as they unfolded (Jacknis 1988). Since this groundbreaking study, visual ethnography has developed the visual with philosophical and epistemological underpinnings that support a reflexive approach, where the visual is regarded as an equally meaningful element of ethnographic research.

4. While I acknowledge that Rubin and Rubin position their research approach as feminist, I am uncomfortable with their use of language, as this connotes a power relationship, with the researcher being the one who giveth but also the one who taketh away.

5. See <www.walkinglab.org>, last accessed 14 January 2020.

6. There are thousands of Aboriginal communities and this generalisation of all Aboriginal culture is based on the research and writings of Myers (1986), Tawa (2002), James (2008) and Long (2008).

7. See <https://www.tarapage.org/placemaking>, last accessed 14 January 2020.

8. 'At MAI we work for free to spread the word about research in feminism and visual culture. All our authors publish their work for no fee. We don't charge our readers. Nothing motivates us but our commitment to raising consciousness about gender politics in arts and media.' See <https://maifeminism.com/>, last accessed 14 January 2020.

CHAPTER 6

The Ethics of Working the Spaces Between

Practice research, underpinned by new materialism, embraces new and different ways of researching; a making and remaking. But this approach also disrupts the practices and discourses that make and remake the identities of researcher as subject and participant as research object; what is of interest is not the subject or object of the research but the space between, the withness. In this chapter I explore and examine how these spaces can be worked, how these intra-actions enable this continuous making and remaking or reproduction and renegotiation of 'identities', and how ways of working the between are not predetermined or planned because they are shared places of discovery and learning (Page 2012a). These concerns, issues and questioning of care are not specific to place-worlds – they are entangled with wider, global discourses and power relations. This chapter plunges into the complexity, the colour, texture and messiness of the ethics of new materialist practice research, and attempts to address researching with care: mind, body, spirit with matter.

Ethics and New Materialist Practice Research

At a postgraduate research level, regardless of country, institution and so on, all students are required to fill in a form and address questions about who they will be researching with (the participants/informants/ subjects, depending where and how the research is positioned) and the ways identities and data will be protected. I am also fairly confident in stating that most researchers in universities would follow a fairly similar procedure. As Boden et al. claim, 'the new ethics regimes taking root in universities sediment rules and codes in centralised policies, bureaucratic procedures and processes that delimit academic freedom to roam critically and creatively' (2009: 728). Obviously, for funding applications and scientific research there are additional layers, paperwork, procedures and so on. The Arts and Humanities Research Council (AHRC),

Biotechnology and Biological Science Research Council (BBSRC) and Economic and Social Research Council (ESRC) are the main funding bodies in the UK that share ethical guidance. The ESRC website states that research ethics

> refers to the moral principles and actions guiding and shaping research from its inception through to completion, the dissemination of findings and the archiving, future use, sharing and linking of data. While research ethics has a long history, originating with medical ethics and then extending to other forms of research with humans, it also has a history of evolution and development. Research ethics in the social sciences initially drew on the 'patient protection' model of medical research, but has more recently broadened in scope to include consideration of benefits, risks and harms to all persons connected with and affected by the research and to the social responsibilities of researchers.[1]

Is this it? Is this what ethics is in research? A procedural exercise concerned with risk, benefit and protection of the individual and institution from accusations of mistreatment that is manifested in signatures on an informed consent form and ticks in boxes?

Levinas's (2000) idea of ethics is responsibility for the other. Similarly, hooks's (2000) approach of entangling pedagogy with political struggles against domination is linked with the ethical imperative of assuming responsibility for the other. But what, who is this other? Traditionally, when researching we perform particular practices and discourses that produce particular ways of knowing that construct particular identities; the researcher as research subject (Self) and that which is studied, the participant, informant and so on, as the research object (Other) (Ellis and Bochner 2000). Hall asserts that 'identities are constructed through, not outside difference' (1996: 5) so it is only through the relation to the 'Other', 'that which is distinct from, different from, or opposite to oneself' (*OED*), that identities are made. This relationship of identities being made through practices and discourses can be illustrated by linking Self and Other with a hyphen (Self-Other), where the hyphen 'separates and merges personal identities with our inventions of Others' (Fine 1994: 131). But this practice of 'Othering', where researchers are speaking 'of' and/or 'for' participants, reflects a desire for mastery and domination, and perpetuates the concepts of 'universal truths, scientific neutrality and researcher dispassion' (Fine 1994: 131) and objectivity (Atkinson et al. 2007). hooks (2000) asserts that being responsible for the other requires that we do not allow the subjectivity and singularity of the other to be captured by political arrangements that treat individuals as objects rather than subjects. In other words we need to *not* deny the relationship, the between of Self and Other, and, as previously stated, the entanglement, the event, the action between matters and how we work this space between, more of Self 'with' Other.

In the Introduction I reworded a Freire quote, replacing 'of the' with 'with'. I use 'with' to connote an entanglement; messy, not structured or ordered, non-hierarchical, non-binary and open to potentials and possibilities. But I also use 'with' to visually denote the 'space between', just as Fine explains the use of the hyphen of Self-Other. Whitehead uses withness as a 'togetherness of things' (1938: 225) and Sweet (2008) uses withness to describe indispensable relationships. Sweet explains that witness comes from the Greek word *marturos*, from which we get the word martyr. 'Witnesses are people who are willing to be martyrs, to "witness unto death". But before the apostles could be "witnesses to him," they first had to simply "be with him," to be "Withnesses"' (2008: 20). Shotter (2010) also uses the term withness in discussing the dialogical of human relations and moving beyond language to include the embodied experience. Shotter refers to dialogical thinking as withness and defines it as 'a form of reflective interaction that involves coming into living contact with an other's living being, with their utterances, with their bodily expressions, with their words, their works' (2008: 186). For Shotter, the practice of withness is 'a knowing to do with one's participation within a situation, with one's "place" within it, and with how one might "go on" playing one's part within it – a knowing in which one is as much affected by one's surroundings perhaps even more than one affects them' (2011: n.p.). But with and withness are not only the state of being connected with persons, but also with things. This enables a working of new materialist thought as it undoes tired binaries, where things, materials, are acknowledged and included in exploring and understanding how we know and learn; so 'being with . . . in this world is not a commodity; it's an ongoing ethical engagement with the world' (Spector 2015: 448). Taking hooks's and Levinas's premise, as responsibility of and for other and the acknowledgement of the entanglement of Self 'with' Other, with things-with stuff, ethics and being ethical is a way of being in the world that needs to be made and remade, where we have care, to take care, to be 'with' care.

Puig de la Bellacasa discusses the complexity and all-pervasion of care in our lives and how care, caring, carer are 'burdened words, contested words and yet they are very common in everyday life, as if care was evident, beyond particular expertise or knowledge . . . it passes with, across, throughout things' (2017: 1). But what is care? If you Google 'care' the definition that comes up is that it is a noun where there is 'provision of what is necessary for the health, welfare, maintenance, and protection of someone or something' and where 'serious attention or consideration [is] applied to doing something correctly or to avoid damage or risk'. Tronto's much-quoted definition is that care 'includes everything that we do to maintain, continue and repair our world so that we can live in it as well as possible. That world includes our bodies, our selves and our environment, all of which we seek to interweave in a complex, life-sustaining web' (1993: 103). Interestingly Tronto's work explores the politics of care where care is not just about a moral positioning but involves affective, practical and material agencies and consequences that are interconnected, or I would reword, intra-acting. To live with care, to research with care, to practise with care is where we are learning and teaching the practices of how to be and the ways to be in this world: mind, body, spirit and matter with care.

Barad also maintains that we cannot separate these matters of care and the care of matter from research, that they are inseparable, and that 'ethics . . . are always already threaded through the very fabric of the world' (2012: 69). So ethics, or with care, is not an addition or adjunct that gets bolted on to our research interests: 'Being is threaded through with mattering and so epistemology, ontology, and ethics are inseparable and so matters of fact, matters of concern, and matters of care are entangled with one another. Or to put it in yet another way: matter and meaning cannot be severed' (Barad 2012: 69).

This ethic of 'worlding' comes from the new materialist recognition of 'skin not as a barrier-boundary but as a porous, permeable sensorium of connectivity with/in a universe of dynamic co-constitutive and differential becomings' (Taylor 2016: 15). This inseparability is not Othering, separating Self from Other, or individuating bodies, that is, getting inside someone else's skin. This is about making connections and commitments where we take responsibility and accountability for these relationalities of which we are part – the practising of withness. This responsibility is where we respond to, not impose or assume, and where we listen, acknowledge, recognise, take care and are responsive to the other, who is not separate from the self. As Barad states, 'This way of thinking ontology, epistemology, and ethics together makes for a world that is always already an ethical matter' (2007: 44).

While Barad positions these understandings within quantum entanglements, MacCormack underpins these entanglements with Spinoza's conception of the corporeality of the mind, where there is no mind without body, no individual without others, and most importantly, 'no thought or theory without materiality' (2012: 4). However, again we cannot assume that by taking up this position the questions and practising of care are automatically achieved; that this is an easy fix or solution. To care, to take care, to research 'with' care is not a final achievement:

> There are no solutions; there is only the ongoing practice of being open and alive to each meeting, each intra-action, so that we might use our ability to respond, our responsibility, to help awaken, to breathe life into ever new possibilities for living justly. The world and its possibilities for becoming are remade in each meeting. (Barad 2007: x)

As discussed in Chapter 5, the processes of research are made and remade consistently, but these are also entangled with the practices and processes of ethics, of care. This means that when we are researching with and learning with, we need not only to be open and attentive to each meeting, each event, but attentive to how we are being taught and what and how we are learning in these spaces between. A new materialist ethics must be 'situational, emergent and unique, located in capacity and action, play out in living bodies as the point of ethical address, and be orientated to practices that are a positive affirmation of life' (Taylor 2016: 15). But it must also be pedagogic, where we are open to learning and being taught, where the practising of care is a continual, responsive process; as Bennett asserts, 'to be (anything, anyone) is also to be following (something, someone), always to be in response to call from something, however nonhuman it may be' (2010: xiii).

This idea of care as responsiveness, as a practice, is explored by Puig de la Bellacasa, where care is conceived as a necessary practice of everyday life, 'care as a doing' (2017: 160), although I would reframe this doing to making; care as a making but also remaking. This idea of care as an act of making and remaking arises in practice research; where practice research, specifically art practices, can enable understanding and learning of the between of bodies with matter, and the many ways we take care of these bodies and these materials. There is a tendency for new materialist researchers to lean towards creative-arts practice research, that is, visual, sensory, movement, sonic, poetic and creative writing practices (Coleman et al. 2019; Barrett and Bolt 2013), because it is ideally located to meet the needs of this ethic of responsiveness, where it is OK not to know but to be open to possibilities. This is because 'practice becomes interference, always diffractive, multiple, uneasy and intense' (Taylor 2016: 19), and as a result disrupts/questions the ways of making practice research, because it 'does not name, but enunciates the very place of the materialist dialectic that no human science has yet approached' (Kristeva 1980: 220).

As an example of disrupting the 'usual' ways of researching and disseminating, Beckie Coleman, Helen Palmer and I collaborated in developing and conducting practice workshops that aimed to explore the new materialisms through interdisciplinary and precarious practice research (see Coleman et al. 2019). Through not offering the usual presentation of papers, we planned the workshop to enable a sharing and learning 'with', where participants experimented with creative practices including embodied mapping, creative writing and collaging. Our aim was to enable translations of ideas across different media, and diffractions of new materialist thinking through materials and material-discursive entanglements. In the context of new materialist arguments that understand matter as a process of materialisation, the workshops attempted to explore the question of how different materials materialise matter differently.

In disrupting the usual practices of a conference, we asked participants to engage and actively participate prior to the workshop-conference event. We called these pre-workshop making-doings, where interested participants were asked to be attentive to the sensory – feelings, sights, sounds, taste, and so on – and to collate/collect matter from/with a 'journey' they did regularly. This matter could be writings, notes, photographs, video, recordings, objects-things-materials and so on collected from the route. We asked participants to bring these materials to the workshop, where we aimed to support and enable questioning, exploring and understanding through mapping the embodied ways in which we understand bodies with place/s.

The participants took these embodied-material mappings and fragmented them into units of lexical matter, and through a series of exercises these units were distributed around the workshop space, culminating in the translation of the initial material into poems and strings of language. These constructions were then taken apart and put together in different ways, creating material renderings of new semantic pathways and showing how language itself is material in a number of ways. The participants were then supported in exploring the embodied concepts created through journeying and mapping, and words and poetry, through collaging. This involved collating images, words, colours, and drawing lines or figures that expressed the aesthetics and themes found in the previous movement work. We asked participants to pay attention to these materials (paper, scissors, glue, pens), as well as the specific practices through which they were transformed (cutting, tearing, folding). The workshops ended with a collective reflection on and sharing of the practices we used and are using.

Through our workshops we were asking questions related to aspects of subjectivity and/or embodiment through engaging with different media. We saw these workshops as ways to support emerging methods for putting new materialist thinking to work, to enable our developing approaches. However, what we were also asking was for participants, fellow scholars and academics to trust us, to be with us and the materials as active participants in sharing and learning; but also to be open to the potentials of this 'not usual' way of presentation at a conference. Not only were we asking participants to prepare and engage with socio-materials prior to the conference, in the workshop we were also engaging in performative socio-material practices that for many would have been unfamiliar and could possibly cause feelings of unease and uncertainty. We discussed these ethical questions and from these discussions we made choices and decisions regarding materials, such as participants bringing materials and various iterations from places they were familiar and comfortable with, and using 'everyday', 'ordinary', familiar materials such as post-its and magazines in the workshops. But these ethics also involved each of us being positioned within the workshops as both leaders and participants who 'cared'. Because when questions, issues or concerns were raised we 'cared', and we were open to learning and being taught, where we practised care, together, by being continually open and responsive to the bodies with matter. What was also required was for each of us, as the workshop 'leaders', to care for and take care of each other for each other in the development, preparation, organisation and making of these research-creation events. So, many questions of care but also of positioning.

Positioning and New Materialist Practice Research

When considering care-ethics, an essential question we need to ask of ourselves concerns positioning; where are you? Because practice research, underpinned by new materialist thought, disrupts and embraces new and different ways of researching the practices and discourses that make and remake the identities of researcher as subject, and participant as research object. How can we 'work' these intra-actions, these spaces between that can enable this continuous making, remaking and negotiation of 'identities'? As discussed previously, the relationship, the between of Self and Other, and the entanglement, the event, the action between is what matters, and is also essential in the matter of ethics. In the matter of care we are working this space between; the 'with' between Self and Other; Self with Other.

Because of my existing practice as an artist, it is important that the research process is me 'with' participants, making, researching, teaching and learning from and 'with' each other, and that the identities of artist, researcher, teacher, participant, learner are fluid, entangled and blurred. Atkinson's work on teacher and learner identities in institutional art education suggests that these are largely constructed according to the particular discourses and practices employed in such contexts. This essentially means that the performance of particular discourses and practices leads to the production of specific identities, the learning of identities. However, these identities also involve positioning and power relations that 'activate or produce certain kinds of individuals' (Atkinson 2002: 97).

So using particular methodologies and methods involves performing particular practices and discourses that produce ways of knowing that make particular identities; the researcher as research subject (Self) and that which is studied, the participant, as the research object (Other). When this happens, the researcher is positioning themselves as separate from the research object; we are not acknowledging or even recognising the impact that we are having on the participants or the impact that the participants are having on us – in other words the pedagogic. We are not being attentive or open to learning 'with' because,

> as subjects, people have the right to define their own reality, establish their own identities, name their history. As objects, one's reality is defined by others, one's identity created by others, one's history named only in ways that define one's relationship to those who are subjects. (hooks 1994: 18–19)

Pink maintains that it 'is not so much as to study other people's . . . values and behaviours, but to collaborate with them to explore and identify (and learn) these' (2009: 58). Otherwise we are denying the relationship, the between of Self with Other, and perpetuating practices and discourses that dominate and oppress; but we are also lacking reflexivity.

> On my first day I sat in a corner, quietly watching, observing the children and the teacher and occasionally writing notes. Then a few of the younger students started to ask questions of me and immediately an older student told them to stop being nosey and then apologised for them. However, very quickly I started to become just a part of the classroom and the school life, nothing special.
>
> After two days of 'just observing' the students would come to me to ask for help or to check their work, yep I still do not like maths. The Principal asked me whether I would teach some art lessons with the students. But is this what I should be doing, I feel really strange about this. Do I get actively involved or just stay in my corner and say no to helping out. I am feeling really wobbly about

what I am doing. Is this how I want to research or be as a researcher, am I meant
to shut off me as an artist teacher and not be involved, just watch.

I just can't do that. Stuff my research plan and what I planned and should
be doing and how I should be doing it. I will just see what happens. I will hang
out at school, teach, help, get involved and see what happens. I am not going to
get all caught up with research plans, questions, methods and data. I will just
see what happens, I'm just going to be. (Research notes)

In letting go of particular fixed constructs of research and researcher, I
became more open to opportunities to actively participate in/with the
school community: doing playground duty, relating with the children,
having lunch with the staff in the staffroom, talking about the weather,
events in the community, working with the principal and teaching assistants in designing and teaching lessons. Through all of these practices
and by being open, flexible and responsive, my methods and practices
as researcher came closer to my philosophy and my practices as an artist teacher.

Probyn (1993) and Butterwick (2001) are particularly critical of the
way in which reflexivity can be approached and the perceived lack of
detailed documentation of the reflexive process. Probyn maintains that
the effectiveness of reflexivity depends on the way in which it is practised: 'what exactly a self-reflexive self is reflecting upon . . . where that
self is positioned and whether it is a physical or textual entity' (1993:
62). Stoller (1989; 1997), Seremetakis (1994), Okely (1994) and Pink
(2009) also acknowledge that reflexivity is an embodied 'process that
involves . . . engaging not only with the ideas of others, but in learning
about their understandings through her or his own . . . experiences'
(Pink (2009: 14). In other words, for reflexivity to be effective we need
to embody reflexivity; be aware of and engage with how our bodily
socio-material experiences are produced through research encounters
and how these may assist in our understanding and learning. As Geurts
states:

> We often find ourselves drenched – not just in discourse and words, but in sen-
> sations, imaginations and emotions . . . And yet, if we have become drenched,
> those we work with may also be soaked through and through. Such moments
> open up space, or sound a call, to body forth fine-tuned accounts. (2003: 386)

However, to be bodily reflexive we must learn, know and understand
our own corporeality and also intra-corporeality.

Pink (2009) asserts that our bodily subjectivity is the awareness of
our own sensory knowledge, values and practices, such as how we cate-
gorise and classify our senses culturally and/or personally. For example,

in the West we divide the senses into vision, hearing, touch, taste and smell. However, Howes and Classen stress that 'other cultures do not necessarily divide the sensorium as we do, the Hausa have two senses and the Japanese five, and these senses do not coincide with modern western ones' (1991: 257–8). But we also need to be aware that there are differences between and within cultures: in terms of gender, ethnicity, generations, materially and so on; and so these categories may be used in different ways and also mean different things. Howes and Classen maintain that embodied subjectivity may be examined before starting the research, but I also assert that it can be learned during the research.

In the study presented in Chapter 1 I had an embodied knowledge of this particular place-world, but at the same time I did not. Like Hockey (2006) with respect to long-distance running and Hahn (2007) with Japanese dance, I had embodied experiences of similar place-worlds before I began the research; similar, but not the same. Consequently, I possessed knowledges and understandings of the sociocultural-material practices of this place-world. But I was also able to learn from and with the participants' (knowledge, beliefs, values), and this enabled me to not only learn different placemaking practices but also to have a deeper critical consciousness of my own embodied socio-material knowledges and practices. This embodied and material pedagogy began before I started researching with, but was also learned while I was researching with.

Our corporeal subjectivity should also be understood with other identity indicators such as gender, sexuality, ethnicity, age and so on. But it is very important that we do not fix these subjectivities, as they shift depending on the socio-material, the what, how and where we are researching and learning. Our identities, our ways of knowing and learning, are continually being made, remade and negotiated in collaboration with the socio-material. It is through these practices of researching 'with' and working the spaces between that we can learn and begin to answer 'where are you'? Not only an ethical question of positioning but the acknowledgement of the importance of 'where' in the entanglement of the practices, making and pedagogy of practice research.

Ethics and Placemaking

To 'take care' in the researching of placemaking, the first step is positioning, the very acknowledgement of place; the importance of 'where' in the research. As Tuck and McKenzie state

> it is typical for place to be superficially addressed in social science inquiry. Many social science professional mores require researchers to clearly define what was learned and how it was learned. When is important too . . . Where, however, is not always given much attention, beyond a few notes at the outset. (2015: 8)

In a lot of social science research, the 'place' of the research is constructed in terms of the research setting or the research site; it is the surface that life happens on or from which data are collected (Massey 1994). Jorgensen (1989) discusses the importance of certain qualities of the research setting that need to be considered, such as visibility and openness. A visible setting is where information about the community is accessible, and an open setting is where access to the community and its members requires little negotiation. The use of this language, or simplified descriptors such as urban, rural and so on, with little or no examination, positions/ makes the place of the research a mere backdrop, rather than integral to and entangled with the research.

The basis for all ethnographic research is fieldwork, and a key assumption within classic ethnography is that the field or being in the field is 'there'; a distant locale away from home (Johnson 1975). This assumption is embedded in the long tradition of ethnographic practice, where researchers travelled to exotic locations to be within and study a culture (Bateson and Mead 1942; Freilich 1970; Gow 1995; Pink 1997; Price 2005); this practice and discourse positions/makes the field 'there', 'Other'. To disrupt this practice of Othering, and position/make place integral to the research, we can use 'place' not only theoretically but also methodologically and ethically to remake/reconceptualise the field as 'place-world'. I have been drawn to these issues and questions regarding our attachments to place, particularly the placemaking practices of our childhood, of home, because of my own experiences and understandings of belonging-disbelonging. But there are many ethical questions and considerations to be made when you want to research the place-world of home.

Home, a sense of belonging, as defined in Chapter 3, is where your practices, your ways of being, enable you to feel at ease, comfortable, to have a connection with a group, place or country. But home is not necessarily the place you grew up in, nor where your family is, nor where you are from – group, place, country. Knowles (2000) and Pink (2000) have both explored the ethical issues of the places of their research being home and home being the place of their research from the position of the 'transnational' – one who has lived in one place but chooses to live in another place and 'the impact of their own transnationalism on their research' (Knowles 2000: 54). To understand this relationship, as researchers we need to be reflexive about our relationship with home and also the place of research. In other words, what are we doing and why are we doing it with home. Knowles (2000) claims that this understanding can come from examining our autobiography: a selection of stories about life, experiences and memories that positions us in the world. Just as we need to be corporeally reflexive, as discussed above, we also need to be reflexive of our own senses of belonging; to engage with and examine how our own senses of belonging/placemaking are made and learned, and how these may support and enable us to understand those of others.

The place-world of remote Australia, the bush, was the focus of this research assemblage, but it was and also is my home, even though I do not currently live there. The senses of belonging I have with this place were learned from past practices and also through/with familial relationships that maintain my entanglements with this place-world. However, entangled with these practices and relationships of belonging are my reasons for not living there, my senses of disbelonging, of discomfort and not fitting in. My research on the practices and pedagogies of placemaking enabled me to examine and explore these tensions, the between of belonging and disbelonging. But in exploring these tensions and feeling of ease/unease I also needed to address care for myself. One way to achieve this was through my knowledges and understanding of the roles and social positions within this particular place-world.

Jorgensen claims that in society all members are defined by their social location, 'where they are located in relation to, and in association with, other members of their community' (1989: 53); so where they are positioned is relational to other members of the community-culture, place-world. According to Jorgensen and Stacey, the extremes of social location are outsider and insider, and these exist on a continuum. They also argue that in qualitative research the social location of a researcher within a community determines what can be described, the types of description and the opportunity to describe (Jorgensen 1989; Stacey 1994). For this research assemblage you could argue that I slid between these two extremes, from complete outsider (having not lived in this particular place-world) to almost insider (as I had previously lived in a similar place-world), and so I have some understanding and knowledge of placemaking practices and pedagogies.

Jorgensen (1989) maintains that the social location of the researcher is pivotal in accessing meanings, because comments, behaviours and actions that may appear to be meaningless from the social location of an outsider may be highly significant to an insider. Jorgensen also

asserts that insider meanings are not usually accessible or displayed
for outsiders, as they are primarily available to people to whom these
meanings constitute a way of life. Elliot (1988) also asserts that gaining
access to members of a small, relatively tight-knit community can be
particularly difficult, as people are more inclined to share their insider
world of meaning and action with a person who is, or has been, a mem-
ber of the community, as one parent shared with me:

> You cannot just step into a small town, a small community and we tell you
> everything then and there. You step into a small town and you be yourself. You
> learn to mingle and get on with people. You should just sit down, shut up, see
> what is happening, say nothing, do nothing, go nowhere. That is what you have
> got to do. Come in and suss it out.

Stacey (1994) asserts that one of the reasons for this is that in small
communities, social roles and expectations are learned early, and outsiders must create roles for themselves or play those roles already in the
local repertoire, as was explained to me by the Principal of the local
school:

> Here your professional life and your personal life are bound up together . . .
> What people see you as in this community is your job and you will always be
> that. You are never just you. You are your job all the time . . . You are seen that
> way all the time. Your personal life intermingles with your professional life and
> you have to work out the pecking order and where you can fit.

In considering and questioning how can we research with care, we
can position ourselves not only as researchers but also be open to taking on and learning roles that exist and are known in the place-world.
But we can also be open and willing to share skills, experiences and
knowledge to demonstrate that we are not an exploitative interloper,
there just to get what we need, to take and then leave. We can work the
space between where we have something to give and contribute, but we
are also open to learning with. Wenger reiterates the importance of the
identity that an outsider takes on:

> newcomers are forging their own identities; they do not necessarily want to
> emphasise discontinuity more than continuity. They must find a place in rela-
> tion to the past. In order to participate, they must gain some access – vicarious
> as it is maybe – to the history they want to contribute to they must make it part
> of their own identities. (2005: 157)

This is not to say that this positioning, this working the space
between, is easy or without anxiety. Even though I understood and had

learned the placemaking practices of a particular place-world, I was still very apprehensive because it had been some time since I had spent time in/with a similar place-world; one that has a lot of space and not many people: 'the bush'. This is because, as Wagner asserts, people who have socialised in large metropolitan settings have difficulty grasping the dynamics of 'face to face societies' (1979: 141), where everyone has knowledge of all the members of the community; as one parent explained to me, 'Everyone knows you and what you are doing, it's all the time.' Because of my learned placemaking practices, I was also able to share that I was no stranger to the issues of living in a similar place-world: 'Oh, you worked at Heatherton, you understand how it is.' However, I also knew that I would never be considered a complete insider, and that there was likely to be a high level of curiosity and even possibly mistrust about what I was doing and why I was really there.

But interestingly and very surprisingly, my concerns were unfounded. No one was overly concerned with my research or exactly what I was doing and why I was doing it. They were interested in me, but more me in relation to them, my positioning: 'So, tell me about yourself?', and 'Why on earth did you choose us and why here?' According to Goffman's seminal text (1959), people are often more concerned with what kind of person you are than with the research itself, and they will try to gauge how far a person can be trusted and what they might be able to offer as an acquaintance or friend. According to Hammersley and Atkinson (1995), because of my lack of social location in this place-world, I would be positioned as a complete outsider, and this would adversely affect the insider knowledge I was privy to. In other words I would not learn anything, or it would be very limited.

But the contrary happened. What I initially thought was just 'small talk' quickly escalated into conversations that were almost confessional. I was being confided in and a lot of personal information, thoughts and feelings about relationships with others in the community, issues, concerns and quite deep feelings about futures and living in this place-world were shared with me. Initially, I was incredibly uncomfortable with this, as it was in complete opposition to everything I had read and previously discussed regarding doing 'fieldwork' in small communities, social location, outsider–insider and so on (Stacey 1994). While surprised, I also felt a great responsibility because not only was I being trusted, I was also being entrusted.

In analysing and critically reflecting on why these very honest outpourings happened, I maintain that is because of the intra-actions, the entanglement of the positions of insider–outsider. I was insider as I took on a known social role (that of teacher) and I shared my own experiences and practices of growing up and living in similar place-worlds. I was also outsider, as I did not live and work in this particular place-world, and so I did not have allegiances or alliances: 'It's OK I can tell you this because you don't know them.' But I was also outsider because I was going to leave this place-world. So what was shared with me would also leave: 'See, I knew you would understand, you get this, I feel so much better talking about this. I suppose you won't be here much longer will you? When are you leaving?' Through working the between of our social positioning, which is not predetermined nor planned, and by being open and attentive to the surprises of researching 'with care', we can enable shared places of discovery and learning (Page 2012a).

The ethics of new material practice research is to research with care, to take care socio-materially, and not separate from the practices and processes of researching, making and learning. Mind, body, spirit with matter we can make and take responsibility and consciously engage in disrupting the practices and discourses that dominate and oppress, to work the spaces between.

Note

1. See   <https://esrc.ukri.org/funding/guidance-for-applicants/research-ethics/frequently-raised-questions/what-is-ethics/>, last accessed 14 January 2020.

Conclusion

Journey, 'an act of travelling from one place to another' (*OED*). Some consider the use of journey to be clichéd; to be honest I am one of those people, and I usually roll my eyes when I hear it. You may also hear an audible sigh. However, the term 'cliché' is defined as an 'overused phrase' (*OED*), and perhaps 'journey' is similarly stereotyped; but maybe this is because it is a very appropriate metaphor. Because an act of travelling can involve literal movement from one place to another; however, it could also be a metaphorical movement, as in the fluidity of learning and understanding, or what Atkinson (2011) refers to as punching into new learning spaces. Interestingly, this dual premise of journey involves the practices of the body. Therefore, as I near the destination of this particular journey, literally and metaphorically, I reflect on the what? and, so what? of this research assemblage, *Placemaking: A New Materialist Theory of Pedagogy*.

I have examined and explored the theoretical and methodological approaches to researching how we make and learn place, underpinned by new materialist thinking. As I have continually stated, it is through our socio-material practices, everyday making, that we know, understand, learn and ultimately make place. Whether we are walking, talking, working, making photographs or films, commuting, doing the washing up or reading, it is through these embodied ways of knowing and learning that we make place. We know and learn these bodily socio-material practices and dispositions (Bourdieu 1992; de Certeau 1984) early in our lives. It is these ways that teach members of a community, a culture or a society to relate in ways consistent with the practices of their group, place or country, and consequently to feel at ease, to have a sense of belonging. De Certeau also maintains that the repetition of these practices enables ways of overcoming alienation and can be used to forge a group and a national identity. But, as also discussed, these socio-material practices and pedagogies can also be used to exclude, where the absence of matter has power to teach and we learn disbelonging.

Place is made and learned with bodies, with the socio-material, and these embodied and material pedagogical practices make meanings that can be used in very powerful yet subtle and nuanced ways. These ways are not only sociopolitically-materially-culturally made, performed and learned; they are part of who we are, our very being. This is because to be human is to already be materially with place, and to be materially with place is to be human, the entanglement of bodies with the socio-material of place-worlds. The main premise of this assemblage is that place is the very experiential fact of our existence, but it is also a necessary one, as it enables the making of meaning and socio-material relations; we know and learn place through embodied and material pedagogies, and we also know and learn place from just being with place-worlds.

Shove states that research that explores sociocultural processes and involves conducting cultural analysis is usually preoccupied 'with the explicit, the visible and the dramatic' (2003: 1). I argue that this may be because embodied perception and memory – feelings, sensing and so on – can be fleeting, hard to describe, to verbalise, and sometimes hard to pin down to the specific. However, regardless of how difficult it is to convey or articulate these affects and effects, the evoking and sharing of a place-world can not only enable an understanding and learning of the embodied and material ways of knowing a particular place-world, but also how through embodied and socio-material practices place is made and learned. This is significant because these practices

> should be seen as a strong undercurrent in everyday life, gaining their power from their invisibility and their being taken for granted . . . this then means that there is a need for a greater interest in the backstage, the prosaic construction of props and preparation rather than the stage itself. (Löfgren and Wilk 2007: 9)

This may then contribute to a more profound but also a subtle examination of embodiment, 'one which is grounded in, and contributes to, theoretical ideas on the body as central to the performance and construction of . . . identity' (Little and Leyshorn 2003: 269), by producing new analytical insights and also developing the theoretical relationship of the pedagogy of between 'where and who'.

Learning the socio-material placemaking practices of a particular place-world, I was also able to explore and examine the practices of 'exclusion, marginalization and . . . the cultural construction' (Little and Leyshorn 2003: 269) of a particular place-world, 'the bush'. I also learned how artistic, linguistic, poetic and geopolitical socio-materials and discourse are used in a very specific and particular way in the making of national identity. However, the children's ways of making and learning place enabled an understanding of this place-world, that is continually made and remade through the everyday socio-material practices of the body. These embodied practices and pedagogies contest the fixed cultural constructions of the bush as lacking and a disadvantaged place-world. This also demonstrates that place and placemaking are complex and dynamic, and that there is no one single, overriding construction, reality or meaning. This can result in an empowering and an emancipation of those who live in these place-worlds, as they can then become places of opportunities and potentials.

This knowledge and understanding of the importance of the where also contributes to the discourses of the loss of connection with place or displacement. Casey (1993) and Augé (2008) maintain that the rise of society searching for a sense of place is because of our increasingly 'placeless' or non-place-world. This placelessness, Cresswell states, is because of a 'combination of mass communication, increased mobility and a consumer society . . . that leads to an accelerating erosion of place . . . and a rapidly accelerating homongenization of the world' (2004: 43).

This idea is explored by Paul Kelly (b. 1955), an Australian singer-songwriter, through the song 'Every Fucking City' (2008), which focuses on a personal journey following a lover through Europe:

> We argued on the channel train to Paris
> The vin rouge helped us make it sweet again
> But by the time that we got down to Lyon
> Everything I said was wrong and you cursed me in the rain
> We split up for a while in Barcelona
> We met up six days later in Madrid
> I was hoping that the break would make things go a little better for us
> And for a little while it almost did
> Now I'm in a bar in Copenhagen
> And I'm trying hard to forget your name
> And I'm staring at the label on a bottle of cerveza
> And every fucking city feels the same
>
> You said to call you when I got to London
> A French girl told me that you'd left a note
> I said to her 'I like your accent' and she thought I sounded funny
> So we ended up drinking in Soho
> Foolishly I followed you to Dublin
> Like a ghost I walked the streets of Temple Bar
> And all the bright young things were throwing up their Guinness in the gutters
> And once I thought I saw you from afar
> Now I'm in a nightclub in Helsinki
> And they're playing La Vida Loca once again
> And I can't believe I'm dancing to this crap but I'm a chance here
> And every fucking city sounds the same

> At a cafe in the port of Amsterdam
> An e-mail from you said you'd gone to Rome
> For a minute I thought maybe but my funds were running low
> And anyway it sounded like you weren't alone
> So I headed north until I got to Hamburg
> A chilly city suits a troubled soul
> And on the Reeperbahn I paid a woman far too much
> To kick me out before I'd even reached my goal
> Now I'm in a restaurant in Stockholm
> And the waiter here wants me to know his name
> And I can order sandwiches in seven different languages
> But every fucking city looks the same
> Arriverderci, au revoir, auf wiedersehen, hasta la vista baby
> Yeah, every fucking city's just the same.

Through Kelly's embodied learning of a modern day 'grand tour'[1] of Europe he concludes that there is little difference between Europe's cities: 'Yeah, every fucking city's just the same.' The ubiquity and homogenisation of the socio-material that Kelly conveys can be largely attributed to the processes of globalisation and technology. As Relph maintains, these 'encourage placelessness, that is, a weakening of the identity of places to the point where they . . . look alike and feel alike and offer the same bland possibilities' (1976: 90). These discourses of disbelonging and placelessness or displacement make place that is lacking, and as previously asserted, these socio-material practices and pedagogies have the power to exclude, isolate and be used politically. Because place is pivotal to who we are as humans, placemaking can become an even more powerful political force. As Cresswell states, 'the very fact that place is such a crucial site of contestation points towards its fundamental role in human life . . . The basic unavoidability of place in human life makes it a very important object of politics' (2004: 122) and of power relationships, because through disconnectedness comes ignorance and harm.

As I stated previously, a journey is defined as an act of travelling from one place to another, literally and/or metaphorically; and for me journeying has similarities to the premise of place: ongoing, fluid and dynamic, there is no fixed destination or end. Through this continuing journey of questioning, exploring and examining the spaces between who we are, how we are and where we are, additional queries have come to the fore. Within the hegemonic structures of academic institutions, how do we share and communicate without a reliance on text-language, how do we go beyond the usual? How do we share the unseen, the fleeting and the felt? The answers to these questions lie in our willingness to 'work' and embrace the between, where 'theory-as-practice-as-process-as com-plication intentionally unsettles perception and knowing through living inquiry' (Irwin and Springgay 2008: xxi).

Through exploring and examining the small, hidden and sometimes taken for granted embodied-material ways of making and learning place we can disrupt the premise of place as a singular or fixed, some-thing to be owned, controlled or excluded from. We need to learn, understand and value the everyday, artistic, individual and collective socio-material ways we know and learn 'place and, more particularly, [become] part of [with] place' (Casey 1993: 33). We need to learn from Indigenous cultures, and from our childhood practices, and acknowl-edge that we are 'owned by the places we inhabit'; and also 'own up to the complexity and mutuality of place' (Malpas 2007: 331) and being human. This book contributes to this discourse as it demonstrates that ways of making and learning place are powerful, complex, dynamic, and that there is no single, overriding, fixed meaning or idea of place.

So when someone says that 'It's only geography' or 'It's just geog-raphy', it is usually said as a dismissive throwaway comment, that no matter the moving, or going from one place to another, the geography, the place, does not matter. But it does matter. The matter of where is more than a site or backdrop, and there is more than the superficiality of difference. The very matter of place-worlds and our intra-actions mean that practices and pedagogies of placemaking are essential knowledges in understanding who we are as individuals, communities, cultures and nations. These knowledges, understandings and pedagogies enable a way of being with the world that is ethical; a humanness, to take care and to be 'with' care.

Note

1. 'n. historical a cultural tour of Europe conventionally undertaken by a young man of the upper classes' (*OED*).

Bibliography

ABS (Australian Bureau of Statistics) (2010a), *ABS Views on Remoteness*, Canberra: Australian Bureau of Statistics.

ABS (Australian Bureau of Statistics) (2010b), *National Regional Profile: Bamorrow* [name changed], Canberra: Australian Bureau of Statistics.

ABS (Australian Bureau of Statistics) (2011), *Australian Population Grid*, <http://www.abs.gov.au/ausstats/abs@.nsf/mf/1270.0.55.007>, last accessed 14 January 2020.

ABS (Australian Bureau of Statistics) (2013a), 'Australian social trends: Population: Population distribution: Population characteristics and remoteness', in Australian Bureau of Statistics (ed.), *Australia Now*, Canberra: Australian Bureau of Statistics.

ABS (Australian Bureau of Statistics) (2013b), *ASGC Remoteness Classification: Purpose and Use*, Canberra: Australian Bureau of Statistics.

ABS (Australian Bureau of Statistics) (2015), *Regional Statistics Queensland*, Canberra: Australian Bureau of Statistics.

ABS (Australian Bureau of Statistics) (2016a), *Regional Statistics Queensland*, Canberra: Australian Bureau of Statistics.

ABS (Australian Bureau of Statistics) (2016b), *Remoteness Australia*, <https://www.abs.gov.au/ausstats/abs@.nsf/Latestproducts/1270.0.55.005Main%20Features5July%202016?opendocument&tabname=Summary&prodno=1270.0.55.005&issue=July%202016&num=&view=>, last accessed 30 January 2020.

ABS (Australian Bureau of Statistics) (2018), *Australian Social Trends: Population–Population Distribution*, Canberra: Australian Bureau of Statistics.

ABS (Australian Bureau of Statistics) (2019), *Year Book 2019*, Canberra: Australian Bureau of Statistics.

AIATSIS (Australian Institute of Aboriginal and Torres Strait Islanders Studies) (2012), 'Native title corporations: prescribed bodies corporate', <https://aiatsis.gov.au/research/research-themes/native-title-and-traditional-ownership/prescribed-bodies-corporate>, last accessed 30 January 2020.

Alaimo, S., and Hekman, S. (eds) (2008), *Material Feminisms*, Bloomington: Indiana University Press.

Alcoff, L. (1991), 'The problem of speaking for others', *Cultural Critique*, Winter 1991–92, pp. 5–32.

Areses Huertas, A., Frimet, B., Johnston, J., McGeer, N., and Page, T. (2012), 'Finding your way: the purpose and relevance of writing for artist researcher teacher practices', *Writing in Creative Practices*, 5(1), pp. 45–72.

Aristotle (1983), *Physics, Books III and IV*, Oxford: Clarendon Press.

Aristotle (2000), *Categories*, Project Gutenberg, <http://www.classicallibrary.org/aristotle/categories/index.htm>, last accessed 13 January 2020.

Atkinson, D. (2002), *Art in Education: Identity and Practice*, Dordrecht: Kluwer.

Atkinson, D. (2011), *Art, Equality and Learning: Pedagogies against the State*, Rotterdam: Sense Publishers.

Atkinson, P., Delamont, S., and Housley, W. (2007), *Contours of Culture: Complex Ethnography and the Ethnography of the Complex*, Lanham, MD: Altamira Press.

Augé, M. (2008), *Non-places: An Introduction to Supermodernity*, London: Verso.

Australian Commonwealth Schools Commission (1988), *Schooling in Rural Australia*, Australian Capital Territory (ACT): Curriculum Development Centre.

Back, L., and Puwar, N. (2012), 'A manifesto for live methods: provocation and capacities', *Sociological Review*, 60(1), pp. 6–17.

Baldwin, T. (2004), 'Introduction', in M. Merleau-Ponty, *The World of Perception*, Abingdon: Routledge, pp. 1–33.

Ball, M. S., and Smith, G. W. H. (1992), *Analyzing Visual Data*, Beverly Hills: Sage.

Bang, M., Curley, L., Kessel, A., Marin, A., Suzukovich, E. S., and Strack, G. (2014), 'Muskrat theories, tobacco in the streets, and living Chicago as Indigenous land', *Environmental Education Research*, 20(1), pp. 37–55.

Banks, M. (1992), 'Which films are ethnographic films?', in P. I. Crawford and D. Turton (eds), *Film as Ethnography*, Manchester: Manchester University Press, pp. 116–29.

Barad, K. (1998), 'Getting real: technoscientific practices and the materialization of Reality', *A Journal of Feminist Cultural Studies*, 10(2), pp. 87–128.

Barad, K. (2001), 'Re(con)figuring space, time and matter', in Marianne DeKoven (ed.), *Feminist Locations: Global and Local, Theory, Practice*, New Brunswick, NJ: Rutgers University Press, pp. 75–109.

Barad, K. (2003), 'Posthumanist performativity: toward an understanding of how matter comes to matter', *Signs*, 28(3), pp. 801–31.

Barad, K. (2007), *Meeting the Universe Halfway: Quantum Physics and the Entanglement of Matter and Meaning*, Durham, NC: Duke University Press.

Barad, K. (2012), 'Interview with Karen Barad', in R. Dolphijn and I. van der Tuin (eds), *New Materialism: Interviews and Cartographies*, Ann Arbor: Open Humanities Press, pp. 48–70.

Barrett, E. (2007), 'Introduction', in E. Barrett and B. Bolt (eds), *Practice as Research: Approaches to Creative Arts Enquiry*, London: I.B. Tauris, pp. 1–13.

Barrett, E., and Bolt, B. (eds) (2007), *Practice as Research: Approaches to Creative Arts Enquiry*, London: I.B. Tauris.

Barrett, E., and Bolt, B. (eds) (2013), *Carnal Knowledge: Towards a New Materialism through the Arts*, London: I.B. Tauris.

Bateson, G., and Mead, M. (1942), *Balinese Character: A Photographic Analysis*, New York: New York Academy of Science.

Becker, H. S. (1958), 'Problems of inference and proof in participant observation', *American Sociological Review*, 23, pp. 652–60.

Becker, H. S. (1986), 'Photography and sociology', in H. S. Becker (ed.), *Doing Things Together*, Evanston: Northwestern University Press, pp. 223–41.

Bennett, J. (2010), *Vibrant Matter: A Political Ecology of Things*, Durham, NC: Duke University Press.

Berger, T. (2016), 'Place, Imaginary, Identity: Place Ethnography in Truth or Consequences, New Mexico', dissertation, University of New Mexico.

Berger, J., and Mohr, J. (1975), *A Seventh Man*, New York: Viking.

Berger, J., and Mohr, J. (1982), *Another Way of Telling*, London: Writers and Readers.

Bickerton, A. (ed.) (2004), *Australian–English, English–Australian*, London: Abson Books.

Birkerts, S. (1986), 'Place: a fragment', in T. Frick (ed.), *The Sacred Theory of the Earth*, Berkeley: North Atlantic, pp. 53–5.

Blackman, L. (2008), *The Body*, Oxford: Berg.

Bloom, L. R. (1998), *Under the Sign of Hope: Feminist Methodology and Narrative Interpretation*, Albany: State University of New York Press.

Boden, R., Epstein, D., and Latimer. J. (2009), 'Accounting for ethos or programmes for conduct? The brave new world of research ethics committees', *Sociological Review* 57(4), pp. 727–49.

Bolt, B. (2004), *Art beyond Representation: The Performative Power of the Image*, London: I.B. Tauris.

Bolt, B. (2013), 'Introduction: toward a new materialism through the arts', in E. Barrett and B. Bolt (eds), *Carnal Knowledge: Towards a New Materialism through the Arts*, London: I.B. Tauris, pp. 1–13.

Bourdieu, P. (1977), *Outline of a Theory of Practice*, Cambridge: Cambridge University Press.

Bourdieu, P. (1984), *Distinction: A Social Critique of the Judgment of Taste*, Cambridge, MA: Harvard University Press.

Bourdieu, P. (1990a), 'Structures, habitus, practices', in P. Bourdieu (ed.), *The Logic of Practice*, Stanford: Stanford University Press, pp. 55–79.

Bourdieu, P. (1990b), *In Other Words*, Cambridge: Polity.

Bourdieu, P. (1992), *Language and Symbolic Power*, Cambridge: Polity.

Bourdieu, P. (1993), *The Field of Cultural Production*, Cambridge: Polity.

Bourdieu, P., and Bourdieu, M. C. (2004), 'The peasant and photography', *Ethnography*, 5(4), pp. 601–16.

Braidotti, R. (2000), *Metamorphasis: Towards a Materialist Theory of Becoming*, Cambridge: Polity.

Braidotti, R. (2013), *The Posthuman*, London: Polity.

Brewster, A. (2007), 'The stolen generation: rites of passage: Doris Pilkington interviewed by Anne Brewster', *Journal of Commonwealth Literature*, 42(1), pp. 143–59.

Brighouse, T., and Woods, D. (2006), *Inspirations: A Collection of Commentaries and Quotations to Promote School Improvement*, London: Continuum.

Broomhall, F. H. (1991), *The Longest Fence in the World*, Sydney: Hesperian Press.

Bull, M. (2000), *Sounding Out the City: Personal Stereos and the Management of Everyday Life*, Oxford: Berg.

Burnell, B. A. (2003), 'The real world aspiration of work bound rural students', *Journal of Research in Rural Education*, 18(2), pp. 104–13.

Burns, R. B. (1997), *Introduction to Research Methods*, Melbourne: Longman.

Butler, J. (2003), 'Performativity's social magic', in R. Shusterman (ed.), *Bourdieu: A Critical Reader*, Oxford: Blackwell, pp. 113–28.

Butterwick, S. (2001), 'We've got nothing/everything to lose: lessons learned from an anti poverty action research project', *Adult Education Research Conference Proceedings*, East Lansing: New Prairie Press, pp. 1–7.

Byrnes, P. (1994), 'Priscilla', *Sydney Morning Herald*, 8 August.

Calhoun, C. (2000), 'Pierre Bourdieu', in G. Ritzer (ed.), *The Blackwell Companion to Major Social Theorists*, Oxford: Blackwell, pp. 696–730.

Candy, L. (2006), *Practice-based Research: A Guide*, Sydney: Creativity and Cognition Studios, University of Technology.

Carey, P. (2000), *True History of the Kelly Gang*, St Lucia: University of Queensland Press.

Carter, P. (2004), *Material Thinking: The Theory and Practice of Creative Research*, Carlton: Melbourne University Publishing.

Casey, E. S. (1993), *Getting Back into Place: Toward a Renewed Understanding of the Place World*, Bloomington: Indiana University Press.

Casey, E. S. (1998), *The Fate of Place. A Philosophical History*, Berkeley: University of California Press.

Chaplin, E. (1994), *Sociology and Visual Representation*, London: Routledge.

CIA (Central Intelligence Agency) (2010), *The World Fact Book*, <https://www.cia.gov/library/publications/the-world-factbook/geos/us.html>, last accessed 13 January 2020.

Clements, P. (2011), 'The recuperation of participatory arts practices', *International Journal for Art and Design Education*, 30(1), pp. 18–30.

Clifford, J., and Marcus, G. E. (eds) (1986), *Writing Culture: The Poetics and Politics of Ethnography*, Berkeley: University of California Press.

Coleman, R. (2009), *The Becoming of Bodies: Girls, Images, Experience*, Manchester: Manchester University Press.

Coleman, R. (2017a), 'Developing speculative methods to explore speculative shipping: mail art, exchange and futurity', in Alex Wilkie, Martin Savransky and Marsha Rosengarten (eds), *Speculative Research: The Lure of Possible Futures*, London: Routledge, pp. 130–44.

Coleman, R. (2017b), 'A sensory sociology of the future: affect, hope and inventive methodologies', *Sociological Review*, 65(3), pp. 525–43.

Coleman, R. (2019), 'Glitter: a methodology of following the material', *MAI: Feminism & Visual Culture*, 4, special issue, 'Feminist New Materialist Practice: The Mattering of Methods', <https://maifeminism.com/glitter-a-methodology-of-following-the-material/>, last accessed 30 January 2020.

Coleman, R., Page, T., and Palmer, H. (2019), 'Introduction', *MAI: Feminism & Visual Culture*, 4, special issue, 'Feminist New Materialist Practice: The Mattering of Methods', pp. 1–10, <https://maifeminism.com/feminist-new-materialisms-the-mattering-of-methods-editors-note/>, last accessed 30 January 2020.

Coleman, R., and Ringrose, J. (eds) (2013), *Deleuze and Research Methodologies*, Edinburgh: Edinburgh University Press.

Coles, A. (ed.) (2000), *Site-Specific City: The Ethnographic Turn, Volume 4: de-, dis-, ex-*, London: Black Dog Publishing.

Collier, J., and Collier, M. (1996), *Visual Anthropology*, Albuquerque: University of New Mexico Press.

Collingwood, R. G. (1945), *The Idea of Nature*, Oxford: Oxford University Press.

Connerton, P. (1989), *How Societies Remember*, Cambridge: Cambridge University Press.

Coole, D., and Frost, S. (eds) (2010), *New Materialisms: Ontology, Agency, and Politics*, Durham, NC: Duke University Press.

Cresswell, T. (2004), *Place: A Short Introduction*, Oxford: Blackwell.

Crossley, N. (1996), *Intersubjectivity: The Fabric of Social Becoming*, London: Sage.

CSIRO (Commonwealth Scientific and Industrial Research Organisation) (2001), *Australia, State of the Environment Report*, Canberra: Department of Natural and Cultural Heritage.

Danaher, P. A., Moriarity, B. J., and Hallinan, P. M. (2001), 'Occupational travellers and regional youth: actor-network theory and policy categories', in G. Danaher (ed.), *Issues of Regional Youth: Proceedings of the Issues of Regional Youth Conference*, Mackay: Central Queensland University, pp. 63–79.

de Certeau, M. (1984), *The Practice of Everyday Life*, trans. S. Rendall, Berkeley: University of California Press.

de Waal, E. (2011), 'With these hands', *Financial Times Weekend*, 12–13 March.

Dean, T., and Miller, J. (2005), *Place*, London: Thames and Hudson.

Deleuze, G. (1995), *Negotiations*, New York: Columbia University Press.

Deleuze, G., and Guattari, F. (1980), *A Thousand Plateaus: Capitalism and Schizophrenia*, trans. B. Massumi, Minneapolis: University of Minnesota Press.

Dermody, S., and Jacka, E. (1988), *The Screening of Australia: Anatomy of a National Cinema*, Sydney: Currency Press.

Descartes, R. (1970 [1734]), *Philosophical Letters*, trans. A. Kelly, Oxford: Clarendon Press.

Descartes, R. (1983 [1644]), *Principles of Philosophy*, trans. J. Veitch, Dordrecht: Reidel.

DH&AC (Department of Health and Aged Care) (2001), *Measuring Remoteness: Accessibility/Remoteness Index of Australia (ARIA)*, Canberra: Department of Health and Aged Care.

DIP (Department of Infrastructure and Planning) (2019), *Bamorrow* [name changed] *Regional Plan*, Brisbane: Queensland Government.

Dolphijn, R., and van der Tuin, I. (eds) (2012), *New Materialism: Interviews and Cartographies*, Ann Arbor: Open Humanities Press.

Downey, G. (2005), *Learning Capoeira: Lessons in Cunning from an Afro-Brazilian Art*, Oxford: Oxford University Press.

Downey, G. (2007), 'Seeing with a "sideways glance": visuomotor "knowing" and the plasticity of perception', in M. Harris (ed.), *Ways of Knowing: New Approaches in the Anthropology of Experience and Learning*, Oxford: Berghahn, pp. 222–41.

Dressman, M. (2006), 'Teacher, teach thyself: teacher research as ethnographic practice', *Ethnography*, 7(3), pp. 329–56.

Drewe, R. (1991), *Our Sunshine*, Sydney: Pan Macmillan.

Education Queensland (2003), *Rural and Remote Education Framework for Action 2003–2005*, Brisbane: Queensland Government Department of Education.

Education Queensland (2006), *Rural and Remote Education Framework for Action 2006–2008*, Brisbane: Queensland Government Department of Education.

Education Queensland (2008), *Workforce Management and Teacher Transfer*, Brisbane: Queensland Government Department of Education.

Edwards, D. (1998), *Rosalie Gascoigne: Material as Landscape*, Sydney: Art Gallery of New South Wales.

Elliot, J. (1988), 'Educational research and outsider–insider relations', *Qualitative Studies in Education*, 1(2), pp. 155–65.

Ellis, C., and Bochner, A. P. (2000), 'Autoethnobiography, personal narrative, reflexivity: research as subject', in N. K. Denzin and Y. S. Lincoln (eds), *Handbook of Qualitative Research*, Thousand Oaks: Sage, pp. 733–68.

Ellis, J. (2008), 'Mad for Oz', *Metro*, 12 November.

Ellsworth, E. (2005), *Places of Learning: Media, Architecture, Pedagogy*, Abingdon: Routledge.

Emmison, M., and Smith, P. (2000), *Researching the Visual*, New York: Sage.

Evans, T. (2003), 'Beating around the bush: reflections on the theme', *Journal of Research in Rural Education*, 18(3), pp. 170–2.

Feld, S. (1982), *Sound and Sentiment*, Philadelphia: University of Pennsylvania Press.

Feld, S., and Basso, K. H. (1996), 'Senses of place', in S. Feld and K. H. Basso (eds), *Senses of Place*, Santa Fe, NM: School of American Research Press, pp. 3–11.

Fetterman, D. M. (1989), *Ethnography: Step by Step*, Thousand Oaks: Sage.

Fine, M. (1994), 'Working the hyphens: reinventing self and other in qualitative research', in N. K. Denzin and Y. S. Lincoln (eds), *The Landscape of Qualitative Research: Theories and Issues*, Thousand Oaks: Sage, pp. 70–82.

Flannery, T. (2002), 'The Day, the Land, the People', Australia Day Address given at the Conservatorium of Music, Sydney, 23 January, <https://www.australiaday.com.au/events/australia-day-address/dr-tim-flannery/>, last accessed 14 January 2020.

Foster, H. (1996), 'The artist as ethnographer', in *The Return of the Real*, Cambridge, MA: MIT Press, pp. 171–204.

Frank, R. (1969), *The Americans*, New York: Aperture.

Freilich, M. (1970), 'Mohawk heroes and Trinidadian peasants', in M. Freilich (ed.), *Marginal Natives: Anthropologists at Work*, New York: Harper and Row, pp. 185–250.

Freire, P. (1970), *Pedagogy of the Oppressed*, Harmondsworth: Penguin.

Freire P. (2000), 'Interview: Paulo Freire: discussing dialogue', in T. Finkelpear (ed.), *Dialogues in Public Art*, Cambridge, MA: MIT Press, pp. 276–93.

Gale, F. (ed.) (1983), *We Are Bosses Ourselves: The Status and Role of Aboriginal Women Today*, Canberra: Australian Institute of Aboriginal Studies Press.

Gale, F. (2005), 'The endurance of Aboriginal women in Australia', in J. Hillier and E. Rooksby (eds), *Habitus: A Sense of Place*, Aldershot: Ashgate, pp. 356–70.

Ganesh, J. (2018), 'A gourmand's guide to globalisation', *Financial Times Weekend*, 8–9 September.

Gayton, D. (1996), *Landscape of the Interior: Re-explorations of Nature and Human Spirit*, Gabriola Island: New Society.

Geertz, C. (1973), *The Interpretation of Cultures: Selected Essays*, New York: Basic Books.

Genzuk, M. (2003), 'A synthesis of ethnographic research', in Center for Multilingual Multicultural Research (ed.), *Occasional Papers Series*, Los Angeles: Center for Multilingual, Multicultural Research Rossier School of Education, University of Southern California.

Geurts, K. L. (2003), 'On embodied consciousness in Anlo-Ewe worlds: a cultural phenomenology of the fetal position', *Ethnography*, 4(3), pp. 363–95.

Gibbs v. *Capewell* (1995), Australian Federal Court, 128 ALR 577.

Gibson, J. (1966), *The Senses Considered as Perceptual Systems*, Boston: Houghton Mifflin.

Gill, N. (2005), 'Life and death in Australian heartlands: pastoralism, ecology and rethinking the outback', *Journal of Rural Studies*, 21, pp. 39–53.

Gilmore, R. W. (1999), 'Queer publics: transforming policy, scholarship and politics', plenary session talk given at 'Local Politics and Global Change: Activists and Academics Thinking about a Queer Future', Center for Lesbian and Gay Studies, City University of New York.

Giroux, H. A. (2003), 'Public pedagogy and the politics of resistance: notes on a critical theory of educational struggle', *Educational Philosophy and Theory*, 35(1), pp. 5–16.

Goffman, E. (1959), *The Presentation of Self in Everyday Life*, Harmondsworth: Penguin.

Gow, P. (1995), 'Land people and paper in Western Amazonia', in E. Hirsch and M. O'Hanlon (eds), *The Anthropology of Landscape: Perspectives on Place and Space*, Oxford: Clarendon Press, pp. 43–62.

Graham, M. (1999), 'Some thoughts about the philosophical underpinnings of Aboriginal world views', *World Views: Environment, Culture, Religion*, 3(2), pp. 105–8.

Grasseni, C. (2004), 'Video and ethnographic knowledge: skilled vision and the practice of breeding', in S. Pink, L. Kürti and A. I. Afonso (eds), *Working Images*, London: Routledge, pp. 15–30.

Grunewald, D. A. (2003), 'The best of both worlds: a critical pedagogy of place', *Educational Researcher*, 32(4), pp. 3–12.

Hahn, T. (2007), *Sensational Knowledge: Embodying Culture through Japanese Dance*, Middletown, CT: Wesleyan University Press.

Hall, S. (1996), 'Introduction: who needs identity?', in S. Hall and P. du Gay (eds), *Questions of Cultural Identity*, London: Sage, pp. 1–17.

Hammersley, M., and Atkinson, P. (1995), *Ethnography, Principles in Practice*, London: Routledge.

Handley, K., Sturdy, A., Fincham, R., and Clark, T. (2006), 'Within and beyond communities of practice: making sense of learning through participation, identity and practice', *Journal of Management Studies*, 43(3), pp. 641–53.

Haraway, D. (2003), *The Companion Species Manifesto. Dogs, People and Significant Otherness*, Chicago: University of Chicago Press.

Hardy, T. (1996 [1887]), *The Woodlanders*, London: Wordsworth Editions.

Harper, D. (2003), 'Framing photographic ethnography: a case study', *Ethnography*, 4(2), pp. 241–66.

Harris, M. (2007), 'Introduction: ways of knowing', in M. Harris (ed.), *Ways of Knowing: New Approaches in the Anthropology of Experience and Learning*, Oxford: Berghahn, pp. 1–16.

Heaney, S. (1984), *Preoccupations: Selected Prose 1968–1978*, London: Faber and Faber.

Heidegger, M. (1959), *An Introduction to Metaphysics*, New Haven: Yale University Press.

Heidegger, M. (1962), *Being and Time*, New York: Harper.

Hekman, S. (2010), *The Material Knowledge: Feminist Disclosures*, Bloomington: Indiana University Press.

Hickey-Moody, A. (2015), 'Manifesto: the rhizomatics of practice as research', in A. Hickey-Moody and T. Page (eds), *Arts, Pedagogy and Cultural Resistance: New Materialism*, Lanham, MD: Rowman and Littlefield, pp. 169–92.

Hindmarsh, J., and Pilnick, A. (2007), 'Knowing bodies at work: embodiment and ephemeral teamwork in anesthesia', *Organization Studies*, 28(9), pp. 395–416.

Hobbs, D. (1994), The rural context for education: adjusting the images', in M. W. Galbraith (ed.), *Education in the Rural American Community: A Lifelong Process*, Malabar, FL: Krieger, pp. 21–43.

Hockey, J. (2006), 'Sensing the run: the senses and distance running', *Senses and Society*, 1(2), pp. 183–201.

Holland, P. (2000), '"Sweet it is to scan . . .": personal photographs and popular photography', in L. Wells (ed.), *Photography: A Critical Introduction*, London: Routledge, pp. 117–64.

Holliday, R. (2000), 'We've been framed: visualising methodology', *Sociological Review*, 48(4), pp. 503–21.

Hones, S. (2008), 'Location, context and perspective in American studies', *Comparative American Studies*, 6(4), pp. 313–28.

hooks, b. (1981), *Ain't I a Woman? Black Women and Feminism*, Boston: South End Press.

hooks, b. (1984), *From Margin to Center*, Boston: South End Press.

hooks, b. (1990), *Yearning: Race, Gender and Cultural Politics*, Boston: South End Press.

hooks, b. (1994), *Teaching to Transgress: Education as the Practice of Freedom*, New York: Routledge.

hooks, b. (2000), *All about Love: New Visions*, New York: William Morrow.

hooks, b. (2009), *Belonging: A Culture of Place*, New York: Routledge.

Howes, D. (2003), *Sensual Relations: Engaging the Senses in Culture and Social Theory*, Ann Arbor: University of Michigan Press.

Howes, D. (ed.) (2005), *Empire of the Senses: The Sensual Culture Reader*, Oxford: Berg.

Howes, D., and Classen, C. (1991), 'Conclusion: sounding sensory profiles', in D. Howes (ed.), *The Varieties of Sensory Experience: A Sourcebook in the Anthropology of the Senses*, Toronto: University of Toronto Press, pp. 257–88.

HREOC (Human Rights and Equal Opportunity Commission) (2000a), *Recommendations*, Canberra: Human Rights and Equal Opportunity Commission.

HREOC (Human Rights and Equal Opportunity Commission) (2000b), *Education Access*, Canberra: Human Rights and Equal Opportunity Commission.

HREOC (Human Rights and Equal Opportunity Commission) (2000c), *Emerging Themes*, Canberra: Human Rights and Equal Opportunity Commission.

Huggan, G. (1991), 'Maps, dreams and the presentation of ethnographic narrative: Hugh Brody's "Maps and Dreams" and Bruce Chatwin's "The Songlines"', *A Review of International English Literature*, 22(1), pp. 57–69.

Hughes, J. (ed.) (1989), *Australian Words and their Origins*, Melbourne: Oxford University Press.

Hugo, G., Griffith, D., Rees, P., Smailes, P., Badcock, P., and Stimson, R. (1997), *Rethinking the ASGC: Some Conceptual and Practical Issues*, Adelaide: National Key Centre for Teaching and Research in Social Applications of Geographical Information Systems.

Hunter, H. (2019), 'Holding the herbarium', *MAI: Feminism & Visual Culture*, 4, special issue, 'Feminist New Materialist Practice: The Mattering of Methods', <https://maifeminism.com/holding-the-herbarium/>, last accessed 30 January 2020.

Husserl, E. (1970 [1936]), *The Crisis of European Sciences and Transcendental Phenomenology*, Evanston: Northwestern University Press.

Ingold, T. (2000), *The Perception of the Environment*, London: Routledge.

Ingold, T. (2013), *Making*, Abingdon: Routledge.

Ingold, T., and Vergunst, J. L. (eds) (2008), *Ways of Walking: Ethnography and Practice on Foot*, Aldershot: Ashgate.

Irwin, R. L., Bickel, B., Triggs, V., Springgay, S., Beer, R., Grauer, K., Xiong, G., and Sameshima, P. (2009), 'The city of Richgate: a/r/tographic cartography as public pedagogy', *International Journal of Art and Design Education*, 28(1), pp. 61–70.

Irwin, R. L., and Springgay, S. (2008), 'A/r/tography as practice-based research', in M. Cahnmann-Taylor and R. Siegesmund (eds), *Arts-based Research in Education: Foundations for Practice*, New York: Routledge, pp. 103–24.

Ivinson, G., and Renold, E. (2013), 'Valley's girls: re-theorising bodies and agency in semi-rural post-industrial locale', *Gender and Education*, 25(6), pp. 704–21.

Jacknis, I. (1988), 'Margaret Mead and Gregory Bateson in Bali: their use of photography and film', *Cultural Anthropology*, 3(2), pp. 160–77.

Jagodzinski, J., and Wallin, J. (2013), *Arts-based Research: A Critique and a Proposal*, Rotterdam: Sense Publishers.

James, D. (2008), 'An Anangu ontology of place', in F. Vanclay, M. Higgins and A. Blackshaw (eds), *Making Sense of Place: Exploring Concepts and Expressions of Place through Different Sense and Lenses*, Canberra: National Museum of Australia, pp. 109–20.

Johnson, J. M. (1975), *Doing Field Research*, New York: Free Press.

Jolley, N. (1984), *Locke and Leibniz: A Study of the New Essays on Human Understanding*, Oxford: Clarendon Press.

Jones, I. (1995), *Ned Kelly: A Short Life*, Port Melbourne: Lothian.

Jones, R. (2000), *Development of a Common Definition of, and Approach to Data Collection on, the Geographic Location of Students to be Used for Nationally Comparable Reporting of Outcomes of Schooling*, Canberra: Ministerial Council on Education Employment, Training and Youth Affairs (MCEETYA).

Jorgensen, D. L. (1989), *Participant Observation: A Methodology for Human Studies*, Beverly Hills: Sage.

Kant, I. (1929 [1747]), 'Thoughts on the true estimation of living forces and criticism of the proofs propounded by Herr von Leibniz and other mechanists in their treatment of this controversial subject, together with some introductory remarks bearing upon force in bodies in general', in J. Handside (ed. and trans.), *Kant's Inaugural Dissertation and Early Writings on Space*, Chicago: Open Court, pp. 3–15.

Kant, I. (1985 [1786]), *Metaphysical Foundations of Natural Science*, in *Kant's Philosophy of Material Nature*, Indianapolis: Hackett, pp. v–223.

Kant, I. (1988 [1768]), 'Concerning the ultimate ground of differentiation of regions in space', in *Kant: Theoretical Philosophy 1755–1770*, ed. D. E. Walford and R. Meerbot, Cambridge: Cambridge University Press, pp. 361–72.

Kaufman, A. S., and McLean, J. E. (1998), 'An investigation into the relationship between interests and intelligence', *Journal of Clinical Psychology*, 54(2), pp. 279–95.

Kawagley, A. O., and Barnhardt, R. (2010), *Alaska Native Education. Views from Within*, Fairbanks: University of Alaska.

Knowles, C. (2000), 'Here and there: doing transnational fieldwork', in V. Amit (ed.), *Constructing the Field: Ethnographic Fieldwork in the Contemporary World*, London: Routledge, pp. 54–70.

Knudsen, B., and Stage, C. (2015), *Affective Methodologies*, Basingstoke: Palgrave Macmillan.

Kontturi, K. K., Tiainen, M., Nauha, T., and Angerer, M. L. (2018), 'Practicing materialism in the arts', *RUUKKU: Studies in Artistic Research*, 9, special issue, <http://ruukku-journal.fi/en/issues/9/editorial>, last accessed 13 January 2020.

Koro-Ljungberf, M., and Greckhamer, T. (2005), 'Strategic turns labeled "ethnography": from description to openly ideological production of cultures', *Qualitative Research*, 5(3), pp. 285–306.

Kottak, C. (2006), *Mirror for Humanity*, New York: McGraw Hill.

Kristeva, J. (1980), 'Giotto's joy', in *Desire in Language: A Semiotic Approach to Literature and Art*, ed. L. S. Roudiez, trans, T. J. Gora and L. S. Roudiez, Oxford: Blackwell, pp. 210–36.

Kusenbach, M. (2003), 'Street phenomenology: the go-along as ethnographic tool', *Ethnography*, 4(3), pp. 455–85.

Lalor, P., and Bodey, M. (2006), 'Obituary: Steve Irwin. Committed to the lore of nature', *The Australian*, 5 September.

Lammer, C. (2007), 'Bodywork: social somatic interventions in the operating theatres of invasive radiology', in S. Pink (ed.), *Visual Interventions: Applied Visual Anthropology*, Oxford: Berghahn, pp. 91–119.

Largey, G., and Watson, R. (2006), 'The sociology of odors', in J. Drobnik (ed.), *The Smell Culture Reader*, Oxford: Berg, pp. 29–40.

Lassiter, C. (1987), 'Relocation and illness: the plight of the Navajo', in D. M. Levin (ed.), *Pathologies of the Modern Self: Postmodern Studies on Narcissism, Schizophrenia and Depression*, New York: New York University Press, pp. 221–30.

Lave, J., and Wenger, E. (1991), *Situated Learning: Legitimate Peripheral Participation*, Cambridge: Cambridge University Press.

Law, J., and Urry, J. (2004), 'Enacting the social', *Economy and Society*, 33(3), pp. 390–410.

Law, J., Ruppert, E., and Savage, M. (2011), 'The double social life of methods', Centre for Research on Socio-cultural Change, working paper no. 95, <http://www.open.ac.uk/researchprojects/iccm/library/164.html>, accessed 13 January 2020.

Lawson, H. (1901), *The Country I Come From*, London and Edinburgh: Blackwood.

Lee, T., and Ingold, T. (2006), 'Fieldwork on foot: perceiving, routing, socializing', in S. Coleman and P. Collins (eds), *Locating the Field: Space, Place and Context in Anthropology*, Oxford: Berg, pp. 67–85.

Legat, A. (2008), 'Walking stories; leaving footprints', in T. Ingold and J. L. Vergunst (eds), *Ways of Walking: Ethnography and Practice on Foot*, Aldershot: Ashgate, pp. 1–19.

Leibniz, G. W. (1956 [c. 1714]), 'Metaphysical foundations in mathematics', in *Philosophical Papers and Letters*, ed. L. Loemker, Chicago: University of Chicago Press, pp. 666–74.

Lévi-Strauss, C. (1995), *Saudades to Brasil: A Photographic Memoir*, Seattle: University of Washington Press.

Levinas. E. (2000 [1991]), *Entre nous: Thnking of the Other*, trans. M. B. Smith and B. Harshav, New York: Columbia University Press.

Little, J., and Leyshorn, M. (2003), 'Embodied rural geographies: developing research agendas', *Progress in Human Geography*, 27(3), pp. 257–72.

Locke, J. (1975 [1689]), *An Essay Concerning Human Understanding*, Oxford: Clarendon Press.

Löfgren, O., and Wilk, R. (2007), 'In search of missing processes', *Ethnologia Europaea*, 35(1–2), pp. 5–12.

Long, S. (2008), 'Slowly down the Georgina: Aboriginal cultural heritage and lineal place complexes', in F. Vanclay, M. Higgins and A. Blackshaw (eds), *Making Sense of Place*, Canberra: National Museum of Australia, pp. 121–34.

Low, K. (2005), 'Ruminations on smell as a socio-cultural phenomenon', *Current Sociology*, 53(3), pp. 397–417.

Lowrie, T. (2007), 'Learning engagements in distance and rural settings: four Australian cases', *Learning Environments Research*, 10(1), pp. 35–51.

Luck, J. T. (2003), 'Does geography shape the nature of an educational innovation?', *Journal of Research in Rural Education*, 18(3), pp. 152–8.

Lund, K. (2005), 'Seeing in motion and the touching eye: walking over Scotland's mountains', *Etnofoor: Anthropological Journal*, 18(1), special issue, 'The Senses', pp. 27–42.

Lury, C. and, Wakeford, N. (2012), *Inventive Methods: The Happening of the Social*, London: Routledge.

Lury, C., et al. (2018), *Routledge Handbook of Interdisciplinary Research Methods*, London: Routledge.

MacCormack, P. (2012), *Posthuman Ethics: Embodiment and Cultural Theory*, Farnham: Ashgate.

MacDougall, D. (2006), *The Corporeal Image: Film, Ethnography and the Senses*, Princeton: Princeton University Press.

Mackellar, D. (1908), 'My Country: A Poem', *The Spectator* (London), 5 September, p. 329, <http://www.dorotheamackellar.com.au/>, last accessed 30 January 2020.

Malpas, J. E. (2007), *Place and Experience: A Philosophical Topography*, Cambridge: Cambridge University Press.

Manning, E. (2009), 'Taking the next step, touch as technique', *Sense and Society*, 4(2), pp. 211–26.

Manning, E., and Massumi, B. (2011), *Thought in the Act. Passages in the Ecology of Experience*, Minneapolis: University of Minnesota Press.

Marcus, G. E. (1998), *Ethnography through Thick and Thin*, Princeton: Princeton University Press.

Marks, D. (1995), 'Ethnography and ethnographic film: from Flaherty to Asch and after', *American Anthropologist*, 97(2), pp. 339–47.

Massey, D. (1994), *Space, Place and Gender*, London: Polity.

Massey, D. (1997), 'A global sense of place', in T. Barnes and D. Gregory (eds), *Reading Human Geography: The Poetics and Politics of Inquiry*, London: Arnold, pp. 315–23.

Massey, D. (2005), *For Space*, London: Sage.

McGrath, B. (2001), 'A problem of resources: defining rural youth encounters in education, work and housing', *Journal of Rural Studies*, 17(4), pp. 481–95.

McKenzie, P., Harrold, R., and Sturman, A. (1996), *Curriculum Provision in Rural Secondary Schools*, Melbourne: Australian Council for Educational Research.

McLeod, J. (1987), 'The concept of culture', *Unicorn*, 13(2), pp. 68–74.

Mead, M. (1975), 'Visual anthropology in a discipline of words', in P. Hockings (ed.), *Principles of Visual Anthropology*, The Hague: Mouton, pp. 3–10.

Measham, T. (2006), 'Learning about environments: the significance of primal landscapes', *Environmental Management*, 38(3), pp. 426–34.

Merleau-Ponty, M. (1962 [1945]), *Phenomenology of Perception*, London: Routledge and Kegan Paul.

Merleau-Ponty, M. (1963 [1942]), *The Structure of Behaviour*, Boston: Beacon Press.

Meyer, M. A. (2008), 'Indigenous and authentic: Hawaiian epistemology and the triangulation of meaning', in K. Denzin, Y. S. Lincoln and L. T. Smith (eds), *Handbook of Critical and Indigenous Methodologies*, Thousand Oaks: Sage, pp. 217–32.

Mills, C., and Gale, T. C. (2003). 'Transient teachers: mixed messages of schooling in regional Australia', *Journal of Research in Rural Education*, 18(3), pp. 145–51.

Murray, S. (2008), 'Digital images, photo-sharing, and our shifting notions of everyday aesthetics', *Journal of Visual Culture*, 7(2), pp. 147–63.

Myers, F. (1986), *Pintupi Country, Pintupi Self: Sentiment, Place and Politics among Western Desert Aborigines*, Berkeley: University of California Press.

Nast, H. J., and Pile, S. (1998), *Places through the Body*, London: Routledge.

Nelson, R. (1987), 'Postmodern meaning of politics', paper presented at the annual meeting of the American Political Science Asssociation, Chicago, September.

Nelson, R. (2013), *Practice as Research in the Arts. Principles, Protocols, Pedagogies, Resistance*, Basingstoke: Palgrave Macmillan.

Newton, I. (1962 [1729]), *Mathematical Principles of Natural Philosophy and his System of the World*, trans. A. Motte, Berkeley: University of California Press.

Nieuwenhuis, M. (2016), 'The emergence of materialism in geography: belonging and being, space and place, sea and land', *Social Science Information*, 55(3) pp. 300–20.

Nolan, S. (1948), 'The "Kelly" paintings by Sidney Nolan', *The Australian Artist*, 1–4 July, p. 20.

Oakley, A. (2000), *Experiments in Knowing: Gender and Method in Social Sciences*, Cambridge: Polity.

Okely, J. (1994), 'Vicarious and sensory knowledge of chronology and change: ageing in rural France', in K. Hastrup and P. Hervik (eds), *Social Experience and Anthropological Knowledge*, London: Routledge, pp. 45–64.

Okely, J. (1996), *Own or Other Culture*, London: Routledge.

O'Neill, M., Giddens, S., Breatnach, P., Bagley, C., Bourne, D., and Judge, T. (2002), 'Renewed methodologies for social research: ethno-mimesis as performative praxis', *Sociological Review*, 50(1), pp. 69–88.

Page, T. (2002), 'The Place of Childhood', unpublished manuscript.

Page, T. (2003), 'Conceptions of Senior Visual Art Education Programmes in a Rural and Remote High School', MEd thesis, The Creative Industries Research and Application Centre, Queensland University of Technology.

Page, T. (2006), 'UK06', unpublished manuscript.

Page, T. (2007), 'Conceptions of art education programmes in a rural and remote cultural context', *Studies in Art Education*, 49(1), pp. 42–58.

Page, T. (2012a), 'A shared place of discovery and creativity. Practices of contemporary art and design education', *International Journal of Art and Design Education*, 31(1), pp. 67–77.

Page, T. (2012b), 'Place and Belonging: Ways of Knowing and Learning in the Australian Bush', PhD thesis, Goldsmiths, University of London.

Page, T. (2018), 'Teaching and learning with matter', *Arts*, 7(4), 82, <https://www.mdpi.com/2076-0752/7/4/82/htm>, last accessed 30 January 2020.

Page, T. (2019), 'Embodied poetic methods to learn placemaking', *MAI: Feminism & Visual Culture*, 4, special issue, 'Feminist New Materialist Practice:

The Mattering of Methods', <https://maifeminism.com/embodied-poetic-methods-to-learn-placemaking/>, last accessed 30 January 2020.

Page, T., Adams, J., and Hyde, W. (2011), 'Emerging: the impact of the Artist Teacher in Contemporary Practices MA on students' pedagogical and artistic practices', *European Journal of Teacher Education*, 34(3), pp. 277–95.

Palmer, H., and Chalkin, V. (2019), 'Bodies ad absurdum and the queer clownifesto', *MAI: Feminism & Visual Culture*, 4, special issue, 'Feminist New Materialist Practice: The Mattering of Methods', <https://maifeminism.com/bodies-ad-absurdum-and-the-queer-clownifesto/>, last accessed 30 January 2020.

Paterson, A. B. (1987), *Banjo Paterson's Poems of the Bush*, Sydney: J. M. Dent.

Paterson, A. B. (1998), *Waltzing Matilda*, Sydney: HarperCollins.

PCAP (Priority Country Area Program) (1996), *Priority Country Area Program*, Brisbane: Education Queensland.

PCAP (Priority Country Area Program) (1997), *Cultural Activities Project*, Longreach: North West PCAP.

PCAP (Priority Country Area Program) (1998), *Cultural Activities Project: Evaluation Survey Results*, Longreach: North West PCAP.

Pile, S., and Thrift, N. (1995), 'Conclusions: spacing and the subject', in S. Pile and N. Thrift (eds), *Mapping the Subject: Geographies of Cultural Transformations*, London: Routledge, pp. 371–80.

Pilkington Garimara, D. (1996), *Follow the Rabbit-proof Fence*, Brisbane: University of Queensland Press.

Pink, S. (1997), *Women and Bullfighting: Gender, Sex and the Consumption of Tradition*, Oxford: Berg.

Pink, S. (2000), '"Informants" who come "home"', in V. Amit (ed.), *Constructing the Field: Ethnographic Fieldwork in the Contemporary World*, London: Routledge, pp. 96–119.

Pink, S. (2004), *Home Truths: Gender, Domestic Objects and Everyday Life*, Oxford: Berg.

Pink, S. (2005a), 'Applications of anthropology', in S. Pink (ed.), *Applications of Anthropology: Professional Anthropology in the Twenty-first Century*, Oxford: Berghahn, pp. 3–26.

Pink, S. (2005b), 'Dirty laundry: everyday practice, sensory engagement and the constitution of identity', *Social Anthropology*, 13(3), pp. 275–90.

Pink, S. (2006), *The Future of Visual Anthropology: Engaging the Senses*, Abingdon: Routledge.

Pink, S. (2007a), 'Sensing Cittaslow: slow living and the constitution of the sensory city', *Sense and Society*, 2(1), pp. 59–77.

Pink, S. (2007b), *Doing Visual Ethnography*, London: Sage.

Pink, S. (2008), 'An urban tour: the sensory sociality of ethnographic place making', *Ethnography*, 9(2), pp. 175–96.

Pink, S. (2009), *Doing Sensory Ethnography*, London: Sage.

Plummer, K. (1983), *Documents of Life: An Introduction to the Problems and Literature of a Humanistic Method*, London: Allen and Unwin.

Plumwood, V. (2005), 'Belonging, naming and decolonisation', in J. Hillier and E. Rooksby (eds), *Habitus: A Sense of Place*, Aldershot: Ashgate, pp. 371–91.

Porteous, D. (1990), *Landscapes of the Mind: Worlds of Sense and Metaphor*, Toronto: University of Toronto Press.

Price, S. (2005), 'The end of innocence', *Sunday Times Magazine*, 9 October, pp. 32–9.

Probyn, E. (1993), *Sexing the Self*, London: Routledge.

Prosser, J. (1998), 'The status of image based research', in J. Prosser (ed.), *Image-based Research: A Sourcebook for Qualitative Researchers*, London: Falmer Press, pp. 97–112.

Puig de la Bellacasa, M. (2017), *Matters of Care. Speculative Ethics in More than Human Worlds*, Minneapolis: University of Minnesota Press

Radway, J. (1999), 'What's in a name? Presidential address to the American Studies Association', *American Quarterly*, 51(1), pp. 1–32.

Rapley, T. (2004), 'Interviews', in C. Seale, G. Gobo, J. F. Gubrium and D. Silverman (eds), *Qualitative Research Practice*, London: Sage, pp. 15–33.

Reed, J. (1948), 'Introduction', in *The Kelly Paintings of Sidney Nolan 1946–47*, Melbourne: Velasquez Gallery.

Relph, E. (1976), *Place and Placelessness*, London: Pion.

Roberts, P. (2004), *Staffing an Empty Schoolhouse: Attracting and Retaining Teachers in Rural, Remote and Isolated Communities*, Sydney: New South Wales Teachers' Federation.

Robinson, K. (2008), 'Outback dreams', *Sunday Times Magazine*, 7 December, pp. 1–19.

Rodaway, P. (1994), *Sensuous Geographies: Body, Sense and Place*, London: Routledge.

Rodman, M. (2003), 'Empowering place: multivocality and multilocality', in S. Low and D. Lawrence-Zuniga (eds), *The Anthropology of Space and Place: Locating Culture*, Oxford: Blackwell, pp. 204–23.

Rose, G. (1993), *Feminism and Geography: The Limits of Geographical Knowledge*, Cambridge: Polity.

Rose, G. (1996), 'Place and identity: a sense of place', in D. Massey and J. Pat (eds), *A Place in the World? Places, Cultures and Globalisation*, Oxford: Oxford University Press, pp. 87–131.

Rose, G. (2012), *Visual Methodologies*, London: Sage.

Rosenthal, T. G. (2002), *Sidney Nolan*, Sydney: Thames and Hudson.

Rubin, H. R., and Rubin, I. S. (2005), *Qualitative Interviewing: The Art of Hearing Data*, London: Sage.

Ruby, J. (1981), 'Seeing through pictures: the anthropology of photography', *Camera Lucida: The Journal of Photography Criticism*, 3, pp. 19–32.

Ruby, J. (2000), *Picturing Culture: Essays on Film and Anthropology*, Chicago: University of Chicago Press.

Russel, P. (2005), *Recognizing Aboriginal Title: The Mabo Case and Indigenous Resistance to English-settler Colonialism*, Toronto: University of Toronto Press.

Sands, R. G. (1996), 'The elusiveness of identity in social work practice with women: a postmodern feminist perspective', *Clinical Social Work Journal*, 24(2), pp. 167–86.

Sayers, E. (2019). *The Materiality of Skateboarding. Motion as Material*, <https://tenderfoot.co.uk/invitations-archive/motion-as-material-front/>, last accessed 14 January 2020.

Schneider, A., and Wright, C. (2010), 'Between art and anthropology', in Arnd Schneider and Christopher Wright (eds), *Between Art and Anthropology: Contemporary Ethnographic Practice*, Oxford: Berg, pp. 1–21.

Scudder, T. (1979a), *Expected Impacts of Compulsory Relocation on Navajos*, Philadelphia: Institute for the Study of Human Issues.

Scudder, T. (1979b), *No Place to Go: Effects of Compulsory Relocation on Navajos*, Philadelphia: Institute for the Study of Human Issues.

Seale, C. (1998), 'Qualitative interviewing', in C. Seale (ed.), *Researching Society and Culture*, London: Sage, pp. 202–32.

Seddon, T. (1993), *Context and Beyond: Reframing the Theory and Practice of Education*, London: Falmer Press.

Seremetakis, L. (1994), 'The memory of the senses: historical perception, commensal exchange and modernity', in L. Taylor (ed.), *Visualizing Theory*, London: Routledge, pp. 214–29.

Shaviro, S. (2009), *Without Criteria: Kant, Whitehead, Deleuze, and Aesthetics*, Cambridge, MA: MIT Press.

Shaw v. *Wolf* (1999), Australian Federal Court, 163 ALR 205.

Shepard, P. (1982), *Nature and Madness*, San Francisco: Sierra Club Books.

Shor, I. (1992), *Empowering Education: Critical Teaching for Social Change*, Chicago: University of Chicago Press.

Shotter, J. (2008), *Conversational Realities Revisited: Life, Language, Body and World*, Chagrin Falls, OH: Taos Institute.

Shotter, J. (2010), *Social Construction on the Edge: 'Withness'-Thinking and Embodiment*, Chagrin Falls, OH: Taos Institute.

Shotter, J. (2011), 'More than cool reason: "withness-thinking" or "systemic thinking" and "thing about systems"', <http://www.systemicgathering.org/2011/07/more-than-cool-reason-withness-thinking-or-systemic-thinking-and-thing-about-systems/>, last accessed 2 May 2019.

Shove, E. (2003), *Comfort, Cleanliness and Convenience: The Social Organization of Normality*, Oxford: Berg.

Sidoti, C. (1999), 'Rights for all: a human rights perspective on regional planning', address given to *Planning in the Hothouse*, 27th National Congress Darwin, September.

Simmel, G. (1997), 'Sociology of the senses', in *Simmel on Culture: Selected Writings*, ed. D. Frisby and M. Featherstone, London: Sage, pp. 109–20.

Singh, K. S. (ed.) (1992), *Visual Anthropology and India: Proceedings of a Seminar*, Calcutta: Anthropological Survey of India.

Solnit, R. (2001), *Wanderlust. A History of Walking*, London: Verso.

Spector, K. (2015), 'Meeting pedagogical encounters halfway', *Journal of Adolescent and Adult Literacy*, 58(6), pp. 447–50.

Spender, D. (1988), *Writing a New World: Two Centuries of Australian Women Writers*, London: Pandora.

Spinney, J. (2006), 'A place of sense: a kinaesthetic ethnography of cyclists on Mont Ventoux', *Environment and Planning: Society and Space*, 24(5), pp. 709–32.

Springett, S. (2015), 'Going deeper or flatter: connecting deep mapping, flat ontologies and the democratizing of knowledge', *Humanities*, 4, pp. 623–36.

Springgay, S. (2008), 'An ethics of embodiment, civic engagement and a/r/tography: ways of becoming nomadic in art, research and teaching', *Educational Insights*, 12(2), pp. 1–11.

Springgay, S. (2011), '"The Chinatown Foray" as sensational pedagogies', *Curriculum Inquiry*, 41(5), pp. 636–56.

Springgay, S. (2015), 'Approximate rigorous abstractions: propositions of activation for posthumanist research in education', in N. Snaza and J. Weaver (eds), *Posthumanism and Educational Research*, London: Routledge, pp. 76–88.

Springgay, S. (2016), 'Learning to be affected in contemporary art', *Portal: Journal of Multidisciplinary International Studies*, 13(1), pp. 1–6.

Springgay, S., Irwin, R. L., and Leggo, C. (2008), *Being with A/r/tography*, Rotterdam: Sense Publishers.

Springgay, S., and Truman, S. E. (2017), 'A transmaterial approach to walking methodologies: embodiment, affect and a sonic art performance', *Body and Society*, 23(4), pp. 27–58.

Springgay, S., and Truman, S. E. (2018), *Walking and the More-than-Human: WalkingLab*, London: Routledge.

Springgay, S., and Truman, S. E. (2019a), 'Queering temporalities, activating QTBIPOC subjectivities and world-makings: walking research-creation', *MAI: Feminism & Visual Culture*, 4, special issue, 'Feminist New Materialist Practice: The Mattering of Methods', <https://maifeminism.com/walking-research-creation-qtbipoc-temporalities-and-world-makings/>, last accessed 30 January 2020.

Springgay, S., and Truman, S. E. (2019b), 'Research-creation walking methodologies and an unsettling of time', *International Review of Qualitative Research*, 12(1), pp. 85–93.

Stacey, M. (1994), 'From being a native to becoming a researcher', *Studies in Qualitative Methodology*, 4, pp. 53–80.

Stankiewicz, M. A. (2001), 'Community/schools partnership for the arts: collaboration, politics, and policy', *Arts Education Policy Review*, 102(6), pp. 3–10.

Stewart, R. (2007), 'Creating new stories for praxis: navigations, narrations, neonarratives', in E. Barrett and B. Bolt (eds), *Practice as Research: Approaches to Creative Arts Enquiry*, London: I.B. Tauris, pp. 123–33.

Stokes, P. (1992), 'The family photograph album: so great a cloud of witnesses', in G. Clarke (ed.), *The Portrait in Photography*, London: Reaktion, pp. 193–205.

Stoller, P. (1989), *The Taste of Ethnographic Things: The Senses in Ethnography*, Philadelphia: University of Philadelphia Press.

Stoller, P. (1997), *Sensuous Scholarship*, Philadelphia: University of Philadelphia Press.

Stoller, P. (2004), 'Sensuous ethnography, African persuasions and social knowledge', *Qualitative Inquiry*, 10(6), pp. 817–35.

Stroker, E. (1987), *Investigations in the Philosophy of Space*, Athens: Ohio University Press.

Stuart, E. (1993), *Impressionism*, Port Melbourne: Lothian.

Styres, S., Haig-Brown, C., and Blimkie, M. (2013), 'Toward a pedagogy of land: the urban context', *Canadian Journal of Education/Revue Canadienne de l'Education*, 36(2), pp. 188–221.

Styres, S., and Zinga, D. (2013), 'The community-first land-centered theoretical framework: bringing a good mind to Indigenous education research', *Canadian Journal of Education/Revue Canadienne de l'Education*, 36(2), pp. 284–313.

Sulkunen, P. (1982), 'Society made visible – on the cultural sociology of Pierre Bourdieu', *Acta Sociologica*, 25(2), pp. 103–15.

Sullivan, G. (2005), *Art Practice as Research: Inquiry in the Visual Arts*, Thousand Oaks: Sage.

Sutton, D. (2006), 'Cooking skill, the senses and memory: the fate of practical knowledge', in E. Edwards, C. Gosden and R. B. Phillips (eds), *Sensible Objects*, Oxford: Berg, pp. 87–118.

Sweet, L. (2008), *11 Indispensable Relationships You Can't Be Without*, Colorado Springs: Cook Communications.

Taguchi, H. L. (2012), 'A diffractive and Deleuzian approach to analysing interview data', *Feminist Theory*, 13(3), pp. 265–81.

Tawa, M. (2002), 'Place, country, chorography: towards a kinesthetic and narrative practice of place', *Architectural Theory Review*, 7(2), pp. 45–58.

Taylor, C. A. (2016), 'Edu-crafting a cacophonous ecology: posthumanist research practices for education', in C. A. Taylor and C. Hughes (eds), *Posthuman Research Practices in Education*, New York: Palgrave Macmillan, pp. 5–24.

Thirton [name changed] State School (2019a), *Parents' Handbook*, Thirton: Thirton State School.

Thirton [name changed] State School (2019b), *School Procedural Handbook*, Thirton: Thirton State School-Education Queensland.

Thompson, J. B. (1992), 'Editor's Introduction', in P. Bourdieu, *Language and Symbolic Power*, Cambridge: Polity, pp. 1–31.

Thrift, N. (1996), *Spatial Formations*, London: Sage.

Tolia-Kelly, D. P. (2007), 'Fear in paradise: the affective registers of the English Lake District landscape revisited', *Senses and Society*, 2(3), pp. 329–51.

Trewin, D. (2001), *ABS Views on Remoteness*, Canberra: Australian Bureau of Statistics.

Tronto, J. C. (1993), *Moral Boundaries: A Political Argument for an Ethic of Care*, New York: Routledge.

Tuan, Y.-F. (1977), *Space and Place: The Perspective of Experience*, Minneapolis: University of Minnesota Press.

Tuck, E., and MacKenzie, M. (2015), *Place in Research. Theory, Methodology and Methods*, New York: Routledge.

Tuck-Po, L. (2008), 'Before a step too far: walking with Batek hunter-gatherers in the forests of Pahang Malaysia', in T. Ingold and J. L. Vergunst (eds), *Ways of Walking: Ethnography and Practice on Foot*, Aldershot: Ashgate, pp. 21–34.

Turnbull, C. (1961), *The Forest People*, New York: Simon and Schuster.

Turpin, T., Iredale, R., Ngui, M., Harrison, B., and Fox, C. (2003), *Evaluation of the Human Rights and Equal Opportunity Commission National Inquiry into Rural and Remote Education*, Wollongong: University of Wollongong.

Tyler, S. A. (1986), 'Postmodern ethnography', in J. Clifford and G. E. Marcus (eds), *Writing Culture: The Poetics and Politics of Ethnography*, Berkeley: University of California Press, pp. 122–40.

Tynan, B., and O'Neill, M. (2007), 'Individual perseverance: a theory of home tutors' management of schooling in isolated settings', *Distance Education*, 28(1), p. 95.

United Nations (1948), *Universal Declaration of Human Rights*, Paris: United Nations General Assembly.

van der Tuin, I. (2014), 'Diffraction as a methodology for feminist onto-epistemology: on encountering Chantal Chawaf and posthuman interpellation', *Parallax*, 20(3), pp. 213–44.

van House, N., Davis, M., Takhteyev, Y., Good, N., Wilhelm, A., and Finn, M. (2004), 'From "what?" to "why?": the social uses of personal photos', Berkeley Technical Report, University of California, Berkeley, <http://people.ischool.berkeley.edu/~vanhouse/photo_project/pubs/vanhouse_et_al_2004a.pdf> last accessed 30 January 2020.

Vannini, P. (ed.) (2015), *Non-representational Methodologies: Re-envisioning Research*, London: Routledge.

Wagner, J. (ed.) (1979), *Images of Information: Still Photography in the Social Sciences*, Beverly Hills: Sage.

Walker, R. (1993), 'Finding a silent voice for the researcher: using photographs in evaluation and research', in M. Schratz (ed.), *Qualitative Voices in Educational Research*, London: Falmer Press, pp. 74–92.

Walton, J. (1993), 'Interpretations of Australian rurality and their implications', in R. C. Petersen and G. C. Rodwell (eds), *Essays in the History of*

Rural Education in Australia and New Zealand, Darwin: William Michael Press, pp. 129–41.

Wenger, E. (2005), *Communities of Practice: Learning, Meaning and Identity*, Cambridge: Cambridge University Press.

White, R. (1981), *Inventing Australia: Images and Identity, 1688–1980*, Crows Nest, NSW: Allen and Unwin.

Whitehead, A. N. (1938), *Modes of Thought*, New York: Macmillan.

Whitehead, A. N. (1978 [1926]), *Process and Reality: An Essay in Cosmology*, New York: Free Press.

Willis, P., and Trodman, M. (2002), 'Manifesto for ethnography', *Cultural Studies Critical Methodologies*, 2(3), pp. 394–402.

Wilson, R. (1997), *Bringing Them Home: National Inquiry into the Separation of Aboriginal and Torres Strait Islander Children from Their Families*, Canberra: Human Rights and Equal Opportunity Commission.

Wright-Smith, C. (1996), *Education and Success in a Small Town: The High Schools Role*, College Station: Texas A&M University.

Wyn, J., and Stokes, H. (1998), 'Community strategies: addressing the challenges for young people living in rural Australia', in *Learning Communities: Regional Sustainability and the Learning Society: An International Symposium*, Launceston, 13–20 June, Conference Proceedings, pp. 311–21.

Wynhausen, E. (1998), 'End of the road?', *The Australian Magazine*, 20–21 June, pp. 14–21.

Index

Note: Page references in *italics* indicate images; 'n' indicates chapter notes.

EU Authorised Representative:

Easy Access System Europe Mustamäe tee 50, 10621 Tallinn, Estonia

gpsr.requests@easproject.com

Printed and bound by CPI Group (UK) Ltd, Croydon, CR0 4YY

03/04/2026

02083721-0002